D1212491

THE PRESS AND
THE PUBLIC INTEREST

The William Allen White Lectures

EDITED BY WARREN K. AGEE

Director, William Allen White Foundation

Public Affairs Press, Washington, D. C.

INTRODUCTION

"Our Republic and its press will rise or fall together." — *Joseph Pulitzer*

The role of a free, responsible, and aggressive press in making democracy work is the theme of these William Allen White lectures, which have been delivered annually by eighteen of America's leading reporters, editors, and publishers. Although given over a period encompassing almost two decades, the lectures are especially timely today. As early as 1950, the lecturers talked about the problems of increasing secrecy, credibility gaps, and managed news which the nation today is facing and which make the performance of today's press more crucial than ever before. These newsmen chart a course for both press and nation in dealing with these problems.*

"The future of the American democracy is contingent upon the performance of the American press," declared Clark Mollenhoff, Washington correspondent, striking a key note for the series. "If the newsmen of today and tomorrow are diligent workers and balanced thinkers on problems of governing our society, then I have no doubt that the American democracy will survive and flourish as a symbol to the whole world. If the press fails in its responsibility—if it flounders in a quagmire of superficiality, partisanship, laziness and incompetence —then our great experiment in democracy will fail. In one hundred and fifty, one hundred, fifty years—or even sooner—it will be replaced by a more efficient authoritarian form of government, and will be remembered as an interesting but impractical system."

It was H. G. Wells, observed the late Grove Patterson, who once said that the Roman Empire could not endure because there were no newspapers—no method of apprising the outlying peoples of the behavior of the center. "Democracy, then, can continue to function only so long and so far as this channel is not tampered with or dammed or used exclusively by the state. Through it also must flow, in the other direction, from border to center, a stream of analysis, criticism, praise, and, if necessary, condemnation."

Because government will want to conceal information, "and has a right to in some small instances," reporters must "ask sticky questions and keep using their legs," reporter-editor James B. Reston stated.

---

* The years in which the lectures were delivered are the dates indicated in the biographical notes starting on page 217.

In a call for the responsible and aggressive reporting of foreign policy, Reston pointed out that "if public opinion is to retain anything but the power of protest, after the event, the reporter has to move into action much earlier in the development of policy than formerly." The late publisher Roy E. Roberts put it another way: "I have a sneaking feeling a return to hardboiled reporting will kick open more doors to governmental secrecy than all the congressional probes or all the speeches of alarm that can be made." Earl J. Johnson, former United Press International editor, emphasized that "the temptation of news sources to manage the news for their own advantage is resisted most successfully in the presence of competitive reporters." And Wes Gallagher, Associated Press general manager, called for what he termed "perspective reporting." "If we, as journalists, use the tools we have at our disposal to put the news in perspective, then the news will have that ring of authenticity, and we won't have to fear any credibility gap. Nor will the lack of credibility of some news sources rub off on the journalist. The public will have confidence in the journalist not only as a conveyor of vital information, but as the principal guardian of its freedom as well."

The increasing social responsibility of the press is another theme running through the lectures. The late publisher Bernard Kilgore noted with pleasure the disappearance of "the big brassy metropolitan newspaper," which tended toward sensationalism in its treatment of news and had a reputation for irresponsibility. In its place, he said, is coming "the lively, local community newspaper which performs, first of all, the service of pulling its own community together with information about itself and takes a position of editorial leadership in the affairs of that community." Editor Hodding Carter said the job of his newspaper is "to respond to every challenge which bigotry, social and economic revolution, and the shrill demand for conformity" make to the spirit of his community. Defending group, or "chain," newspapers as, among other things, providing for the editorial independence of local editors, publisher Paul Miller observed that, "Newspapers are continuing the effort to wipe out every reason for legitimate criticism—sloppy reporting, mealy-mouthed commentary, cheap gossip, questionable advertising . . . More and more publishers and editors are meeting critics head on." Editor Erwin D. Canham said, "We should make clear to people the difference between the old, special-group, prejudice-serving newspaper and the total public-serving newspaper which is the typical pattern today." And editor Palmer Hoyt, describing how his newspaper combatted "McCarthyism," stated that never before has it been so urgently important that newspapers recognize their responsibilities to provide "balance and stabilization" to the flow of the news. "As a matter of simple fact, our civilization is held together by an extremely tenuous thread, and that thread increasingly needs the strong wax of practical journalism to preserve it, keep it strong, and make it possible for democracy to endure."

The press itself does not escape criticism in the series of lectures. Editor Irving Dilliard issued a call for more editors who read broadly, who criticize others and yet who accept criticism, and who actively seek staff members possessing what William Allen White characterized as "intelligent discontent." Magazine editor and newspaper publisher Gardner Cowles observed that too many newspapers are dull, that they inadequately report changing developments in their communities, and that they often are physically unattractive. "Too many newspaper editors today are too careful, too cautious, too fearful of being controversial, too worried about ruffling the hair of some readers. I don't think any man can become a great editor unless he is willing to become meaningfully involved in the important issues of his community, his state, the nation and the world. And he needs to *care passionately*." Declaring that conscience makes a newspaper different from every other industrial organism in society, editor Norman Isaacs said the kind of professionalism needed by newspaper executives is "one of the spirit." "We need people who seek no material riches. We need people who seek only the richness of usefulness to society. We need men and women who recognize the printed word to be the most powerful weapon in society and who seek to be its servants, not its masters; men and women willing to serve journalism as Schweitzer has served medicine. Men and women who realize instinctively that democracy will rise or fall on the . . . integrity of its journalism."

In other major lectures, editor Ernest K. Lindley reviewed foreign policy and observed that, whereas senators and representatives, cabinet members and cabinetmakers come and go, Washington correspondents remain not only as an institution or a group but as individuals. The late reporter Jules Dubois warned about dangers to press freedom in Latin America, "where the first goal of the Communists or dictators of the right is to gain control of all mass media of communications"; magazine editor Ben Hibbs deplored the influence of the business office on the editor's independence; and newspaper editor Jenkin Lloyd Jones described "the inexact science of truth-telling," involving essentially the difficult business of selecting facts, as a major problem confronting the press.

The lectures are sponsored by the William Allen White Foundation, which was established shortly after the death of the world-famous editor of the *Emporia* (Kan.) *Gazette* in 1944. The goal of the foundation is service to the profession of journalism and the William Allen White School of Journalism at the University of Kansas. Its policies are established by a board of trustees consisting of more than 90 prominent men and women in the United States who are involved in journalism or concerned with its future. The foundation underwrites professional seminars and workshops and recognizes outstanding work by high school and college journalism students. Each year it presents its Distinguished Service in Journalism citation to an American journalist who exemplifies the William Allen White ideals in journalism and who is deemed worthy of the award for service to his profession and community. The award was inaugurated in 1958, but recently the board authorized the granting of the citation to the previous lecturers as well. A Kansas editor also is cited annually for distinguished service in the White tradition.

The publication of this book commemorates the 100th anniversary of the birth in 1868 of William Allen White, whose life and writings summed up the wisdom and the spirit of his age and earned for him the love and admiration of the great and the humble across the nation and around the world. An editor, philosopher, novelist, and politician, White likely will be remembered best by his famous editorials, including "To An Anxious Friend," his 1923 Pulitzer Prize editorial.

"You tell me that law is above freedom of utterance," the prize-winning editorial began, expressing an eternal conflict which is just as pressing today. "And I reply that you can have no wise laws nor free enforcement of wise laws unless there is free expression of the wisdom of the people — and, alas, their folly with it. . . . You say that freedom of utterance is not for time of stress, and I reply with the sad truth that only in time of stress is freedom of utterance in danger. . . . This state today is in more danger from suppression than from violence, because, in the end, suppression leads to violence. . . . This nation will survive, this state will prosper, the orderly business of life will go forward if only men can speak in whatever way given them to utter what their hearts hold — by voice, by posted card, by letter, or by press. Reason never has failed men. Only force and repression have made the wrecks in the world."

WARREN K. AGEE

Director, William Allen White Foundation
William Allen White School of Journalism
University of Kansas, Lawrence, Kansas.

CONTENTS

COPS AND ROBBERS IN FOGGY BOTTOM

By James B. Reston

The conflict between officials and reporters in Washington over what information about foreign affairs should be made public is now becoming an important issue. In a country whose action depends upon consent of the people and whose actions now affect the interests of the whole world, an understanding between reporters and officials on the obligations and rights of the reporter is imperative, but no such understanding exists today.

Instead, responsible officials and responsible reporters, as distinguished from the old-fashioned scoop-artists, gossip-mongers, and saloon-rail journalists, are now playing cops and robbers with each other. The object of the cops seems to be to conceal information. The object of the robbers is to disclose information. The cops seldom ask themselves why they want to conceal the information, and the robbers don't analyze very often why they want to disclose the information. Both sides just go on waging their own private little Cold War behind the gas works and the State Department in Foggy Bottom, to the despair of each other and the detriment of the public.

Secretary of State Acheson's attitude toward the reporters and his strategy in dealing with them is not unlike his attitude and strategy toward the Russians. In both cases he follows an aloof policy of containment. He is determined to block the expansionist tendencies of reporters in fields where he thinks they have no rights. His attitude is the lawyer's approach to a private case: the preliminaries to all public trials should be *sub judice*. The executive branch of the government, he argues, must have the right of uninterrupted private discussion and negotiation among its own officials and with other governments, and until it decides to disclose that information—even if it's about such things as the Hydrogen Bomb—the reporters have no right to violate the government's privacy and report what's going on.

While he does not dislike reporters personally, he apparently thinks they are presumptuous, superficial, often selfish and indifferent to the public interest, irresponsible with secret information, much too distrustful and skeptical of officials, and far too interested in being first with any story rather than being right and careful with what he regards as the main story.

I don't think Mr. Acheson has ever really analyzed these feelings very much, and I doubt whether—knowing as much as he does about the pre-war and post-war State Department—he would himself be unskeptical if he were a reporter but there is a lot in his argument, and it is easy to illustrate.

Several weeks ago, General Omar Bradley accepted an invitation to make a private talk to the members of the Overseas Writers, a group of former foreign correspondents in Washington. In the course of answering questions, the General said that, speaking as a soldier, he could see advantages to rearming the Germans. Within an hour after the meeting, somebody present reported (and distorted) his remarks to an official of the French embassy. By 5:30 of the same afternoon, a French official was at the State Department, seeking an assurance that the United States was not rearming the Germans. And within 48 hours, General Bradley's views on the rearmament of Germany were being openly discussed in the French press.

The net effect of the incident was that the U.S. government was embarrassed by the indiscretion of an American correspondent, doubts were raised in France about the reliability of U.S. policy in Germany, and General Bradley (and every other official who heard about the incident) was highly skeptical of the value of any off-the-record discussions with reporters.

A similar, but even more disturbing, incident occurred at the height of the Soviet pressure on Yugoslavia last year. Various highly secret meetings were held in Washington on what action the United States and Britain should take in the event of a Soviet armed attack on Yugoslavia. One reporter, whose dispatches are widely circulated throughout this country, published a column several days later saying that the U.S. and Britain had decided that they would give aid to Marshall Tito if war broke out, but that they definitely would not go to war for him.

This naturally was interpreted by the Yugoslavs as an invitation to the Russians to take aggressive action against Yugoslavia, and it was properly condemned in Washington as a dangerous and senseless bit of journalistic enterprise.

It is a matter of opinion why such incidents as these occur, but my own view is that they occur partly because an atmosphere of rivalry, perhaps even of hostility, has grown up between reporters and the sources of official information; partly because the exclusive report of an interesting bit of information is still regarded as a triumph in the newspaper business, even if the information is more damaging than beneficial; and partly because the old points of contact and cooperation between reporters and officials are breaking down.

In William Allen White's generation, officials in Washington had plenty of time to see correspondents. The Secretary of State in those days could devote weeks and even months to meditation upon the Newfoundland Fisheries problem. The corps of correspondents was small and dependable. When Henry L. Stimson was Secretary of State in the Hoover Administration, he held a press conference every day and saw correspondents privately and regularly.

This produced understanding both ways, but it is not possible in 1950. Mr. Acheson is lucky if he sees Mrs. Acheson once a day, let alone taking time out for regular private talks with a press corps that is larger than the Senate and House of Representatives combined. If he sees a correspondent privately once or twice a year that is about par for the course. He holds his press conference once a week, but whenever a big story is breaking, the reporters, under pressure to report the facts, cannot see him and can find only with the greatest difficulty, somebody—usually in another country's embassy—who can give them reliable information.

Thus the main link between the reporter and the main source of news is broken at the most critical time. The other link, the off-the-record press conference, has broken down for a variety of reasons. When Mr. Acheson or one of his aides thinks about talking off-the-record to the State Department correspondents today, he has to remember that among those correspondents are the representatives of the Soviet news agency, Tass. He has also to remember that organizations such as the Associated Press now sometimes consider it a useful information and public relations policy to send a summary of his off-the-record remarks to all member newspapers for the private information of their editors. These private memos give a lot of publishers and editors a sense of being in on things, but they terrify government officials and in the long run make them hesitant to say anything to any large group off-the-record.

Even the meetings between top government officials and small groups of, say, 10 or 12 dependable correspondents are breaking down, not because the correspondents have misused or betrayed the information given them in these meetings but because government officials have less and less time, and—as the Cold War gets hotter —are more and more afraid that they'll be blamed for saying something some official in some department thinks they shouldn't have said.

We must be fair about this to the officials. Their problems are varied and perplexing. The consequences of premature disclosure in certain negotiations can be serious. The official reporters of the Soviet government; the American correspondents who would rather be first than be right; the peep-hole journalists, who have trans-ferrd their talents and their mass audiences from obstetrics to politics without any period of gestation — all these are problems. But the people have to be adequately informed in a democracy in spite of these problems, and the government is not doing what it could to keep informing them. The more complex our problems become, the more dangerous they become, then the more they must be explained to the people, but the opposite procedure now prevails. The Fireside Chat — that most useful educational contact between the President and the People — ended just when issues began to get really confused — that is to say, precisely when it was needed the most. As the crises in Germany and in the Far East have become more complex, the official sources of information on these subjects have not opened up, but have tended to close down.

Let me illustrate the public's side of this problem (for in the last analysis it is not the reporter's side at all—we are merely channels of necessary information to the public, and the reporter's convenience or inconvenience is of no more importance than the personal convenience of the official). I referred earlier to General Bradley's speech to the Overseas Writers on the advantages to be gained in rearming Germany. Shortly thereafter, Field Marshal Montgomery of Britain came to Washington and New York and was later quoted in the United Nations as going even further than Bradley in demanding the rearmament of the Germans.

These two statements by the two most distinguished active soldiers in the West naturally raised some serious questions. Secretary of State Acheson had just come back from Germany, and the questions were put to him. His first reply was that the question of rearming Germany had not even been discussed in the Paris meeting of the Council of Foreign Ministers (which he had attended on his way to Germany). This naturally did not satisfy the reporters. They pressed him for a statement of policy on whether the United States intended to permit the rearmament of Germany, but the most he would say was that the government had no such intention at the present time.

The net result of this was to raise serious doubts in the minds of many people about U.S. intentions in Germany, doubts which Mr. Acheson could have removed very easily. He had just approved a few days before the controversy a detailed directive to the U.S. High Commissioner in Germany, John J. McCloy, telling him in the most specific terms that the object of U.S. policy was to keep Germany disarmed, to limit its police forces, to deny to the Germans the privilege to import, own or fly aircraft of any kind, and to scrutinize every individual and group showing any ultra-nationalistic tendencies. Why didn't Mr. Acheson put an end to the controversy by telling the simple facts about his instructions to Mr. McCloy? The previous U.S. directive on Germany had been published, so why not this one? The only answer given — after the *New York Times* got hold of the text itself and published it months later—was that publication "might have embarrassed McCloy in Germany."

The government's handling of its public relations on Formosa and the Far East is another illustration of how inadequate cooperation between responsible reporters and responsible officials can contribute to public confusion, violent controversy, and a fear at home and abroad, that the giant doesn't quite know how to use his strength.

Leave aside the question of what might have been done by the U.S. in China in 1946—though General Marshall would probably have taken a different line with Chiang Kai-shek if his Moscow experience had preceded his China experience, rather than the other way round—but leaving that aside, the State Department said virtually nothing about the impending collapse of Nationalist China from Labor Day 1949 until January of 1950.

Officials there had every opportunity to do so, they complained constantly about statements in the press that their policy in the rest of the Far East was being misrepresented, and they promised to make available summaries of that policy before Christmas of 1949 but they never did. Nor did they say anything else to explain U.S. policy in that part of the world.

As a result, when Senators Knowland of California and Smith of New Jersey came back from the Far East shouting about the doom of Formosa and its importance to the U.S., the public had little basis for judgment on the rights or wrongs of their charges, an angry debate ensued, and Mr. Acheson finally had to jump into it with the complaint that things were getting out of hand.

Even after the decision was made by President Truman in the National Security Council that the U.S. was not going to send troops or military missions to Formosa, the decision was not announced, and the angry argument was allowed to go on in the country for another week before the President decided that it was getting so hot he'd better let the people know that he had decided the issue.

Finally, when it was decided to make a major statement on U.S. policy on the Far East, how was it made? In a national broadcast which could be heard by the people? In a careful, state document which could serve as a guide for the future? It was made in an extemporaneous address at 1:30 one Thursday afternoon to the National Press Club because Mr. Acheson, wanting to be a good guy, had promised the retiring president of that club that he'd make a speech one day before the club president retired.

I happen to believe that our policy on Formosa was right, given the conditions in January 1950. Despite these complaints, I also happen to think that Dean Acheson is incomparably the ablest Secretary of State the United States has had since Henry L. Stimson, but on this question of public information, no contemporary public official has contrived to do so little with so much. Even when he did explain his Far Eastern policy, what did he say? He said that the Russians were "detaching" the four northern provinces from China and "attaching" them to the Soviet Union (which wasn't quite true). He based his whole Formosa policy of noninterference on the thesis that the Chinese were inevitably going to react against the Soviet Union, and that we should not, by going into Formosa, deflect China's wrath from the Russians to ourselves. But all this had been true for years. The Russians did not suddenly go into the northern provinces of China. They were there last year, and if the State Department had made its policy clear about China and Formosa then, much of the divisive argument of late 1949 and early 1950 might have been avoided.

Nothing in recent years in Washington has produced quite so much controversy in the field of what should and should not be published as the Hydrogen Bomb. President Truman was opposed to any public discussion of the bomb or his interest in it. If he had had his way, nothing would have been said in public at all: he would merely have ordered the bomb built, like any other weapon, with no announcement, no discussion, no debate about the responsibilities of American power, or the international control of atomic energy.

It's a good idea not to be dogmatic about this particular case. Very few reporters would be prepared to argue that they had the right to disclose information about powerful new American weapons. Several unusual facts in this particular case, however, are relevant.

First, it was not a reporter who let out this particular cat. As early as December 1946, when John J. McCloy was Assistant Secretary of War, he discussed publicly the possibility of producing a hydrogen bomb 1,000 times as powerful as the Nagasaki bomb. P. M. S. Blackett, the British physicist, among others, discussed the super bomb in a book in 1948, and Senator Johnson of Colorado discussed it in a television broadcast on November 1, 1949.

"Our scientists," Senator Johnson said, "have already created a bomb that has six times the effectiveness of the bomb that was dropped at Nagasaki and they are not satisfied at all. They want one that has 1,000 times the effect of that terrible bomb that was dropped at Nagasaki that snuffed out the lives of 50,000 people ... They have been devoting their time to two things: one, to make a super bomb; and the other to find some way of detonating a bomb before the fellow who wants to drop it can detonate it. We have made considerable progress in that direction."

This extraordinary statement by a member of the Joint Congressional Atomic Energy Committee was naturally reported in the press. Al Friendly of the *Washington Post*, hearing about the broadcast, got hold of the text and printed what Senator Johnson said. The Alsop brothers followed with three columns on the difficult decision facing the President. And the *New York Times* then published a series of articles on the scientific aspects of hydrogen

fusion, and the political and military questions raised within the
Administration prior to the President's decision to order production of the bomb.

During the preliminary debate within the Administration, some
of the men who knew most about the possibilities of the H-bomb
took the position that this was not really a weapon of war alone
but a means of exterminating whole populations. To treat it merely
as a military secret which raised no new political and moral questions seemed to them an extraordinary procedure, and some of
them said so at the time.

These facts raise the question of the newspaper's right and obligations in its most difficult form. Who is to decide whether the
information should be published? What is to be the basis of judgment? Is military security alone to be the test? If the President
is to be the sole judge, is he free to exert this right indiscriminately,
say, to cover up shortcomings or divisions within his own Administration?

I find it difficult to be as positive in answering these questions
as the President is. His attitude is that he must be trusted to decide
such things without interference or pressure from the outside. I
don't know what he expected the papers to do about Senator Johnson's broadcast, but apparently we were supposed to ignore it, and
all the arguments within the government that followed. There
was, however, one aspect of the situation that could not be ignored.
In the middle of the debate before the President made his decision
about the H-bomb, President James B. Conant of Harvard University publicly charged that the Administration had not yet devised "even the first approximation to a satisfactory procedure for
evaluating technical judgments on matters connected with the
national defense."

Mr. Conant was on the original Acheson-Lilienthal Committee
that studied the question of controlling atomic energy. He was an
advisor to the Atomic Energy Commission and he could scarcely
be characterized as a frivolous man. Yet here he was publicly discussing how to solve the very differences at issue on the H-bomb
and asserting: "The simple fact is that many important decisions
are being made in Washington today without adequate evaluation
. . . To my mind we have not yet evolved a satisfactory procedure
for evaluating differences of opinion among technical experts!"

This was in some ways the most disturbing statement made during the entire debate, for while the President was crying for more secrecy, some of his most illustrious and best-informed associates were pointing out the Conant speech to reporters as the real truth of the situation within the government. In these circumstances, was there an obligation to publish, or was this to be kept out of the papers too? And if so, what is the end of such a process in democracy?

What is particularly disturbing about this problem is that the same demands for secrecy are made on less important issues as well, so that when a really big issue comes up it is difficult for the government to make a serious new argument.

There should, of course, be some means by which the responsible reporter and the responsible official could discuss, in private and with mutual confidence, the implications of the President's dilemma over the H-bomb. But it is precisely this lack of mutual confidence which is the problem.

In these circumstances the least we in the newspaper business can do is try to analyze our own faults and try to correct them, but this will not be done, I suggest, by adopting softer standards of reporting. The power of the government is growing all the time and our skepticism will have to grow with it. The power of the executive to decide issues in the secret stage of negotiations with other nations is growing all the time and this, I fear, is going to impose new obligations on reporters and probably bring them even more into conflict with officials than in the past.

What the United States does now in the realm of foreign affairs is almost always done as part of a coalition. When it negotiates agreements in secret, the theory is that the agreement will always be subject to review by Congress, but the power of review isn't what it used to be.

We no longer have a government of "equal powers" in the field of foreign affairs, if we ever did have. The Congress retains all its powers over the purse and it still has the right of review, but the President and the Secretary of State in the executive branch are now more than ever before in a position to call the turn. When the President announces to the world that he wants aid for Greece, the Congress does not really have complete freedom of action; it can only go along with him or repudiate and humiliate him—and it will always hesitate to do the latter. The Congress theoretically could refuse to vote the funds to build the hydrogen bomb, but once the executive branch of the government announced that the bomb effort was going to be made, the Congress had very little practical choice but to go along.

This is an increasing and an important trend, for almost everything the United States does in the field of foreign affairs is now done in collaboration with other nations. Thus the executive is always coming to the Congress with a policy in one hand and a reminder in the other that any major change by Congress would embarrass the United States in its relations with other countries.

Thus, it seems to me, if public opinion is to retain anything but the power of protest, after the event, the reporter has to move into action much earlier in the development of policy than formerly. The State Department would like to keep him out of the picture entirely until the basis of an agreement is reached with other countries and the tentative agreement is sent to Capitol Hill but by then policy has crystalized so much the aggressive reporting might at that point upset a whole series of apple-carts.

It should not be impossible, at some point in most of our negotiations before informal commitments are taken, for our government to indicate the broad lines of the policy it favors, so that there can be some objective discussion of the facts in public. But if the government will not make an effort to try to inform the people, then I think it is the reporter's duty to do the best he can to inform them, and the newspaper's duty to give him time out from routine coverage to enable him to do so.

I am not suggesting that we can conduct diplomacy in the headlines of the world's press, or that the government has no right to private discussions and private negotiations. Obviously it has, and in some cases the secrecy must be total until the negotiations are completed, but in most cases the demand for total secrecy is not made in order to assure the success of the negotiations with the other nations, but to assure the executive of an advantageous position in the presentation of its case in Congress.

I have wondered what a good reporter and philosopher like Bill White would say about this problem if he came to Washington once more. He was a courteous man, but I think if he sat in our press conferences today, he would feel, not that the reporters were pressing too hard, but that they had become a little too courteous, that there were not enough chips on enough shoulders. I think he'd want to know why there was just a handful of the large corps of

Washington reporters probing into these life and death questions of atomic energy, the organization of the armed services, the conduct of our foreign policy, the personalities and characters of the men involved.

As a matter of fact, I think he'd rather enjoy the game of Cops and Robbers in Foggy Bottom and think it was inevitable and healthy. I imagine he would tell us that officials in Washington or Emporia had always sought to hide as much information as possible, especially when they didn't quite know where they were going, and that one of the necessary antidotes to this very human procedure was for brash young men to ask sticky questions and keep using their legs.

He knew that we have at least our share of chumps and scoundrels in the newspaper business and that we shouldn't take ourselves too seriously, but he was less afraid of our scoundrels than their scoundrels, and he didn't want to regulate our folly.

"You can regulate and control every material aspect of human life," he said, "but certain intangibles cannot be checked. The reporter is dealing in one of those intangibles. However narrow he may be, however foolish, however dumb or malevolent or greedy he may be, if he still has his freedom, then he does his work. Then he serves his purpose, and helps, if only by the example of his folly, to mark the course ahead.

"But woe betide this land, sorry the day for this world, when the man who comes into the market place peddling information, even though it is badly damaged goods, even though it smells to high heaven, is held on leash by any hand except by the common sense of fairness and the laws thereunto appertaining. . . ."

2

THE YEARS OF DANGER

By Ernest K. Lindley

When I left Kansas to try my luck in metropolitan journalism, William Allen White gave me a letter of introduction to the Editor of the *New York World*. Unless perhaps he had seen a few of my pieces — quite ordinary pieces — in Henry J. Allen's *Wichita Beacon*, he didn't know whether or not I had any ability or potentialities as a journalist. However, he was generous enough to offer to vouch for all that he knew about me. His letter consisted of two sentences. The first identified me by name and as the son of the Chancellor of the University of Kansas. The second read, as I recall it: "He has long legs and is willing to use them." The latter half of the second sentence was based on unreliable hearsay. Otherwise his letter complied with the best standards of journalistic accuracy and brevity. And you will note the editorial skill with which he insinuated that one little visible fact — the only fact he had to go on in this case — was vastly significant; indeed, so conclusive that nothing more need be said. What more telling testimonial could a young reporter have had from a master of the craft? It was sufficient to put me on a road which led in due time to Washington.

The Washington correspondents appear in too many forms to be classified as a single species. Many of them have curiousity — about the present, the past, and the future. Some of them even predict — often in fascinating detail — what is going to happen next week, next month, or at the next election — with no more than the usual margin of human error. A few of them are dedicated to improving or removing our public officials. No matter how good our public officials are, they are never good enough to satisfy all the Washington commentators. The advice of the Washington correspondents is generous — not only plentiful but made available at the nominal price of a newspaper, a news magazine, or a twist of the radio or television dial.

The Washington correspondents are also, for the most part, a durable lot. Senators and Representatives, cabinet members and cabinetmakers, come and go. Even Presidents come and go — although not so frequently as they used to. But the Washington press and radio corps remains, not only as an institution or a group but as individuals.

A correspondent who has been in Washington, let us say, 18 years — which does not seem a long time to me — is senior in service to most of the legislators and policy-making members of the Executive branch. Of the 435 present members of the House of Representatives, fewer than 30 were in Congress 18 years ago and not more than a dozen others can be said to have any sort of experiences in national or international affairs stretching back that far. Of the 96 members of the present Senate, only five were in the Senate 18 years ago. Four others either were then in the House or had previously served in Congress. Perhaps half a dozen more have had some kind of experience in national or international affairs going back 18 years.

In the executive branch one party has been in power without interruption for nearly 18 years. Yet, apart from the nonpolitical career men, only one member of the present cabinet and one member of the sub-cabinet have served continuously in the government since Roosevelt's first year. Incidentally, 18 years ago Secretary of Defense Marshall — a selfless patriot and one of the greatest citizens the country has ever produced — was a colonel. And two others of similar breed, Eisenhower and Bradley, were majors.

A veteran Washington correspondent looks upon the newer men in public life very much as I should suppose a college teacher looks upon the Freshman class. In each batch of arrivals, he is pleased to see a good many solid citizens — C average perhaps, with a sprinkling of B's and B-pluses. Here and there he sees a potential star. As to the others: he wonders how they managed to get their high school diplomas.

Not only Freshmen, but the Sophomores and the Juniors and sometimes even the Seniors can profit from coaching. And we try to see that they get it. The students sometimes feel that their mentors are too critical — even bilious. Admittedly, we sometimes became a trifle impatient when we see the same mistakes being repeated over and over again. The same old speeches and the same old political tricks also become irksome. Of course, age and

experience do not necessarily produce wisdom — either in public
life or among Washington correspondents or newspaper editors.
Certainly they do not lead to a common viewpoint on public questions. The veterans in public life, and journalism, are as disparate
in outlook as the neophytes. The correspondents may have one
advantage in that they don't have to get re-elected, although
they have to satisfy somebody — a portion of the public or at
least a publisher. The natural laws of politics do not always result
in the survival of the best public servants. Some journalists are
free to express themselves with considerable independence and
forthrightness, without regard to party or special interests. (I doubt,
however, that if more of the politicians were to emulate the journalists in these respects they would suffer as much as they fear.)

Six years have passed since the end of the second world war.
We may wonder, many of us, how, soon after a massive victory,
we managed to fall into another perilous predicament. There is
not much point now in wondering how it came about, except as
we may perhaps locate in the past some lessons of value in the
future. However, the teachings of history are often so complex
that it is hard to be sure what they are; it is, of course, quite
impossible without references to the facts. If we start out with
distorted facts we are hardly likely to reach correct conclusions.

As illustration, we may take the Yalta agreements. They were
made six years ago this week and intended to lay the political
foundation of the postwar world. It was precisely because they
anticipated difficulties, that Roosevelt and Churchill sought definite
postwar understandings with Stalin while all three men were still
fighting the common enemy and we were still at the height of our
military power.

The Yalta agreements covered too many subjects to be
reviewed here. Among the most important — and later the most
controversial — were those on Eastern Europe and the Far East.
It is sometimes said that Roosevelt handed Eastern Europe and
Manchuria to the Russians.

An important fact — indeed, a central fact — with regard to
Eastern Europe at that time is that the Russians already had it,
or most of it. Their armies had to move through Eastern Europe
to reach Germany. They were setting up puppet governments as
they went along. One of Roosevelt's foremost objectives at Yalta
was to see to it that these squatter rights would be only temporary

and would never have legal sanction. In the Declaration on
Liberated Europe, Stalin promised that the provisional governments would include representatives of all democratic parties and
that, in due course, free elections would be held. As to Poland —
an ally — there was a separate and more detailed agreement, with
similar objectives. In regard to all, it was stated, in effect, that the
Big Three jointly, not just Russia, should have responsibility.

In these agreements on Eastern Europe, the Western Allies
gave up nothing which they held or which lay within their physical
reach. Stalin gave up — or promised to give up — part of what
he held. If he had kept his word, most of Eastern Europe would
not now lie in bondage to Moscow.

The ink on these contracts had hardly dried, however, when the
Kremlin violated them, first in Rumania and then in Poland.
These infractions were causing Roosevelt deep anxiety at the time
of his death. Why Stalin ever made the promises if he intended to
break them so soon is not easy to fathom. Possibly when he got
home, his colleagues in the Politburo convinced him that he had
given up too much — that he had been "taken in" by Roosevelt and
Churchill.

In the Yalta agreement on the Far East, Stalin promised to go
to war against Japan not later than three months after the surrender of Germany. Our top military strategists were unanimous
in regarding Russian participation in the wa ragainst Japan as of
the utmost importance. No one knew at that time whether the
atomic bomb could be made, and the first great fire raids on Tokyo
had not yet occurred. (The Chiefs of Staff still wanted Russia in
the war at Potsdam, in July.) They thought Russian help might
save a year or two of war and hundreds of thousands of American
lives. They were especially concerned about the supposedly powerful Kwantung army and the great industrial and agricultural
resources of Manchuria — an important part of the war-making
power of the Japanese Empire. We had no forces available for a
campaign in Manchuria.

In return for entering the war against Japan in good time,
Russia was to get back what it lost in the Russo-Japanese war —
the lower half of Sakhalin island and certain rail and port rights
in Manchuria — plus the Kuriles and recognition of the status
quo in Outer Mongolia, long a Soviet satellite. The contract
stipulated, however, that China should retain full sovereignty in

Manchuria; and Stalin agreed to conclude a pact of friendship and mutual assistance with the National Government of China.

As it turned out, Russian help in defeating Japan was super-fluous. And it is sometimes said that the price paid for Russian participation would have been too high, in any event. Such comment ignores the obvious fact that *without any agreement* Russia could have waited until we defeated Japan and then marched into Manchuria, as well as Korea and the lower half of Sakhalin. The Yalta agreement was in the nature of a limitation on Russian aggrandizement. Excepting perhaps the Kuriles, the Western powers gave up nothing which they held or was within their reach. Stalin agreed to take much less than he could have seized without any agreement.

Unquestionably there were defects in the Yalta contracts — some in language and others probably in substance. On the whole, however, they represented a reasonable adjustment of conflicting interests. This seems to be generally recognized in Great Britain, where they have never become a political issue. Certainly, if they had been so favorable to the Kremlin as it is sometimes contended in retrospect, the Kremlin would not have violated them so extensively. If the Yalta pledge of free elections in Europe is ever made good, we will be entitled to feel that we have won a great victory. We will no longer need to worry much about Communist imperialism.

The notion that we are in trouble because we did not draw our contracts with the Russians a little more carefully — or a little sooner — was in vogue at one time and has not altogether vanished. It was, and is, a dangerous notion because it obscures the true nature of the enemy. It amounts to a plea in extenuation of his crimes.

The real lesson of Yalta is, I think, the obvious one: that Moscow's word is worthless, that the Kremlin will not keep any compact that it can violate to its advantage with impunity, that it can be made to behave only by force. This lesson was fairly evident even before the surrender of Germany. I recall Averell Harriman's coming from Moscow to the San Francisco conference in April, 1945, to sound the alarm, because the Kremlin was already welching on the Yalta Agreements on Liberated Europe and Poland.

There were strong practical reasons for not calling the Kremlin to account before Germany and Japan had surrendered. But it surely was a mistake to dissolve our great wartime military establishment before we had secured the peace. "Bring the boys home" was perhaps the costliest slogan in our history.

One of the great — but, I fear, not universally recognized — virtues of the present Secretary of State is that he understands — far better than do many of his critics — that we cannot bring the enemy to terms without plenty of force and the willingness to use it. He is a lawyer — a very fine one — with considerable experience in diplomacy. But he does not think that the enemy can be cornered by clever argument or a more tightly-drawn contract, or be subdued by tricky diplomatic maneuvers. He recognizes that in handling an adversary of this sort, diplomacy is a very limited instrument, although of course it has not lost its usefulness in dealing with friends. Since he became Secretary of State in January, 1949, Acheson has been the foremost advocate in the government of rearmament — for ourselves and our allies. It is ironic that so many of his bitterest critics are men who have opposed in the past so many measures which increased our strength and that of our allies.

In looking back over the last six years, one can put a finger on probably a few specific mistakes. Personally, I thought our postwar policy in China was wrong and that we should have made a far greater effort to prevent China from falling under Communist control. But among all those who are now bemoaning the loss of China to the Communists, not more than a corporal's guard favored effective action when it might have been taken. Few of them were willing to do more than vote a few additional millions of dollars for Chiang Kai-Shek. They were not willing to send thousands of American officers and noncoms or take the other strenuous actions that every competent observer held to be necessary if Nationalist China were to be saved.

In general, however, we owe our present predicament less to specific mistakes than to attitudes of the mind and weaknesses of spirit. Many of these were quite natural: the let-down after a very considerable effort and strain, the craving to get back to "normalcy." But we were afflicted to an unnecessary degree with myopia and a combination of lassitude and euphoria. In that atmosphere, many people fell under the spell of a double underestimate. They underestimated the enemy and, no less serious, they underestimated our own capabilities. "We can't afford it" became a byword. Some of our chosen representatives seemed to regard the United States as a broken-down invalid. The loudest voices seemed, at times, to be those of the shorter-sighted and flabbier elements in our national life. As late as 1948, when it was already as plain as it is now that we should have been spending billions to build our military strength and that of our allies, they cut taxes again. The practical political effect of that action was to put a temporary ceiling on our efforts to protect ourselves and the free world. It was a blunder of the first magnitude, based on a terrible misreading of the world situation.

And let us not be deceived by assertions that the money could have been found without increasing the total budget by cutting other expenditures. Even then three-fourths of the Federal budget went to paying for previous wars and trying to prevent another one. There was not enough leeway in the remaining fourth to provide the additional funds needed for defense — not even if all the non-war and non-defense activities and services of the Federal government had been obliterated. As much demagoguery is committed in the name of economy as on almost any other subject — which is perhaps not surprising in view of the fact that very few citizens ever have time to read, much less analyze, the Federal budget, even if they can count in the billions. Economy, however, is an instance in which the end is so hard to achieve that many people may feel that almost any means are justified.

In a more intellectual style, the idea that we can't or couldn't afford it, is expressed in the thesis that we should reduce our commitments to match our strength. This is hardly more than a refined way of saying we should continue to appease — and so add to the strength of — the aggressor. The prudent course, if we want to survive, is to increase our strength as much as is necessary to make sure that we do survive. What we can't afford is defeat and annihilation.

The idea that we can't afford to be strong has been shelved, at least temporarily. Of course, there is a limit to our capacity. But it is much higher than our most hypochondriacal representatives thought it was. There is little doubt that we have ample strength to cope with the situation, provided that we use part of it to generate strength into our friends, and so multiply the total strength available to us.

In reviewing the past and the present, we probably should devote a moment to the pilot fisherman — the men who fish for the pilot fish which guide the shark to his prey. Certainly we don't want the pilot fish nosing around in sensitive places — indeed, we would like to exterminate them. Undoubtedly, some people were very slow to recognize the existence of the pilot fish, and slow to realize how diligently and faithfully he works for the shark, and how skillfully he sometimes conceals his stripes.

However, when the net is cast for the pilot fish, it is likely to bring up a lot of other fish, most of them quite innocent creatures, althoug here and there one may look rather odd. It takes experts to distinguish a well-camouflaged pilot fish from harmless and altogether respectable fish. Among the amateur pilot fishermen in Congress, there are not many such experts. Also, like other zealous fishermen, the amateur pilot fishermen like to boast about their catches and are not above spinning tales about the big ones they saw but which got away.

A few of the pilot fishermen have become fanciers of reformed pilot fish — they keep them around as pets, and seem to regard them as the finest forms of marine life. A reformed and repentant pilot fish undoubtedly is much preferable to an unregenerate one. But it is not easy for objective observers to comprehend why it should be regarded as nobler than all the millions of fish which had enough patriotism and ordinary common sense never to work for the shark.

Another curious characteristic of some of the pilot fishermen is that they evince so little interest in the shark. When it has been suggested that it might be a good idea to buy a few harpoons to kill the shark, or at least to drop a net around the beach to keep him out, they have either protested at the expense or scouted the notion that the shark could really bite. Some of them wouldn't even toss a life-line to a man overboard. They seem to regard the pilot fish as more dangerous than the shark.

Despite complacency and lethargy, we have not been inactive or ineffective in these postwar years. Indeed, we have accomplished a great deal. We helped to dislodge the Russians from Iran, where they were trying to inch their way toward the Persian Gulf and Indian Ocean and a grip on the immense oil reserves of the Middle East. We helped to block the Communist thrust toward the Eastern Mediterranean — and the gateway to Africa — through Greece and Turkey. We furnished the help necessary to save Western Europe from chaos and Communist domination by infiltration. We took the lead in organizing the defense of Western Europe against outright military conquest, through the North Atlantic pact and arms aid. We countered the Kremlin's effort to force the West out of Berlin by improvising the air lift. We have held Japan and many other important areas eagerly sought by the Red Axis.

We can take pride in these achievements. Some of them exemplify the highest form of statesmanship: imaginative but firmly rooted in enlightened self-interest — the only kind of self-interest which yields steady dividends.

I think we can say honestly that we assayed the vitality of Asiatic nationalism — at least in part and probably better than did some of the other Western powers. The downfall of Western Imperialism in Asia — only a few vestiges of it remain — closes an epoch stretching back almost to the Age of Discovery. We saw the trend, thought it valid, and encouraged it, not only by example — as in the Philippines — but by prodding the greater colonial powers. The British yielded an Empire barely in time to save most of it for the Commonwealth. The Dutch and the French were a little tardier. Many of the free Asian nations are finding that self-government is not as easy as it looked and that it does not automatically solve economic difficulties. These difficulties are formidable in most of Asia. They appear almost insoluble where the population grows more rapidly than any increase in productivity it is reasonable to expect. But when non-Communist governments are willing to tackle their problems energetically, we would be short-sighted not to lend a helping hand.

On the whole, we have been employing our economic strength to good advantage. I think we may say also that we have scrupulously protected our moral position. Here we have derived some benefits from giving the Kremlin the best of every doubt, from making every concession that could even remotely be justified, and even from turning the other cheek on many occasions. Probably only by doing so could we fully convince ourselves and, gradually, the rest of the free world, that the objectives of the Kremlin are as unlimited and as evil as we know them to be. At every step, we have had to prove to others, as well as to ourselves, that we were overlooking no possibility of peaceful adjustment. There is no satisfactory answer to the reproach that you didn't try all peaceful methods hard enough or long enough before resorting to force. We saw that recently when we were trying to persuade our friends to face up to the Chinese aggression in Korea. By extreme forbearance in these postwar years we have not only held the free world together but strengthened our moral leadership.

Our most serious errors lay, I believe, in dismantling so much of our military power — and, having disarmed so quickly and so far, in not rearming sooner. When we came home after the first world war, we left behind allies with plenty of armed force. In the second world war, the Germans disarmed the French, the Dutch, the Belgians, the Norwegians and others. And the Allies disarmed the Germans and the Italians. Western Europe became a military vacuum, or rather, perhaps, an unarmed hostage on the doorstep of the Soviet Union. The war, followed by the disarming of Japan, left a similar condition in the Far Pacific.

We had the good sense to keep on making atomic bombs and the means of delivering them. Otherwise all probably would have been lost before now. Up to now our atomic weapons have been a counterpoise to the Soviet army — but no more than a counterpoise. The Kremlin knew that if it resorted to direct military aggression, we would reply with the bomb. But if we tried to use the threat of the bomb to bring about a general settlement, the Kremlin had an obvious riposte: to send the Red Army marching into the free fringe of Eurasia.

The most valuable and important section of this fringe is, in many respects, Western Europe. All there is to say about the importance of Western Europe to the free world system and to our own survival has been said many times. It was all said in the debates on interim and the Marshall plan in 1947 and 1948. It was all said again in 1949 in the long debates on the Atlantic pact and arms-aid. It has been said again in the last few weeks — and never better than by the best-known Kansas graduate of West Point. Perhaps the Kansan we honor today would have said it still better. Certainly he would have said it in his unique way. No one can doubt where he would have stood — no one who remembers his service as Chairman of the Committee to Defend America by Aiding the Allies.

Anyone who is not yet convinced probably never will be — unless he should have to take the consequences of his own different advice. Were that to happen, the rest of us would have to suffer, too, and the truth about the experiment might never become known, as the results probably would be compiled by the historians of whatever school happened at the time to enjoy the approval of the Kremlin.

The Soviet atom explosion in September, 1949, was a clear warning that the free world had better make haste in erecting stout defenses — before our own atomic weapons lost their deterring influence on the Kremlin. That is likely to happen when the Russians think they have effective air defenses against our bombers. It may happen when they have enough bombs of their own to wage atomic warfare — perhaps as few as 25. They may think that their power to retaliate with bombs against our friends will inhibit us from using atomic bombs against *them*. We cannot be sure that even a handful of Russian atom bombs would not, as a practical matter, neutralize our immensely larger stockpile.

Until Korea, it seemed to many of us that we were losing the military race. We were moving, but not fast enough. We were poorly prepared to respond to the challenge of overt agression in Korea. It took some courage to respond. And there were risks in doing it. But the consequences of not doing it would have been staggering. The free world almost certainly would have caved in at several points, not only in Asia but probably in the Middle East and parts of Europe.

Some people feared that we were being sucked into a trap: that the Korean aggression was a feint or diversionary prelude to other aggressions. It is quite probable that the Red Axis had planned a number of moves for 1950 and 1951. But if that is so, our response in Korea changed the plan, or at least deferred it. No other move has yet occurred.

From what we know now, we can say with reasonable assurance that we were right to go into Korea in June. We can say with a measure of confidence that we were right also not to make a hasty exit when the Chinese Communists intervened and gave us a setback in Northern Korea. The Chinese Communists are already being made to pay a price for their aggression and in time we may be able to raise the price a good deal higher by a variety of methods.

On the positive side, our response to the challenge in Korea not only saved but injected some vitality into the collective security system. We should not feel discouraged by the fact that some members of the team boggled at the second jump, when the crossbar was raised from three feet to five. Most of them finally got over it. After these successes and with further encouragement, they may be ready for a still higher jump the next time.

Also, out of the Korean aggression has come, at last, a vigorous effort to increase our military power. Our Allies, especially in Europe, also have felt the spur. The rearmament programs now set in motion may transform the whole situation within 18 months or two years. Even if the great war should come in 1951, we will be in better shape to fight it than if the Korean aggression had not occurred and we had not responded to it as we did. It may well be that the Korean aggression — and our reaction to it — have saved our necks.

We have passed through several years of mounting danger. Probably years of danger lie ahead of us. Five, ten, twenty years — who can know? In a way the longer estimates may be the most optimistic. For they usually assume that a greater war can be prevented.

The year 1951 could be the most dangerous of all — not because we and our allies are weaker than we were a year ago. On the contrary, we are stronger. But a year from now, unless somebody stops us, we obviously will be very much stronger. By sometime in 1952, the free world should be ahead in the arms race — the balance of military power may be tilted against the Red Axis — perhaps irrevocably.

Looking at that prospect, the masters of the Kremlin may conclude that 1951 affords them their last chance — for a long time to come, at least. They may be tempted to attack now. Also, they may fear that when the free world has mobilized its strength, it will not be content to stand passively on the defense. Here lies a compelling reason why, in the free world, we should avoid loud talk or hints about so-called preventive war or anything like it.

President Truman and Secretary of State Acheson frequently have been attacked in publications which I shall not name for speaking as if the Communist world and the non-Communist world might live in peace, side by side. That is an utterly impractical notion, these critics say. Those who voice it ought to be thrown out, they say, making way for officials who will proclaim that our objective is to destroy the Communist system at its source.

Now, even if you are convinced that the enemy cannot be tamed or cured and that you can never be safe until you destroy him, is it wise to say so before you are prepared to do it? Whatever their inner thoughts about the future may be, the official spokesmen for the free world should — I submit — be discreet. They ought to say that peaceful coexistence is possible, even if they doubt it or thoroughly disbelieve it.

From where we sit, it is hard to believe that the Politburo will deliberately choose a great war. Unless its defenses against atom bomb carriers are better than we think, Russia would suffer hard punishment. It is hard to see how the Kremlin could expect to win a great war, until it is able to knock out the United States. And almost certainly it does not yet have enough atom bombs to do that.

From where we sit, there appear to be a number of weaknesses behind the iron front of the Communist Empire. Certainly many of the satellite peoples are unwilling prisoners. It is futile for them to try to shoot the jailer when they lack the power to break the lock on the prison door. But it is questionable whether they would zealously defend the prison against some one who might break down the door for them. It is even more questionable if they can be trusted outside the walls — and the same doubt may apply to some of the citizens of the Soviet Union.

Moreover, although they have been producing arms at a tremendous rate, the Russians may be short of a few essential war items such as gasoline.

Stalin has not only saved the Soviet Union but built one of the greatest Empires the world has ever seen. It is not easy to imagine his gambling all he has achieved on a throw of the dice. It would seem more consistent with his renowned wisdom as well as with his own Marxist doctrine, to pause, to sit back and wait for a more opportune time — perhaps when the capitalist system has spiralled down into another great depression.

We do not know how Stalin and his colleagues view these matters. We have no wire recorders in the Kremlin. Not even the most gimlet-eyed keyhole peepers or the longest-eared gossip columnists can tell us what is going on in the minds of the Politburo. The great war might start tomorrow. It may be prevented — forever.

I must confess that it is not easy for me to envisage a long static stalemate between the Red Axis and the free world. It seems doubtful to me that there will ever be a state of affairs justifying the description "peaceful coexistence" — until the Russian regime undergoes a radical change. It is not easy to imagine our feeling secure while an enemy who has avowed his intention to destroy us builds up a stockpile of fission bombs — and fusion bombs — with which he might wipe us out almost at a stroke. It is not easy for me to imagine our feeling secure until the Iron Curtain has been lifted or torn down, until atomic and other super-weapons have been brought under effective international control and until there is freer communication between the peoples of the Soviet Union and the rest of the world. These are not changes which a totalitarian regime can make without risking overthrow or disintegration. We can hope they will come about without a great war but, if we are steadily realistic, we cannot count on it.

I realize that this is an unsatisfactory state in which to leave the future. But there is a limit to the vision, even of a Washington correspondent.

3

NEWSPAPERS AND THE SURVIVAL OF FREE SOCIETY

By Erwin D. Canham

Everywhere in the world today, in some way or other, freedom is in danger. And everywhere in the world freedom of the press, which is a right of the people and not of the press, is also in danger. These dangers, it seems to me, spring from three causes:

• Our failure to make clear to enough people the importance to them, in their daily lives, of the instruments of freedom;

• The efforts of power-hungry men and regimes to destroy freedom;

• The gap between our words and our deeds, the need for doing our job — as the agents of the people — more effectively and responsibly.

In short, freedom itself is in the midst of a crisis of confidence — a crisis of understanding. In this crisis the institution of the press is in the same boat with all the other institutions of freedom. We all face this crisis of confidence. We all need to undertake positive efforts to make clear to the people the importance to them of the institutions we represent. We all need to serve them ever more adequately.

These are truisms which are often expounded to businessmen and to newspapermen when we are in convention assembled and start to beat our breasts. Let us today try to think of the problem in concrete terms.

What has brought about this crisis of confidence? In the case of the free press, and in the case of free institutions, I believe it is because the conditions under which we operate expose us to wide public misunderstanding and unpopularity. Actually conditions of the press — as of free institutions — have changed remarkably for the better, but we have failed to make the fact adequately known to the people either here or elsewhere. On the contrary, we are often attacked for changes which are really improvements.

Newspapering in this country has been revolutionized in the last half-century. (I think many of our other institutions have too.) In the case of newspapers, changing economic conditions have resulted in a decline in apparent competition in a vast majority of American communities. For this we are roundly accused of conspiratorial monopoly. And indeed, from some points of view, the situation is deplorable. We all deeply regret the disappearance of once-great American newspapers.

But what is not usually recalled is the fact that during the same period, the service of American newspapers to their readers has become very much more effective. The news-objectivity of American newspapers, with only a few exceptions, has greatly increased. The typical nineteenth-century newspaper was proudly and violently non-objective. This did not matter when applied to editorials, which are expressions of judgment and opinion anyway. I urge any of the critics of today's newspapers to take a trip into the files. I believe that they will find that the news-adequacy of the columns of almost any American newspaper is noticeably superior to the service of any comparable newspaper at any previous time in American history.

The typical American newspaper has ceased to be the projection of the set of prejudices of a single group of readers. In its news columns at least, it is responsible to the entire community. A few decades ago, the average American newspaper was read by a like-minded group of readers. If it didn't suit them, there was the possibility of changing for another paper. Now which is better: a larger number of newspapers in each of which there is news-distortion and news-prejudice — a multiplicity or error — or a smaller number of newspapers in which an ever-increasing standard of news-objectivity must be maintained? Does truth lie in a diversity of error?

In these days the newspaper which must serve the largest possible number of people in the community does not particularly suit the prejudices of any single segment of them. It is not talking to a like-minded group. Hence it is not particularly popular, and it may have to run the barrage of criticism of the entire community. Nevertheless, it is a far better newspaper — in its news service, at least — than it used to be in the so-called golden age of diversity. The external criticism which it meets can be a very useful disciplinary and muscle-toning influence. We need and can profit by criticism, so long as our response to it is vigorous and constructive. But we should not permit criticism to mount to the pitch where it destroys public confidence. We can meet it only with the facts.

The facts in connection with newspapers are that the public has a basic right to be informed. Only as it is correctly informed can it preserve all its liberties, and maintain a dynamic and free community. The first act of any dictator is to seize control of the channels of information, and to turn them to his thought-control purposes. Laws, even such basic guarantees as the First Amendment to the American Constitution, would not be worth the paper they are written on without public understanding and support. There are splendid paper guarantees of press freedom in the Soviet Constitution. They are worthless, because the people's liberties are kept from them by police power.

The best way to prevent the theft of our freedoms is to make sure the people understand their importance. And so newspapers must continue to explain and to illustrate and to exemplify in their daily service the importance of information to people. We must make clear to people the difference between the old, special-group, prejudice-serving newspaper, and the total public-serving newspaper which is the typical pattern today. We must balance criticism with understanding. It is fine to live in the dog house — if you're a dog — but neither American newspapers nor any other public-serving institution can afford to neglect public misunderstanding of their basic role.

We are living at one of the great turning-points of human history. Either the world will move in the direction of more freedom or of less freedom. Either we will strengthen and broaden — here and elsewhere — the institutions of representative government, political, economic, and social, or we will strengthen authoritarianism and the big state. The conflict in directions is manifest everywhere in the world. What can we Americans do about it as individuals, what can we do about it collectively?

It is my thesis today that within American society we have already evolved the basic institutions which can preserve freedom, but that we do not know what we have done. Still less have we communicated our achievement to other peoples. We have the machinery of communication, but we have not yet learned what it is we must say.

Before I justify this observation, let us take a quick look at the world in which we live. We emerged from the Second World War, six and a half short years ago, with high hopes for a cooperative and peaceful world. I believe that it was utterly inevitable that we should have made an effort to live amicably with the Soviet Union on the basis of trust and confidence.

Indeed, I believe that even now — while we struggle to create a power balance in the world — we should never cease trying to convince the Russians, big and little, that we have no hatred toward them, no designs on their territory, no intention of blotting out their legitimate and large place in the sun. Whatever else we may have to do, we should never obscure to all other peoples the fact that the true meaning of America to the world is neither militaristic nor materialistic, but moral.

However, we learned the hard way that the men in the Kremlin were not willing to accept a moral world. Following hard upon the destruction of German and Japanese military power we dismantled our own military power, all except the atomic bomb. The bomb alone kept, and perhaps keeps, Communist power from spreading farther into the vacuums that surrounded its territories. Successively we resisted the onrush of this power in Greece and Turkey and in Berlin. Through the Marshall Plan we sought to prevent Communist use of the economic plight of most other nations to conquer them. Up to the present, these have been reasonably effective measures.

Then we helped organize the North Atlantic Treaty Organization and we supported western European unification. In Korea, against all the evidence and almost by instinct rather than by rational thought, we resisted Communist aggression. That means that, despite our continuing difficulties in Korea, we have saved Japan. Had Communist power swept in 1950 down the Korean peninsula until it faced Japan across the straits of Tsushima, it would have been exceedingly difficult to prevent Japan's industrial potential and skilled manpower from falling victim to the aggression a few miles away. The same fate would have befallen the even more skilled and potent west German industrial complex had we not resisted in Berlin and prepared the nucleus of a western European force.

Meantime, somewhere along the way, our military technicians appear to have let us down. The jet planes which would have been the match of the MIGs over Korea should have been on the drafting boards some seven years ago. They apparently were not. The long-range bombers which would have been the equal of what they might encounter in Russian skies should have been on the drafting boards. Let me interpolate that one of the best ways never to have to meet those Russian planes is to be ready with superior force if necessary. Instead, we came up with the B-36's, and of them, the less said the better. Perhaps the President and Secretary Johnson, the other politicians, Congress, and public opinion — in which newspapers bear part of the responsibility — were to blame.

Somewhere else along the way, we lost the technical secrets of the atomic bomb. How we lost the atomic bomb — and, indeed, how we got it in the first place — is an interesting and significant study. If Hitler and Mussolini had not applied their barbaric and specious racial doctrines, they would not have driven out of Europe the scientists who brought a good share of the essential secrets of atomic fission with them. Albert Einstein . . . Lise Meitner . . . Niels Bohr . . . Enrico Fermi . . . these were key men and women. They would have been working in Europe if hate had not driven them away. And now did we lose the secrets? First, because we had failed to show Alan Nunn May, Klaus Fuchs, and the pitiful quartet of Gold, Greenglass, and the Rosenbergs that the free system is better than Communist totalitarianism. Second, because along with our British ally we failed to comprehend the possibility of treason. We carried confidence too far. President Roosevelt at the Quebec Conference agreed to accept, without further security check, the British assurances of their scientists. The British failed to take seriously the proof of Klaus Fuchs' life as a communist spy when the Nazis sent it to them. They thought it was an effort to divide the Allies.

In this digression, something of the moral strengths and weaknesses of our system are revealed. As a final footnote, I might add that if Hitler had not been so obsessed with ego, so stubbornly set on his own whims and concepts, the Nazis would have had great quantities of guided missiles before we would have been able to mount and launch the cross-channel landings. It would have been a very different world, all along the way, if these various moral crises had been invariably resolved on the side of reason and perception.

In any event, we find ourselves today in a situation where the physical strength of the anti-communist alliance appears to be growing, but with many setbacks and grave dangers. We need moral tenacity and steadiness and patience in these days more, perhaps, than anything else. We need to understand and to communicate to others the essential terms of the crisis.

What are these terms? What is this crisis? One way to put it is to say that for the last century or more, men have made fabulous progress in conquering nature but have failed to conquer themselves. We have an actual and potential control of our physical environment which raises us far out of our former dependence on materiality. But this very preoccupation with matter and mechanics has seemed to make us more materialistic than ever. Our need and opportunity today is to awaken.

Therefore let me lay before you today the facts to which I believe we should awaken, and some concept of what we should do about it. First, it seems to me we should realize ourselves, and communicate to others, the exact nature of the vast hoax Communism has perpetrated on much of mankind. The biggest of totalitarianism's big lies is the traditional and widely accepted belief that we in the so-called capitalist world are doomed to the defense of the status quo, while Communism is dedicated to change — to revolution.

The fact is that Communism, like totalitarianism of the right as well as of the left, is reaction. Since it says that man must be subordinated to the state, in effect enslaved by the state, it is reaction and tyranny no different from all the dictators which have existed since the dawn of society. Pharaohs . . . caesars . . . czars . . . emperors . . . kings . . . fuehrers . . . commissars . . . they are all part of the pattern of absolutism. They do not set men free; they do not liberate. Our system is based on the rights of man. It does set men free; it does liberate. Not man as a mere selfish anarchistic entity, but man, God's man, as the highest social value in the community — which often means sacrifice of selfish purposes for the good of all.

Our system is not shackled to the status quo. Our enterprisers are continually asking, as a matter of course and condition of survival, if there are not better ways to do tomorrow the tasks they are carrying out today. We are committed to perfectibility, as a social principle. We must therefore refuse to accept dogmatism and the closed mind. We will be saved just to the degree that our minds remain open to criticism, to analysis, to challenge, to improvement.

We it is, therefore, who ought to be and really are the true revolutionaries in the world today. And yet, by propaganda and by our own failures to understand and to communicate, we have let much of the world fall into the delusion that we are defending things as they are. We have lost the battle of slogans and the songs — yes, and of manifestos. We were once very good at slogans and songs and manifestos. They are still implicit in our system. The Declaration of Independence and Lincoln's Gettysburg speech are among the greatest manifestos of history. Even Wilson's Fourteen Points and the Roosevelt-Churchill Four Freedoms were capable of moving men and did. But, of course, manifestos are not enough. We were forced to compromise the principles of the Fourteen Points and the Four Freedoms. Our acts were not consistent with our words. And we lost those battles for men's minds — or largely lost them.

But this time we must win. It is a turning point — a crisis. Let us, therefore, proclaim anew the truths we live by, and let us put our words into deeds. If we are to declare anew the true revolution, let us carry it out. The fact is, of course, that we are carrying it out in part every day.

Take our own unfinished business inside U. S. A. — above all, take our racial problem. No doubt we have lagged seriously and inexcusably in not working out more justice and equality of opportunity for Negroes and for people of other races or religions who sometimes face barriers of prejudice. We must take seriously the degree we fall short of an adequate standard of justice and equality of opportunity; we must dedicate ourselves to the improvement of our works.

But the more important fact is not that we have unfinished business. It is that we have done so much. Considering the scale and economic and social complexity of the Negro position in the United States, it is remarkable that we have come so far in achieving opportunity and justice. That, not our shortcomings, is the historic achievement. This is no excuse and no apology for the gap. It is a plain statement of historic fact. Scarcely anywhere else in the world today can men of diverse races and religions enjoy as much freedom and opportunity as is available in the United States. But it is not good enough, and it will be — it must be — better tomorrow.

There are other ways in which we must convert our commitments into action. Communism is a potent export doctrine. The free system ought to be. We should make available to other nations and peoples the essential elements of our system which can be turned to their use. This does not mean that we should ever try to make others over into our image. Neither the political nor the economic systems which we use are perfectly adapted to the needs of people with other experience, traditions, aptitudes, disciplines. We and our forebearers have had several centuries to learn how to operate our system in its evolutionary progress, starting, say, with Magna Carta. To expect the Indonesians or the Guatemalans to take the American Constitution, engraved on crackling parchment, and apply it effectively, is a fantasy. And yet the Indonesians and Guatemalans need the essence of representative institutions, and of an operative free economic system, adapted to their needs and experience.

One of the most useful things that could be done today — and a beginning has been made — would be to set up international teams skilled in the operation to specific public tasks and make them available to nations with a problem. The United Nations and some of its subsidiary organizations have made an admirable start toward filling this need.

I do not know, and I do not believe anybody knows, just how much freedom a given people can operate, nor through what technique they can do it. But they ought to have the ingredients and the institutions of free society available.

For example, an international team ought to be ready to go on call into some area to assist in setting up a police force which would protect rather than terrorize the community. Another team should be available to show people how to collect taxes fairly and effectively (maybe we could invite such a team to Washington for consultation). There should be a team on setting up an educational system or a sanitation system, or a power plant, or a method of operating the secret ballot and free elections.

These functions are the warp and woof of democracy. Rather than putting the stress on drafting a noble Constitution — and the Soviet and the Argentine Constitutions are excellent documents in many ways — we need to create an international pool of practical knowledge on making the elements of democracy work. You cannot evoke the discipline and tradition, say, of the Scandinavian community by writing it down on a paper. But the Scandinavians, and many others, should be on hand to show other people how it's done — or, rather — how it can be done in terms of specific national or community aptitude and experience.

Just as I believe American newspapers have changed form — and hence need to be redefined and reclarified to the people — so it seems to me that basic changes in the free enterprise or capitalistic system have come about which are little understood. I believe there has gradually come into being a new atmosphere and new techniques of cooperation as well as competition, and a new measure of social responsibility, which makes American enterprise at mid-century a far more effective, fruitful, and operative institution than it was in 1900. I also believe economic power has been tremendously decentralized, which is all to the good. Nowhere in the United States today does such power exist as reposed in the Morgan firm in 1900. Or in the railroads. But the major change, it seems to me, is in the extraordinary speed of voluntary private organization. We have created — without consciously meaning to do so — the workable, effective and far superior alternative to cartels on the one hand or socialism on the other. We have added a measurably new dimension to our economic system.

Voluntary private organization in the United States has opened up channels of interchange of ideas, techniques, skills, friendships which are transcendent in their effect on our economic system. I can remember the day when a textile manufacturer in my native Maine would keep armed guards at the factory gates to keep away any intruder from the competitive mill, and then he might hire spies to try and discover his competitor's trade secrets. Today, if a manufacturer develops a new process, he is likely to be reading a paper about it at the next meeting of his trade association. Or his chief engineer will be describing the process proudly to the meeting of his professional group. Or the chief chemist will have written a learned article about it for a technical journal.

Data to prove my point could be piled up through thousands of examples. In short, we have learned that it is much more effective and beneficial to pool information than it is to hoard it. We have learned that sharing pays off. And that is an extremely important corner to turn in social and economic organization. It has helped measurably to raise standards of American achievement in every field of endeavor. It has not destroyed competition, but has focused the competitive drive toward doing a constantly better job.

As a result, we have generalized achievement. This is not merely a matter of standard of living, although it can most easily be studied in those terms, for a standard of living is merely the symbol of opportunity and achievement. But consider the elements of life and daily experience available to a millionaire on the one hand, and to an ordinary, steadily employed man on the other. The working man can obtain a house that will be as well heated, as clean, as snug and pleasing in its scale as that of the millionaire. He can have as attractive carpets on the floor, pictures on the wall, and chairs to sit in — if he or his wife has taken advantage of the many opportunities to develop good taste. His dinner will be as good, and perhaps better, since his wife will probably be a better cook than whoever the millionaire can employ. His motor-car will be as swift and just about as sleek, his entertainment as diverting, there will be no limits to the cultural opportunities open to him. He can go on his vacation to just about as salubrious a spot, and he probably gets more time to go on a little hunting trip. His wife and daughters will be dressed and groomed so that they are indistinguishable at ten paces from the millionaire's women-folk.

In short, we have gone a very long way toward generalizing opportunity and accomplishment. This means that we have gone a long way toward removing envy as a social element, and that is a great achievement.

I say all this because I believe we have not yet begun to make the case which will save freedom to and for the people of our nation and of the world. We have not adequately sold them on what freedom depends: upon the continuance of a system whose chief dedication is a constant daily challenge of the status quo.

This is the sort of thing that newspapermen and all others should be saying if we are to bring into being the degree of public understanding which will prevent the destruction of freedom. I said at the beginning that there were concerted efforts of power-hungry men and regimes to destroy freedom. We know too well of the conspiracies of totalitarian systems and police states, whether of the left or of the right. They are deep-dyed reaction, no different in essence from all the despots down the ages. They are the true reactionaries. They have an ideological and dogmatic status quo which denies civil liberties. But I do not need to argue the point. We know how such regimes destroy freedom. We are erecting barriers against them.

Far more dangerous is the threat to freedom, partly from ignorance, which comes from within. In the area of information —

of the public's right to know — this danger is very great. All over the United States, from the White House to the county courthouse, public officials fail to understand and accept their duty to let the facts be known. President Truman's recent executive order setting up a system of classifying, and withholding, information throughout all the civilian departments of government, was the most graphis and sweeping blueprint or suppression. The President's avowed purpose — to prevent military secrets from being made public — is challengable. But there is plenty of machinery to protect such information right now. The Executive Order, as in so many other activities of big government, sets up a system capable of gravest abuse. It "threw out the baby with the bath water." It is being vigorously resisted, and, in the face of the outcry, the President has curbed such agencies as sought to use the new system for suppression. But the order is still on the books, and it could be used to draw a cloak over governmental malfeasance at any time.

Such high-level action is reflected throughout national officialdom. In virtually every community in the country, newspapers have had to fight and fight hard in recent years to obtain or retain access to public records. In some instances, it should be pointed out, there is a conflict of rights. An adjustment is necessary between the right of the people to know, and the right of privacy, or the right of an individual to a fair trial. For instance, in demanding the right of access to relief rolls, newspapers have no intention of throwing the relief system back into the dark days of pauper lists and the public poor house. No such revision is necessary. But it is necessary that the public's representative — the newspaper — exercise the right of checking up on how the public's money is being spent. If newspapers don't check up, no independent authority will be able to check up. And no activity of government can degenerate — and ultimately ruin itself — more quickly than the agency which does not have the life-giving benefit of an independent check-up.

For some years the American Society of Newspaper Editors — and this is another illustration of the values of voluntary private organization — has maintained a Freedom of Information Committee. We have had the benefit of the studies of highly expert, specialized counsel. And we have maintained a set of vigilant watchmen throughout the nation, seeking to expose and defeat every instance of a violation of the people's right to know. More important than this defensive struggle, no doubt, is the positive effort to help the people understand why it is vital that their right to know shall not be violated, and to comprehend the newspaper's role in defending it.

But newspapers do not own the right of press freedom. It belongs to the people. Newspapers are merely stewards. Here, then, the retention of freedom depends upon a better discharge of stewardship. I could make — and you could make — another whole speech pointing out the shortcomings of newspapers. Certainly we are imperfect — if we weren't, we would be declining, and newspapers must more effectively accept their responsibility to the entire community. The only alternative to dwindling diversity in the newspaper field is the voluntary and conscientious acceptance of responsibility. Such responsibility cannot be enforced by law. Legal and political restraints upon newspapers, beyond the well-established bounds of libel, slander, obscenity, and so on, can easily destroy freedom. This fact is reasonably well understood.

Newspapers are frequently urged to follow the example of bar associations and medical associations, and set up self-licensing systems. But any license, even though it be imposed by other newspapermen, is repressive and intolerable in the field of ideas. The battle for freedom has to be made on behalf of the worst, rather than for the best. I believe that if the great press martyrs of the past — the great spokesmen for the free world — had been required to obtain a license from a majority of their colleagues, they would have been suppressed before they started. Great ideas are not necessarily popular. Unorthodoxy is often the key to true freedom.

So we cannot look for better performance by newspapers to any kind of official or legal restraints. But we can expect great improvement through the acceptance of voluntary responsibility, spurred by a steady flow of invigorating criticism. There has never been a time when American newspapers were more conscious of the need of self-improvement than they are today. Moreover, the citizen holds a decisive whiphand over newspapers any time he wishes to exercise it. It is the nickel which does — or does not — drop on the newsstand counter. This is not a perfect and total control. It can veto, but it cannot necessarily bring about improvement. Indirectly, it tends to do so. It is one, at least, of the final tests.

And with it, goes the acceptance of social responsibility which has been the keynote of our modern years in American experience. More and more leaders in the fight for freedom have realized that the key to survival is the acceptance of social responsibility. They have acted on that knowledge.

But an endless task lies ahead of us all: it is the task of keeping people alert to the constant dangers to freedom; the task of helping them to understand the effectiveness and the revolutionary character of the instruments of freedom we already have; the need of challenging the status quo and accepting the duty of doing more effectively tomorrow the tasks we perform today.

4

NEW DIMENSIONS IN THE NEWS

By Palmer Hoyt

It would be interesting to know the kind of advice that William Allen White would give young men and young women about to enter journalism today. I am sure that he would agree with me on one thing — never has the opportunity for those entering into newspaper work been as great or as valuable or as challenging as now.

Today, a new importance attaches to the development and proper functioning of the whole field of mass communications. And this is particularly true in connection with newspapers. In fact, one might say that as the mass communications of radio and television develop in variety and extent, thus bringing the world closer together, the newspaper has entered into a new field—the field of balance and stabilization.

As a matter of simple fact, our civilization is held together by an extremely tenuous thread, and that thread increasingly needs the strong wax of practical journalism to preserve it, keep it strong and to make it possible for democracy to endure.

And, may I say, that despite increased costs of almost unbelievable proportions in all fields of newspaper operation, such as newsprint, labor and administrative costs, newspapers generally have continued to do an increasingly competent and conscientious job.

Naturally in the realm of overall American newspaperdom, which embraces the operations of seventeen hundred dailies and eleven thousand weeklies, there are some glaring examples of incompetence, of bad thinking and of worse performance; but in general, it is apparent that the newspapers of this country are increasingly recognizing their responsibilities, the reasons for their responsibilities, and that they propose to meet these responsibilities in the strongest possible way. This is of great importance in our lives — this matter of the recognition by newspapers of their responsibilities — because never has the burden of proof and presentation been so strong on newspapers, and never has it been so clear that nothing will supplant the newspapers as a key fact in our complex civilization.

I was graduated from the University of Oregon School of Journalism in 1923. Just before commencement day, a great and good friend of mine who had loaned me money to finish school, expressed extreme regret that I was going into the newspaper business. I shall never forget his words. The gentleman said, and he was an outstanding success in his own field, "I am sorry you are going into newspapers, because in ten years there will be no newspapers."

And I asked, "Why not?"

He said, "The radio will supplant them. There will be no more newspapers."

History now reveals that the greatest boon to the development of newspapers was this same radio. Certainly it is true that the radio did furnish some competition, competition for available reading time, competition for the advertising dollar, and so on, but the advent of radio forced the newspapers to become better, to become more readable, and to more completely fulfill their obligation to their circulation areas.

There has never been any doubt in my mind but that the increased flow of news through radio newscasts tremendously increased the numbers of newspaper readers.

For many years I was connected with the *Portland Oregonian*, which then operated two radio stations, and as our newscasts increased, so our circulation increased and in the same proportion as the mounting volume of news spoken into the air each day and night.

I see no threat to newspapers in the advent of television. It is virtually impossible for television to enter into competition with newspapers in the presentation of news because of the difficulties of picturization. Of course, there is always the commentator reading a news report. This, however, is hardly so exciting that it becomes a necessary part of the life of any person who is genuinely interested in news and its background.

Right there in that word "background" is one of the obvious responsibilities of the press. It is increasingly necessary for newspapers, without departing from their highly held standards of objective news reporting, to give adequate background about important stories and events so that the reader will be informed and can, in due turn, make his own judgments.

It is true that in the case of television, some economic threat is apparent in the division of advertising funds particularly on the national levels. However, it is equally true that television has been tried in many merchandising efforts and has been found wanting. For example, department stores generally do not depend on television to merchandise their varied stocks. Experiments in New York years ago indicated that mass purchasing can not be left to the bracketed and divided audiences which view television.

Principal economic menace to newspapers at the present time from this new child of mass communications is the diversion of funds on big national accounts. However, this will stabilize itself, and as in the case of radio, television will be responsible for developing vast new sums of advertising money. Increasingly, manufacturer, wholesaler, retailer and purchaser are recognizing that advertising with its information, with this suggestion of the right of choice, with its automatic guarantee of superior products, is one of the least expensive items in the American budget.

Advertising men and dealers in mass communication generally like to talk about "impact," but still the greatest daily impact in the United States is the daily newspaper, forgetting about magazines, news magazines, weekly newspapers, class magazines, trade journals and all other publications that appeal to class audiences.

Today more than 50 million daily newsapers are being circulated to and being read by the public. Exact figures are interesting. In 1951, the daily newspaper circulation reached 53,593,000, which happened to be just 25,000 short of the all time mark of 53,618,000 in 1950. For the record, I might say that at the beginning of 1952 there were 1507 evening papers, 363 morning papers and 564 Sunday papers in the United States. Evening newspapers represented a total circulation of 32,225,000, the highest total ever recorded. Morning papers were slightly off from the preceding year — at 20,457,000. Sunday circulation at the end of 1952 was 45,907,000. Figuring the normal three readers for every paper, it is easy to come to the realization that our daily and Sunday newspaper readership more than equaled our total population of approximately 150 million persons. This, of course, is not equaled elsewhere in the world, all factors considered, and brings clearly to point the fact that the American public is the best informed public in the world.

There is impact for you, impact every day of the year, Sundays and holidays included. There are readers equal to our total population.

This same impact, of course, connotes tremendous responsibility, particularly in this era when new dimensions are entering the news picture. There is the dimension of completeness, more necessary than ever because of the partial and suggestive treatment given the news by radio and television. This emphasizes the great need for newspapers to run key speeches and key addresses, complete publication of vital civic reports and adequate reporting of responsible statements by community leaders. This is more difficult than formerly. Due to the fantastic increase in newsprint prices, every inch of space must be weighed and evaluated by every newspaper editor in the United States.

Then, of course, there are the dimensions of the news itself brought sharply to mind by McCarthyism. May I pause for a moment and analyze McCarthyism. McCarthyism to me has several meanings. First, it is a synonym for irresponsible charges. Second, it is a description of an era: An era in which the charge becomes more important than the trial, the proof or the acquittal.

Historically, there is nothing new about McCarthyism. It is a form of witch hunting which varies in importance in connection with the era in which it is practiced. However, the modern form of McCarthyism was made important by its leading proponent, the Senator from Wisconsin, Joseph E. McCarthy, who has substituted newspaper headlines for proof, and whose reckless charges have shocked and excited the nation.

Elmer Davis, the noted news commentator, has recently stated that to date, Joseph E. McCarthy has yet to prove a single charge. Under the operational plan of McCarthy, plain proof is not essential to his purposes; because each new charge produces a trial in the public prints. This represents a problem for newspapers with which they will have to cope individually. There is no basic law which will insure newspapers against the evils of mccarthyism in handling of headlines and news events. Of the three phases of the problem mentioned, headlines, deadlines and news events, the greatest problem to face is, of course, deadlines. Actually, it works out something like this. Twenty minutes before the press time of a given newspaper, Joseph E. McCarthy accuses John Jones of being a Communist. It just happens that John Jones is not a Communist, but the charge, made under senatorial immunity, is flashed over the wires of one or all of the news services. Then the bannerline. McCarthy says: "John Jones is a Communist". Now let's see what happens to John Jones the "Communist."

As I said, this particular John Jones is not a Communist, so eventually he gets around to a factual denial of these charges and a documentation of his innocence. What happens to the story then? Does it have a banner line? I am afraid that it does not. It gets a small space inside, perhaps on the first classified page.

The problem of fair play is important, both to the newspaper involved and to the future of our freedoms. One newspaper, the *Denver Post,* has taken upon itself the task of making a study of the situation and trying to cope with it. To this end, I have had a number of meetings with my news executives and we have researched the field quite thoroughly.

We have not yet found any golden road to Rome. But at least we have aired the problem and are still airing it, and thus have insured greater precaution in the handling of loose charges, mouthed under an immunity that is rapidly becoming distasteful to our citizens.

Just before I left Denver, I dictated a memorandum which I will share with you. This is the memorandum:

Office memorandum: Ed Dooley, Managing Editor
From: Palmer Hoyt, Editor and Publisher
"In view of the mounting tide of McCarthyism, I would like to review with you certain precautions which may be taken to guard against loose charges, irresponsible utterances and attempts at character assassination by 'spokesmen,' official or otherwise.

"First: Instruct the news staff always to evaluate the source of the charge.

"Second: Ask the news staff to weigh the story and see what they would do with it if official immunity were lacking.

"Three: Discuss with the news staff the general proposition of whether or not the *Post* can withhold publication of this particular moot story until proper proof or a qualifying answer can be obtained from the person, organization or group accused.

"Four: Ask the news staff whether they of their own knowledge know a doubtful charge to be false, and to apply any reasonable doubt they may have to the treatment of the story.

"Five: In connection with the banner lines or other headlines on this type of story, ask the news staff to determine whether wording is used as shock treatment or to summarize the facts.

"It is obvious that many charges made by reckless or impulsive public officials can not and should not be ignored, but it seems to me that news stories and headlines can be presented in such a manner that the reading public will be able to measure the real worth or value and true meaning of the stories.

For example, when it is possible and practical, we should remind the public in case of a wild accusation by Senator McCarthy that this particular Senator's name is synonymous with poor documentation and irresponsible conduct and that he has made many charges that have been insupportable under due process.

"In connection with the play of the story which can not be ignored, it is possible that it can be played down. For example, it might be placed in the middle or lower part of page one, or inside the paper and given smaller headlines. If it must be given a large display, I would advocate and I wish you would consult with your staff as to the advisability of this procedure: The addition of a kicker line such as 'Today's McCarthyism' or 'Mc-Carthy charges today'.

"Please advise your staff that the *Denver Post* is alert to the problem of McCarthyism and we are anxious to take every possible step to protect the innocent and give everyone under the fire of McCarthy or other "official" spokesman every possible chance to defend themselves. If possible, we want to give them that chance in the same story, but in any event as quickly after as possible and with the same news emphasis. I wish that you would instruct the news staff that the *Post* will not consider any story complete and covered until rebuttal and answering statements are printed. Also, please remind the news staff that it is our policy to request of the press associations rebuttals from those under attack, and to ask the associations to use every possible effort to move these mitigating or diluting statements in time for proper play in connection with any McCarthy or similar attacks.

"There are, of course, many similar devices which may be used in connection with one-sided stories, and which will be a matter of judgment on the part of the news editors; such as, a blackface precede or a drop-in in a particular story of accusation saying that similar charges have been made by this source but that no proof has ever been submitted, or calling attention to the fact that those attacked have not had the opportunity to answer or disprove the charges.

"As far as the *Post* is concerned, the accused will be given every opportunity to prove his case and the *Post* stands ready to print rebuttal or comment."

This memorandum was presented to our news staff with the idea that they would share with me the solution of a very real problem, which presently in too many instances makes the front page of an American newspaper a courtroom for the trial of loose, undocumented or unproven charges.

Elmer Davis, hitherto mentioned, holds that truth has three dimensions: the truth, the whole truth and nothing but the truth. So it seems to me the news might have similar aspects as: 1. The news itself as reported; 2. the truth of the news as presented; and 3. timing of the charge and the reply.

All of these three dimensions of the news should and could be properly taken into account by a news editor in determining the play for a story which qualified as a "McCarthy coup".

The danger of mccarthyism is now heightened by the recent threat to investigate American colleges. Whether or not such an investigation will be made and whether or not McCarthy will make it is still moot, but the fact is that the dragging of the intimate life of the American colleges across the screen of public scrutiny is fraught with grave dangers to the whole pattern and practice of freedom. And it is a matter which should be of great concern to any and all persons who prize their American citizenship and its accompanying American franchise of freedom.

Actually, I do not think that the investigation of American colleges and education in general will come to anything.

It is my view that the American jury of public opinion has already passed on Communism. I believe that the American public has viewed the Communists and found them wanting. It is my further contention that the American people want no part of the Communists; that they view them as dangerous; that they view Communism as merely another name for Russian imperialism; that they hold American-born Communists to be traitors and that they ask only that the government of the United States be alert and that through due process that they investigate the Communists and their activities both in and out of government.

The danger would seem to be in an investigation of "communism" in American education generally and in American colleges in particular that it will turn out to be a witch hunt in fact and the quarry will not be the red fox of communism but the free flying eagle of American liberalism.

Educators are now saying that liberal teachers are afraid to voice their views on economic and social subjects lest they be charged with being fellow travelers. Before we close this subject, I would like to say again due process is the answer, and again I want to say that I do not believe that Joseph McCarthy or anyone else can indict the 350 thousand members of school boards in the United States, or the thousands of regents and trustees of the American colleges and universities, or the tens of thousands of American teachers or the millions of American undergraduates.

And, speaking of undergraduates, I want to say that the undergraduates in the schools of journalism are very important to the newspaper business — because these are the men and women who will be journalism leaders of tomorrow.

We have reviewed today some of the problems that face the newspaper business. There are many more. As a matter of fact, the newspaper business will always, and should always, have pressing problems for solution. These problems will always be greater — they will never be less. Their solution will increasingly call for trained minds, dedicated men and women. Where better to get them than from the schools of journalism?

For years, certain publishers, managing editors and city editors took pride in scoffing at school of journalism graduates. Fortunately, these dodo birds are almost extinct. Business, generally, in the United States places a high value on college graduates. Why should journalism be the only branch of American business that denies the value of a college education?

The school of thought that holds that journalism can't be taught is increasingly smaller. The principal advocate of this school was Robert M. Hutchins, one-time president of the University of Chicago. Mr. Hutchins not only had a low opinion of the schools of journalism, but also believed that journalism could not be taught. He, of course, overlooked the obvious fact that journalism has many didactic problems; things that can be taught most advantageously. To sum it all up, we have found on the *Denver*

Post that school of journalism graduates and qualified former students of journalism go farther faster than untrained cubs.

Early in these remarks, I referred to William Allen White. I would like to close with a few quotations from his editorials, which, though written years ago, well point up problems of the day.

Mr. White said:

"The only excuse an editor has for being is that his paper shall print the news. The question that comes to every man running a newspaper is: what is news? That he must settle for himself, and having found a rule, must stick as closely to it as possible. When an editor begins monkeying with his conscience, stretching his rule to shield his friends or to punish his enemies, he is lost. . ."

These words from the great editor's pencil clearly expound the editor's obligation.

In the next quotation, if you will substitute mccarthyism for gossip on the grand scale, you will see that his views are equally sound. I quote:

"Every day matters come up in every community, big or little, that are disagreeable to print. Nasty stories are always afloat. Gossip is always in the air. An editor in a town of one hundred people could fill a six-column daily with gossip alone, if he could keep from being lynched. Much of it would be false and all of it would be unfair. And yet often these matters come up in such a shape that they may not be ignored. And here is where an editor has to set his jaw and go ahead following his conscience without fear or favor. Such times come to every attorney, to every doctor, to every preacher, to every man in every relation of life."

The principles of journalism enunciated by Mr. White in 1903 are as sound today as they were at the dawn of the twentieth century. But here at the mid-century point, the judgment and the conscience of editors are under the severest test in the history of American journalism.

Today, men "with a grievance against his fellow men" are ignoring the courts of law to spread their charges with despicable resklessness under the protective cloak of congressional immunity. They are raising matters "in such a shape that they may not be ignored." They are challenging editors to "set their jaws," to re-examine their consciences.

In 1913, Mr. White rephrased the credo of the *Emporia Gazette*. "What chiefly we are aiming at," he wrote, "is to reflect in good, simple English the events of the day in the light of such truth as providence has given us, and to comment on the events of the day as candidly and as honestly and as understandingly as the good Lord will let us."

That, if you please, is a great expression of the basic function of the American newspaper. And, if that function continues to be followed, this great democracy may face the future with confidence.

5

NEWSPAPERING AS IT SEEMS TO ME

By GROVE PATTERSON

Few experiences in my life as a newspaperman have been more rewarding than the privilege of my friendship with William Allen White. Notwithstanding his nation-wide reputation, justly earned, as America's best-loved editor, the finest thing about Bill White was his immeasurable capacity for friendship. No knight in armor could have been more invincible against an evil foe, yet he was the gentlest, most gracious and generous of men. Little notes that he wrote me from time to time are among my treasured possessions. No man, despite his abilities and his distinguished position in American life and letters, could have been more modest.

I remember once when I was president of the American Society of Newspaper Editors, some highly advertised member was late for his part in the program of the convention. I took my predicament to Bill White. I asked him to go on, despite the lack of previous notice.

"I'll get up and talk," he said, "until you see this character show up at the door — then you cut me off." I did — to the loss of the Society. No American, newspaperman or not, should fail to read *The Autobiograhpy of William Allen White.*

When he was 65, Mr. White wrote a booklet which happily was sent to many of his friends. He called it, *"Thoughts at 65."* In it, among other observations, he wrote, "Out of each friend's eyes I see looking the same essential individual that I saw in childhood and I am sure they all see the same in me. The years have done nothing to that deep, final something that is personality. It is changeless. It has resisted the years and the torture of the flesh; why may it not be immortal — that mysterious spiritual essence that we call personality, for short, the soul?

"Being 65, I shall probably know quicker than most people, and that does not disturb me. I fear vastly more a futile, incompetent old age than I do any form of death. As one grows into his middle sixties, death seems more reasonable than it does in childhood and youth. The thought of death used to terrify me. Now it seems a natural thing, a part of life, just another experience, whatever it is . . . In the meantime, life has been good, a tremendously interesting adventure. I have never had a bored hour in my life. I get up every morning now, wondering what new, strange, gorgeous thing is going to happen, and it always happens at fairly reasonable intervals."

Bill White lived quite a long time after 65, and I do not think the happy pattern of his life changed. Honors and deep satisfactions continued to come to him and he deserved them. For him, life indeed was a spiritual adventure. He went hunting with high hopes, faithful to whatsoever things were of good report, and he came home with a full mind and a light heart.

Before reaching what I might, with some exaggeration, call the main substance of his address, I wish, in the first few minutes, to make to students of journalism a few specific observations and suggestions relating to newspapers, growing out of 48 years' experience. They may be trival but I hope not impractical. I may be giving expression merely to some personal idiosyncrasies.

The man who makes the largest contribution to the day by day impression which your newspaper gives the reader is not the reporter, not the editor. He is the copy reader, the man who writes the heads. It happens that much of my earlier experience was on the copy desk. I spent more time on the copy desk, sometimes cruelly called the convalescent home of reporters who have lost their legs, than I did on the street. I am therefore particularly sympathetic with and particularly critical of copy readers.

These preliminary observations, as well as all the rest, I have put into items. My first item, then, deals with the copy desk. In fairness, let me say at the beginning that many of the faults and failures of copy readers are owing to a lack of time, especially on afternoon papers, and to penurious publishers who do not provide a large enough staff. Nevertheless, copy readers could do so much and often do so little.

Now, the average reporter will write as well as he knows how, which often is not very good. But after all, he has an approximate knowledge of the English language and he puts words together as well as he can, up to the limit of his experience. But a large number of copy readers are men of more maturity, with years of writing behind them. Yet most of them appear to consider themselves as

merely head writers. With a desk that is not defensibly under-
staffed the copy reader should have not only the skill but the
ambition to make a well-written story out of a badly written one.
The English language is so rich in its potentialities, so varied and
arresting and dramatic in its almost endless galaxy of words, that
I cannot understand why a copy reader does not love to play with
it. Of course, if your average reporter could write like Henry
Mencken, or Somerset Maugham, or Ernie Pyle, that would be
better yet, and then your copyreader could be reduced logically and
legitimately to head writing. But there are few such reporters, and
if there were, they would not be reporters for long.

But how can an experienced copyreader let a reporter dangle along
with a 75-word paragraph or an opening sentence that attempts to
cover the background of the anti-trust suit down to the bookkeeper
who eloped with the secretary and the January installment of the
income tax? In short, may I repeat that it is the function of the
copy reader to make a well-written story out of a badly-written
one. If he does not have the skill and the ambition to do that,
he had better go back to selling Fuller brushes.

Then as to the heads themselves, or headlines as the lay public
calls them, too many of them are incredibly bad. True, a more
general use of the hanging indention style has done away with
some of the typographical provocation that resulted in these headline monstrosities which at best would take a man or woman of
liberal education ten minutes to translate into meaning.

Many copyreaders speak and write English only a part of the
time. Presumably they can do it in their homes or in their other
off hours. The rest of the time, in their somewhat precarious
perches on the rim of the desk, they think, speak and write what I
call journalese. Many newspaper readers fortunately can learn to
read and translate it but it takes a deal of doing. Just for one of
the less abstruse examples of journalese let us take the story of
the president of an insurance company who has confessed to rob-
bing the cash drawer because he felt sorry for his invalid mistress
and needed more money. So here goes the head: "Risk firm head
bares girl pity." Then there is the old reliable, or should I say
unreliable, "said head." How I loathe the "said head"! "Ike said
Fearing Red Move." Or that hoary old offender, the "held head."
"GOP win held doubtful."

Now all of these horrible examples of traditional practices are

not wholly to be blamed on the individual copy reader. In newspaper offices throughout America, and I believe there are few
exceptions, there are far too many hard and fast rules for heads and
head writing. Were I again a managing editor, I should abolish
all copy desk rules. I was raised to believe that there must be
a verb or implied action in every head. Everything must be in the
present tense. The verb on the top line must find its subject in
the deck the very latest. Label heads were barred. Oh, how they
were barred! And yet, in story after story, and it is as true now as
it was when I was on the desk, the label head might be the wellnigh
perfect head, while that moronic hybrid of journalese replaces it
because it lives up to the horrible rules.

When I am reading my London or Manchester paper I am vastly
more intrigued by a head which says "The Turnbridge Wells Murder", in one line, than I am by the average American acrobatic
routine head. After a case is established in the minds of the readers
and they have become familiar with its implications, the label head
is perfect. The only reservation I have in recommending label heads
is that some copy readers are far from industrious and may overuse
them as merely an easy way out. A label head that has no invitation or intrigue is only dull.

Now, as to item number two of these preliminary, specific observations. Here most of you will doubtless think I am considerably
more than drastic, perhaps slightly crazy. Probably all of the sports
editors of the country and most of the managing editors will disagree with me. This item concerns my pet aversion — football art
— action pictures of football games. I happen to be a sports fan,
especially a college football fan. The sport pages of the Sunday
paper are loaded with four, five, six or eight column pictures of
running men at what are described as crucial moments in the
game. As a matter of fact, they are frequently cloudy, indeterm-
inate blobs of ink, not half as illuminating, not half as illustrative of
the play as one decently written paragraph. Never do I see the
sports pages of the Sunday edition or any week-day edition, if
there are games to be recorded, clogged up with murky, meaning-
less so-called football art, that I do not think of how much more
valuable and attractive that sports editor's service to his readers
would have been if he had filled that worse than wasted space with
some clearly written text. I venture to say that many sports fans
do exactly as I do. I do not waste 30 seconds trying to make head

or tail out of a lot of dull pictures. I want to read the story. I like the general lead and I like the play-by-play account.

But enjoying my freedom of speech and talking to men and women, many of whom are definitely interested in newspapers, I want to make it very clear that were I again a managing editor — a working editor—I would not give the order to cut down on football art. No. I would give the order to abolish it. Never again would a sports photographer get a free ticket to cover a football game for my newspaper unless he would promise to hamper my sports pages with nothing more than pictures of the rival coaches, the rival captains and perhaps a few stars depending on how starrily they had performed. That is all the football art I ever want to see. Not only is white space too valuable to be thrown away but happily there are too many excellent sports writers who know how to occupy white spaces with snappily contrived stories. Perhaps you gather by this time that I consider football art a waste of space.

The fact is, let me say just here, that as to heads, display of news, art, style of writing and various other factors that go to make up our pages too many newspapers have become the lazy victims of tradition and routine. For example, why is the lead story on the front page always displayed on the right hand side? The moment I pick up a newspaper I start reading from the left side. I think most readers do the same thing. I nearly always read the right hand story last, unless it is a story of extraordinary significance. Recent tests by experts as to the natural habits of the eye show that the eye of the average reader always falls on the left side of the page first.

Then there is the routine of type that is too small. Fortunately some newspapers are getting away from six, seven and eight point and going to nine point which, when I was learning to set type at the case, was called bourgeois. It is still good. Millions of readers, and not just odd dodos, would be delighted with a larger and more readable type face. Six and seven point type provides a cruel and unusual punishment which ought to be prohibited by law.

I come now to the more important aspects of newspaper making. My third item deals with newspaper writing. The easiest writing for any reporter or editorial writer is that which is clothed in big words and long sentences. Anyone who writes at all can learn to do that sort of thing quickly. The best writing, and by all odds the most difficult, is that of a simple style rich in short words and short sentences. It is not easy to keep the ideas up and the language down. But the best writers can do it. The late Charles E. Jefferson, for 30 years minister of the Broadway Tabernacle in New York, was justly famous for what his admiring fellow preachers called an economy of style. That is what reporters need — an economy of style. It is the result of no miracle. One doesn't get it over night. "A bricklayer learns to be a bricklayer by laying bricks," Irvin Cobb used to say, "and a writer learns to write by writing." The piece of that gives the reader the feeling that it was dashed off in a rare moment of inspiration is usually the piece upon which the writer has toiled the hardest and most earnestly.

But now to the substance of the reporter's story. The late Malcolm Bingay, of the *Detroit Free Press,* a great newspaperman, once said: "The news writer must be able to convey to the general public a statement of fact so starkly naked of masquerade that it is immediately understood by the moron and the most erudite college professor; by the ditch digger as well as the bank president; by him who runs and by him who meditates." To the news writer Bingay uttered this word of caution, "Master words without ever letting words master you."

To the item of reportorial writing I bring an observation on what has of late become a controversial subject, the matter of interpretive writing and the matter of objectivity. If by interpretive writing one means the expression of a background of knowledge and understanding of what the story is all about, I am all for it. But if interpretive writing means even the slightest display of personal or slanted opinion, the reporter ought instantly to be demoted to the advertising department or to some related field of commercials and propaganda. But the use of a background of information is not only wholly desirable, but imperative for good reporting.

I recall an instance in relation to a big story when nineteen out of twenty reporters in Washington were unprepared. The day President Roosevelt took the country off the gold standard, only one of a very few reporters in the capital, as far as I remember, knew what the action meant. He was George Benson, now editor of the *Toledo Times.* The story he wrote for his paper at that time, the *Minneapolis Journal,* was clear and understandable. Other reporters were satisfied with hazy handouts.

Apart from legitimate background writing, the reporter has the moral responsibility to adhere, as near as humanly possible, to objective writing. To purvey uncolored information is the newspaper's first and main job. It is the editor's business to make certain that the people have the facts, freed from a writer's bias. There is no crime committed in the field of journalism, not even super-lurid sensationalism, not even inaccuracy, that is more subversive of the principle of free press, more indefensible, than the crime of slanting the news to meet a publisher's policy. I am sorry to say there are a few newspapers in this country the publishers of which contrive to have their slants, their angles, their special hopes and fears and aspirations, woven into the fabric of what ought to be an objective news story. Although total objectivity will always be an unattainable ideal, facts and writers being what they are, a deliberate departure from a sincere effort to be unbiased can make a tragic mockery of the free press and create an unholy weapon in the hands of journalistic gangsters.

Today there are 1,786 daily newspapers in the United States, with a circulation of approximately 54 million. There are 545 Sunday papers with an aggregate circulation of 46 million. There are some 7,800 weekly papers. I rejoice in saying that I believe that all but a very few are seeking to do an honest job of providing accurate information in the news columns and an equally conscientious job of seeking to create an enlightened public opinion through an intelligent use of the editorial page.

My fourth item deals with the actual content of the newspaper. Too many of us have lost our sense of perspective. We have fallen hard for bright trivialities. We have gone Hollywood-happy. Our space is too generously allocated to the Ali Khans and their near-brides, to the Miss Americas and the swimming pool set.

Charlie Kettering, of General Motors, once told me that he didn't want experienced men in his laboratory, because when an improvement was suggested they knew just why it couldn't be done. He wanted inexperienced men who didn't have sense enough to know it couldn't be done. They just went ahead and often did it. I wonder if some of us oldtimers don't need a new kind of young man in our newspaper who is so dumb that he actually doesn't know that circulation comes principally from second-class performance by second class people. Perhaps we need some new ignorance about our business.

We pass over vast areas of important news, rich resources, just because it is routine to do so. May I give you an outstanding example. Most Americans believe in the United Nations and the continued participation of the United States in the organization. Numerous polls indicate that. President Eisenhower again and again has told us that our support of the United Nations must not waver. But what about the United Nations in the news columns? There is plenty about it, practically all concerned with the controversial issues — War or no war. Debates, debates, debates. Name-calling, insults and confusion. Speeches devoted to calling a spade a bull-dozer.

And all the time, the magnitude of the United Nations as the most extraordinary organization for social service on a global scale the world ever saw or ever dreamed of seeing, gets scant attention in the news columns. The divisions, commissions, auxiliaries and committees carry on their great work almost unnoticed. The International Refugee Organization, for example, has taken care of more than a million homeless strangers and displaced persons. Under the International Children's Emergency Fund nearly 50 million children have been vaccinated or treated in an anti-tuberculosis world-wide campaign. Technical aid programs have sent experts into 36 countries. The World Health Organization has relieved the sick all over the earth by preventive medicine. The Educational, Scientific and Cultural Organization has done and is doing an incalculably important work in drawing thoughtful thousands into a wide-spread plan for human betterment.

I mention but a fraction of these concerns. There are numberless columns of fascinating news in the activities of the United Nations but one has to go to pamphlets and reports to find it. Again and again editors make the mistake of overestimating the information of their readers and underestimating their intelligence. Public taste may be low but not half so low as many editors think it is.

My fifth item I label "the responsible editor." In an address some time ago Sir Winston Churchill declared that there is one thing which goes far beyond the advance of science, that reaches beyond the field of logic, that transcends all material things—it is the dignity and the nobility of the human spirit. Journalism is in need not only of an aristocracy of intelligence; it is in need of an aristocracy of spiritual awareness. Morale always trickles down from above; it is not something to be built up from below; it comes down from leadership. The hour has come for the responsible editor to lift the levels of his thinking, to push out the horizons of his imagination and to rise above partisanship and petty considerations. The privilege of a free press imposes upon editors increasing responsibilities in a turbulent world where life becomes day by day more complex and more bewildering.

How many Americans stop to think that this much vaunted freedom of the press is mainly not something granted to and possessed by newspaper owners? It is a privilege granted and guaranteed to all the people by the Bill of Rights of the Constitution. A free press is not a meal ticket for editors and publishers. It is the precious possession of every citizen. It is his protection against ill-meaning masters who would forge the chains of slaves in darkness. It is the responsibility of the editor and publisher to protect the people from the assaults of evil. As I have said, today's newspaperman owes to a society, often unappreciative, a lesser concern with the trivialities of the news and a greater concern for national conscience, social, economic and political, and for those international relationships which tend to world peace.

Peace is the major objective in this changing world. Furthermore, today's newspaperman ought to be definitely mindful of a greater responsibility in the field of religion and indicate a keener understanding of those aspirations of the spirit which lift man above his tiresome involvement in the urgent but lesser concerns of an upset world. It is the responsibility of editors to learn to make a more important employment of those unique facilities which the newspaper business furnishes for reaching into the lives and stimulating the actions of men.

The institutions of democracy rest upon the foundation of a free press. The thoughtful editor long ago came to the conclusion that he faced the opportunity of making a newspaper into something more than a newspaper. He seized the opportunity of making it into an institution for constant service in the community. He should know now that he faces an even greater opportunity, the profound duty, of making the newspaper the chief agent for enabling representative government to function. From my observations in Europe I am convinced that practically all the evils inherent in totalitarianism, in whatever nation they have come to pass, could have been prevented or destroyed in 60 days if there had been a free press, administered by properly responsible editors.

Democracy has been too often superficially defined as the rule

of the majority. The glory of democracy is not that it is the rule
of the majority. The glory of democracy is that it is the one type
of government upon the earth which provides for the continuing
rights of a minority not in power. What could be more despotic,
more tyrannical, than a majority in power, without provision for
the rights of the minority? The American newspaper is peculiarly
the medium for the expression of the minority because it is not
under the control of government.

I have said that the average American citizen does not think
through the meaning of a free press, its significance in representative government. It probably occurs only to a minority that the
institutions of democracy do indeed rest upon a system which opens
and keeps open a channel for human expression, a channel through
which flows, from the center of government, the stream of information which makes it possible for democratic organization to function over the farflung territory of a nation. H. G. Wells once said
the Roman Empire could not endure because there were no newspapers—no method of apprising the outlying peoples of the behavior of the center.

Democracy, then, can continue to function only so long and so
far as this channel is not tampered with or dammed or used
exclusively by the state. Through it also must flow, in the other
direction, from border to center, a stream of analysis, criticism,
praise and, if necessary, condemnation.

After nearly 50 years in journalism, I venture to speak somewhat
critically of editors, of myself and others engaged in the business of
making newspapers. Daniel Burnham, great architect, once said:
"There is no magic in little thoughts." We editors in these difficult
times are called upon to have a renewed faith in the calling to
which we are devoted.

The most constructive suggestion that can come to any man is
the idea of personal responsibility for corporate action. Our newspapers can rise no higher than ourselves. We must impose upon
ourselves the censorship of good taste. We must be restricted—but
only by truth and decency.

If we are to have a free press, we must furnish a responsible press.
With other publications and with the radio, we are largely responsible for the creation of that irresistible giant which is public
opinion. It is a terrible responsibility. We are engaged in widening
the horizons of men's thinking. There is surely something of

human progress, something eternally purposeful in this effort. I wish editors would write over their doors those words of Thomas Jefferson, carved in stone and set above the entrance to the University of Virginia: Enter by this gateway to seek the light of truth, the way of honor, and the will to work for man." How thoroughly William Allen White would have approved of those words.

I have the faith to believe that this is the spirit which animates the better part of the leadership of American journalism. May we ever speak freely, but God give us to speak only after thinking, with common sense and with true tolerance. I say "true tolerance." I am beginning to think that much which passes for tolerance is over-rated. It is merely the total absence of convictions. It is so easy to be a good sport in matters we do not care about.

And now to another major responsibility. The hour has come for the publishers of this country to sense the high desirability of making a specific constructive effort to raise the standards of American journalism. I am so glad to learn—and I learned a lot more about it today than I knew before—of the splendid program of the William Allen White Foundation engaging in research, in institutes, in sponsoring internships for reporters, in trying to find out what we lack as editors and how we may better prepare ourselves and prepare those who are coming after us.

I am happy to say that such an ideal on a nationwide scale is right now being translated elsewhere into actuality. The American Press Institute, a project of American publishers, is in its eighth year of service to the working press, to the men who determine the standards of our journalism. As an affiliate of the Graduate School of Journalism at Columbia University—and I know all of you who are interested in the William Allen White Foundation and in your own great School of Journalism will be interested in this—I am convinced the seminars of the Institute are having a profound effect on the thinking and product of editors, managing editors, city editors, reporters and publishers.

Journalism needs new techniques—new spiritual convictions and new inspiration. I should like to see editors and men of other professions, too, brought here by the William Allen White Foundation, not that they may be brushed up in their techniques (they're already good in that in most cases) but that they may be given inspiration— that they may indeed be brought to lift the levels of their thinking and push out the horizons of their imagination.

Finally, to what is perhaps the most important conception of the newspaper's responsibility. We Americans, along with others, have lived in recent years, through two world wars and another only somewhat less limited, and what have we learned from them? Only one thing—how to make a superior preparation for a third. Sometime ago I was privileged to have a talk with General Lucius Clay in London and later in Berlin. He said: "There is only one guarantee of peace—a mighty America, a strongly armed western Europe and the continuing consciousness on the part of Russia of our striking power."

This is not peace. It is only an armed truce. So long as our productive power remains greater than that of Russia, it may last for some years. But so long as the two mightiest nations on the earth build higher and higher their stockpiles of guns and bombs and men and ships, the day of the explosion will surely come. I am profoundly convinced that lasting peace can never come to rest upon the race track of competitive armament.

It must be perfectly obvious to anyone who thinks about it carefully, as it was to President Eisenhower who put it in a speech, that durable peace can finally come in but one way, namely, by universal disarmament. The fact that there is a United Nations commission devoted to the study of ways and means of guaranteed disarmament must give satisfaction to all but cynics and those whose imaginations are dead. Furthermore, Americans can take comfort and, indeed, inspiration from the resolutions that have been introduced in the Congress which call upon the United States government to make disarmament the definite and continuous aim of its foreign policy.

We talk much about the four freedoms, but the one we editors need most desperately is the fifth, the freedom of the imagination. For lack of imagination too many editors do not sense the vitality of those projects looking to world federation and disarmament. In my opinion, newspapers, in the call to promote peace by methods other than the preponderance of arms, face the heaviest responsibility in our history. True peace can come only if we are able "to create an ocean of public opinion on which to launch the ship of a great idea." This is the new and greater responsibility of American newspapers in this changing world.

And now my sixth and last item—a final word to you young

men and women who are expecting to make a career of newspapering. There is no satisfaction in life greater than the satisfaction of independent, self-expression. Perhaps you will be fortunate enough to own and edit a country weekly. To me that is almost the best job of all. After his early experience on the *Kansas City Star,* how quickly Bill White must have come to love Emporia and his little paper, later to become a daily, nationally known.

I think there is no more useful and spiritually rewarding job in any village than the job of being editor of one's own paper. Usually the editor is the most influential man in town, his income is probably among the largest and surely he has more fun than anybody else on earth. In time, if he is a smart young man with a few ideas and more ideals, he will be able to do more for more people than any of his fellow citizens.

A country editor can be just about anything he wants to be in his home town. If he has character, if he uses such talents as he has, there will come a day when he can sit behind his porch boxes on a summer evening and look back upon his life, the friends he has married and buried in his columns, praised and chastised, as on an old-fashioned garden. Life will look good to him, for he will have made it good.

If a young man has not brought out of college a deep curiosity to know, to find out, he has made little progress in education, and still less is he fitted for newspapering. Unless he has acquired from the right sort of teaching, good reading and study, or some strong spiritual inheritance, the profound desire to make his life count for something, toward the bettering of the times in which he lives, unless he feels something like a spiritual call to be a newspaperman, he might better seek success in some more ordinary work. For journalism is not an ordinary business. Not only does it partake of the dignity of the profession of the law, teaching and medicine, but it contains, or should contain, some of the spiritual elements of the ministry.

A man without ideals at the head of any newspaper is a poor influence and may be a definitely harmful member of society. Newspapermen, like sophomores, are frequently cynics. They are cynics because they do not know. They only think they know. One learns many regrettable things about his neighbors and fellow citizens during long experience in newspaper work. Reports by cynicism and disillusionment only reflect their own shallowness, their lack of real insight and deep experience of life. I want no part of cynical, over-sophisticated reporters and editors. One of the secrets of the charm of William Allen White lay in the fact that he believed in people, sought the good in them, and found it.

What shall you emphasize in your preparation for journalism, even more important than such practical aspects as are included in your newspaper laboratory? Above all, you should know history, political science and economics. Especially must you know history. If you do not know what men have done in the past, you are unable to judge the meaning, the significance of what they do now. History furnishes a set of checks and measures by which one learns to judge the present by the trials of the past. And so I put history, political science, economics—especially history—ahead of English. After all, one learns to write by writing.

I say again, don't even consider going in for a newspaper career as you would into a business to make money. Go into it only if you think you have something to say—and must say—and want to make a contribution to a better society. Business, profession, or trade—I say it is a calling.

What better can I do in closing than to give a personal testimony! I came out of college with certain ideals. They are, I am sure, pretty much the same ideals and principles that you have or are acquiring here at the University of Kansas. They were the ideals of decency, service and justice possessed by the great man for whom this school is named. In nearly 50 years I confess freely that I have all too often departed in practice from those ideals and principles but I say that in all those years I have felt no need to abandon them nor have I had any inclination to do so. A popular play of a few years ago declared that "you can't take it with you." I say to you, "you CAN take it with you." I say to you that if you have faith in God and your deepest convictions, the temporary disillusionments of newspapering shall not prevail against your faith.

"Ideals are like stars. You cannot succeed in touching them with your hands. But like the seafaring man on the desert of the waters, you can choose them as your guide, and following them, reach your destiny."

6

CONSCIENCE AND THE EDITOR

By Norman E. Isaacs

It is very doubtful that William Allen White ever heard my name. But, needless to say, my generation of newspapermen certainly knew of Mr. White. He was more than a great journalist. And more than a great American. To us, William Allen White was a symbol—a symbol of honor and decency and social conscience in a profession which we loved, but which so often showed its tarnished side.

I would like to think that Mr. White would approve of my being here. In his eyes, I might be one of the many happier examples of the kind of America which he loved and about which he wrote with such grace and charm and insight.

Born across the sea and with a greater part of my boyhood spent in our neighboring nation to the north, I have been able to spend my working life in the calling of my choosing and to have achieved a little measure of success.

Mr. White was already a noted journalist when I was born. He was 58 when I was just breaking in with a deep—and, fortunately, abiding—affection for the printed word. He was a sturdy 68 when I became a youthful "cub" managing editor.

Mr. White then was looking back on fifty years of newspapering and describing it as "a gorgeous adventure . . . happy, gay and free."

He pictured it as a half century of "much anxiety, a little pain, many hours of sorrow, but through it all the self-respect that makes for tolerance and understanding, for joy and some semblance at least of usefulness; the net of which is happiness."

Looking back on my own quarter of a century, I can vouch for the accuracy of his summary. Those of us separated from him by a generation and more still see it as a magnificent adventure. And even those of us who have suffered the hours of agony that go with living through the death of a newspaper that was part of us can still see the "happy, gay and free" side of it.

And all of us who have managed to keep a sense of conscience about our calling are happy in the feeling of usefulness despite the discontents we feel about the quality of our work and the total effect of our performance.

For the basic and fundamental premise of editing a newspaper today has not changed one whit from those days when William Allen White was winning recognition and honor for the manner in which he operated the *Emporia Gazette*.

We hear a great deal about the tremendous improvements in newspapering. And there have been great strides these last fifty years. There are new technical improvements being adopted constantly. We have improved in all of the ways in which the genius of science has opened the doors.

Our personnel has improved correspondingly on all levels of journalism. Our staff people today are better educated than those of a generation ago. For the most part, they are better behaved. And almost all of them come into our profession with high and shining ideals.

Fortunate, indeed, is the young college graduate who wins a place on a good newspaper. There he soon learns that these great technical advances are simply a modern tool to do the basic job better— that the essential quality of good newspapering remains the same as it was a generation ago: That a newspaper has a mission, and a character and courage.

If we have produced a group of cynics it is those who have entered journalism only to find that the technical advances are little more than a handsome facade—that it covers up a shell: a functioning technological unit going through the mere motions.

We have heard entirely too much these past several years about newspaper economics; too much about the threat of radio and television competition, which is again purely an economic consideration; and entirely too little about our moral values, which are, after all, what newspapering is all about.

Certainly, the profit factor is a vital one. Without it, we can have no independent press. A newspaper's owner, therefore, is rightfully entitled to a *reasonable* return on his money.

Most of the journalistic troubles we have today can be traced to three groups of people within the profession:

1. Editors and publishers who have somehow lost the saving grace of humility, whose consciences have become elastic, who have

permitted editorial judgments to slop over into the news columns, who use their newspapers to play favorites, who—to put it indelicately—have too often permitted their minds to become something like concrete: all mixed up and permanently set;

2. Owners of newspapers who still seem to think that great profits are possible out of their newspapers if only certain economies can be practiced, mostly by cutting down on news space, and squeezing news expenses; owners who are not newspapermen by calling, who neither understand nor accept the fact that it is immoral to inflict upon their communities newspapers which are biased, incomplete, inefficient and which keep the citizens uninformed about matters which the citizen has a right to have; and

3. Those employees of newspapers—news employees—who have become so fascinated with their Guild activities that they pay less attention to newspapering than to their union activities; and who have lost, in the process, their objectivity about life; and who have confused newspapering with mass-production of some sort or another to the extent that initiative and enterprise are all but stifled on those papers where they operate.

The economic facts of newspapers life are interesting in themselves. The trends of the last few years are such as to raise hopes that within another generation newspaper ownership may largely be concentrated in the hands of men of conscience who regard journalism as a professional calling.

For newspapering has ceased to be alluring for the financial speculator. To establish a newspaper today takes millions of dollars. Those already in newspapering can make a respectable and reasonable return. Men of good sense have long since become accustomed to the reality of the situation.

The mortality rate in newspapering has been high these past several years, which only underlines this point I am making about profits. And the indications are that if the country were to run into economic difficulties, more than a few newspapers will join the list of the departed.

In short, the tren dto newspaper monopoly continues. Today, in more than 90 per cent of the cities of America, there is only one newspaper.

And this alone poses the moral question clearly for all newspaper executives. In all these instances, we have become virtually the sole fountain of information for our communities. Does not conscience demand that we give all that we have to protect these wells of information from taint and corruption?

It seems to me a duty far more vital and compelling than the preoccupation with technical progress which grips so many in our profession these days.

The new engraving process, the teletypesetter, the improvements in matrices, all these are well and good, but yet all of them have served only to place more emphasis on speed and standardization. More and more newspapers are squeezing themselves into the pattern in which the mechanical contrivances threaten to dominate the whole enterprise. We cannot and we must not tolerate a journalistic process which produces only a robot press.

We are standardized enough as it is and if we allow centralized editing, we will only be opening the door to still further—and justifiable—criticism of the American press.

Criticism of the press has been going on for years, as much from within as from outsiders. A good deal of this inside-the-craft criticism has been sound and intelligent. In his time, Mr. White himself wrote some of the most scathing of comments about the ethical conduct of those whom he considered to be prostituting a noble profession, either for reasons of greed or personal bias.

Unfortunately, the reaction of a majority of editors and publishers has always been more heated and ill-informed than wise. Some of our colleagues deplore public criticism of the press by editors. This is the kind of nonsense that simply invites still more criticism. As Aldous Huxley has put it, facts do not cease to exist because they are ignored.

Let us, for a moment, consider one pertinent example of how the press behaves. Let us consider the performance of newspapers in the 1952 presidential campaign. I am not one of those who accepts the "one-party-press" phrase. I consider it to be a gross overstatement and, therefore, a self-defeating one. There are enough ruggedly independent newspapers, and enough of them are powerful, to make the blanket labelling an absurdity.

The facts are clear enough. It is true that a very large proportion of the press has allied itself editorially with one of our two major parties. While I do not relish this preponderance of support for one party, it does not seem to me that the press' honor is thereby endangered. The real threat is in what I referred to earlier — the insidious contamination of news columns with editorial bias.

In the 1952 campaign, a majority of our newspapers, I believe, acted with fairness and equity and performed their news duties with honor. But there were sufficient newspapers which conducted themselves with vulgar and boorish displays of one-sidedness to make it clear that all was not well within journalism.

Some of these newspapers were guilty of the most outright form of campaigning in news space; some were guilty of news suppressions. It was obvious not only to us in the profession, but to readers who were deeply offended.

It seemed to many of us that some form of study was called for in order to ascertain with some accuracy how much of this type of distortion had occurred so that we could be at once better prepared to answer our critics, who would have the public believe that all were guilty, and in order that we ourselves could assess our collective and individual conduct.

Nevertheless, all of the proposals made were rejected by the newspaper profession. Some of the arguments made against such studies were on utterly specious reasoning. And some were presented on sincere and perfectly valid grounds.

To many of us, the best argument presented was on the admitted practical difficulties. And there were obviously many. Going back over burned ground is always hard. It is posin ga great problem to re-assess a news-judgment situation a year or more old. The time and costs involved in this type of re-evaluation would be immeasurably greater than if a current study could have been made.

Since that campaign two and a half years ago, countless editorials have been written in defense of the press. Let a newspaper which supported the Eisenhower ticket make some criticism of the administration and you can almost bet on it that this will be cited as conclusive proof that those who have talked about a "one-party press" are thus revealed to be liars and charlatans. Perhaps some of them are, but this doesn't prove it.

Let's be honest with ourselves. We have another campaign coming up next year. I propose that right now we formulate plans for a nationwide, on-the-spot study of the press' performance in the 1956 presidential campaign.

How to do it? We have five major newspaper organizations—the American Newspaper Publishers Association, the American Society of Newspaper Editors, the Associated Press Managing Editors Association, the National Editorial Association, and Sigma Delta Chi.

Each of these organizations could make contributions, according to their means, to a committee which could be organized quickly to coordinate and direct such a study.

There need be no great debate about how to arrive at the makeup of such a committee. One way of doing it might be to choose a seven-man committee. This might be done by first taking the presidents of the four associations serving in the field of journalism education — the Association for Education in Journalism, the Association of Accredited Schools and Departments of Journalism, the American Society of Journalism School Administrators and the American Council on Education for Journalism. Add to this the directors of our two noted in-service training groups, the American Press Institute and the Neiman Foundation. And, if I were the one who had the choice, my selection for a seventh man, to serve as chairman of the group, would be Mr. Kent Cooper, the famed "KC" who served American newspapering for so many years as the guiding genius of The Associated Press.

I feel sure that the journalism schools and departments of the country, given proper directions by those skilled in communications research, could then do an intelligent and objective study of our total performance *as we do it* in 1956.

Let us have an end of abuse of each other on grounds of motive. Let us find out what the facts are in this situation.

Have we anything to gain from such a study? Everything!

If we are, as we claim to be, men of conscience who are issuing fair newspapers then the facts will be so clear that we can adequately refute all the charges of bias that are made. More important we will demonstrate to the nation that we who use our editorial columns and the power of our printing presses to criticize others are willing to be weighed on our total performance in the "goldfish bowl" which we advocate for all others.

Let us not forget that we, too, have been on trial before the American public for a long time. Let us now start answering some of the $64 questions ourselves, instead of merely writing editorials about other men who decline to be questioned.

I take the opportunity of this rostrum to make this proposal because it seems to me to typify the spirit of William Allen White. He was one editor who was never afraid for one moment to stand up and be counted.

It is a curious thing, the twists that make men's names live. And of one thing you can be sure. It isn't the dollar that a man is ever remembered by—unless he has put the dollar to some humanitarian purpose.

Men's memories live because they have stood for something constructive, something courageous, some nobility of the spirit.

The other day, I had occasion to comment on something that had struck me as I was reading up on Mr. White's era in journalism. I mentioned something odd that I had run into connected with the name of Frank Munsey. Two of our brightest young reporters looked puzzled. I asked if they had ever heard of Munsey and they shook their heads.

I explained to them that Munsey was known as the destroyer of newspapers. In describing Munsey, I went to Oswald Garrison Villard, who worte that "the striking fact is that in his own narrative, Munsey voiced no ideal or aim save . . . to publish something and to earn much money by doing so."

What had struck me as the curious thing was that in the journalism history books which I checked, more attention was focused on William Allen White's savagely bitter comment about Munsey than to the man's career.

And I got the odd feeling that Mr. White's editorial "Rest In Trust," is about all that will keep Mr. Munsey's name alive. What a tragic memory to leave behind!

It is equally tragic that we have in journalism today some men who worship the dollar more than they do principles.

Mr. White wrote that editorial because he was angry to the core about the elevation of the dollar sign above the spirit of journalism. Yet we can't forget that Mr. White himself was a sound and prudent businessman. Nevertheless, to him being an editor took precedence.

Making his newspaper pay its way was important, but he epitomized Thomas Carlyle's great phrase: "Everywhere in life the true question is not what we *gain*, but what we *do*."

If this could only become one of our guiding principles!

It would bring the day of professional operation that much closer.

Many of us in newspapering have lifted our voices in behalf of such a professional attitude. Three years ago, here in his William Allen White Lecture, Mr. Edwin Canham of the *Christian Science Monitor*, spoke eloquently against the idea of licensing journalists.

I agree with him that any license, even if granted by other

newspapermen, would be repressive and intolerable. Mr. Canham made the point that if the great press martyrs of the past had been forced to depend on license being issued by a majority of their colleagues, they would have been suppressed before they ever started.

At one time, Mr. White advocated licensing, but I am sure that had he been alive to hear Mr. Canham, he would have instantly agreed with his argument.

Licensing in itself means nothing. The Bar and Medicine, in many instances known to newspapermen, have shown themselves extraordinarily reluctant to revoke licenses even when the offenses against professional conduct have been flagrantly outrageous. Journalists could hardly be expected to operate at a higher and more rigorous standard of ethics.

The kind of professionalism we need is one of the spirit. More of our people must come to it — more and more and more — if we are ever to attain our proper stature as servants of the people.

And this goes not only for owners of newspapers and for editors, but for every staff member, too. It means not only the members of the American Newspaper Publishers Association, but the members also of the American Newspaper Guild.

It is a favorite pastime of vocal editors, like me, to throw the book at the wayward publisher. For too long, however, we have paid too little attention to the Guild. It is by no means exempt from the same criticisms which we editors deserve and receive, or the criticisms which we direct at publishers.

It is true that the Newspaper Guild helped the working newspaperman tremendously in raising his pay standards. It is a fact that the Guild — or in some cases the fear of Guild organization — helped bring about improvements in hours and working conditions.

But it is equally true that the Guild has been just as much a degrading influence on the spirit of professional journalism as has been the arrogant and greedy publisher. The Guild denies it with vehemence, but the facts clearly indicate that Guild policies were as much responsible for the death of several newspapers as were the managements' policies.

The Guild is a mixture of the highest of good intentions and the worst of methods. For every bit of material good it has accomplished, it has placed on the other side of the scales the evil of stultification of the spirit of journalistic enterprise.

Under the belief—sincerely held, I might add—that it is defending legitimate labor union rights, the Guild has built a record of protecting the incompetent and the misfit.

Even granting the fact that an employer usually gets the kind of employees he deserves, the Guild has nonetheless instilled in far too many newspapermen a spirit of vindictiveness and an attitude of suspicion.

At various times I have worked with the Guild. My record, I think, was one of fairness. I was no pushover, but I tried, at least, to be fair. On some occasions, I have publicly defended the guild against what I considered unjust accusation. Once or twice, the Guild has made kind comment about me. So I hope that what I say today will fall on some ears not completely unreceptive.

Not all Guild members agree with the Guild's policies. Many of them are "captive" members. The union shop clause, which is another term for closed shop regardless of all the fancy argument, is merely another form of licensing.

What it imposes on newspapermen is the shop steward checking up to make sure they are turning in their overtime slips; the grievance committee taking up hours to argue for some staff member whom they all know themselves to be two-thirds incompetent; long drawn-out negotiations in which the office politicians vie with each other to show what important people they are and to demonstrate how tough they can be with the boss.

A newspaper with a decent and intelligent management needs no Guild. Unfortunately, however, not all managements are decent. In these cases, where newspapers are run on backward and penurious lines, the staff's only recourse sometimes is the Guild.

And the Guild has to exist if for this reason alone. The Guild has a perfect right to try to organize newspapermen. It should continue to press for higher wage standards — and for better working conditions.

But it has long seemed to me that it could do these things without resort to the spiritual tyranny of the union shop, the shop stewards, and all the other union techniques which may be suited to making automobiles, but which serve only to destroy a part of newspaper originality.

It's time for the Guild to come of age, too.

All of us — publishers, editors, business managers, circulation directors, promotion managers, staff men of all types — have got to get back to the fundamentals of newspapering.

We've got to stop looking for a gimmick or an angle. They mean nothing. The fortunes poured into cheap promotions, into contests, into stunts of all varieties, have produced nothing but cheapness.

Recently, in *Editor & Publisher*, I read a report of a talk by an advertising executive to newspaper advertising representatives and I have not read such utter nonsense and claptrap in years.

This gentleman was deploring modern newspapering. He called it static and unchanging. It bores people, he said. He said that newspapers had become "dependent entirely on the news that somebody else makes."

And he recommended that we go out and "make" the news. On television and radio, he said, opinions are given freely. People are interested in opinions. They are controversial. And while he did not say so, I got the distinct impression that he was advocating an even greater freedom in news writing latitude.

What he said was that newspapermen must "bite the dog" and bring back the "scoop" and the "extra" to win public interest.

This is the kind of advice we don't need. The "scoop" isn't quite as dead as the dodo-bird, but it's close. And so is the extra.

What the gentleman has forgotten is that radio revolutionized journalism. Radio is a medium of instantaneous transmission. Radio helped kill the extra. One doesn't want an extra with three paragraphs of bulletin material, already heard on every radio station in the nation. What the reader wants from his newspaper is the *complete* story. He doesn't want opinion. He wants interpretation. He has a right to his own opinions. And the public, I hardly think, wants us to go out and start making our own news. The day of Cardiff Giant is dead, too, I hope.

Wha twe need are good newspapers. And this is the best newspaper promotion in the world. Just, plain *good* newspapers.

And what is a good newspaper?

First of all, it's an *honest* one. It prints the news without playing sides. It tells what happened as objectively as it knows how.

Second, it's an *adequate* newspaper. It is one that isn't trying to squeeze nickels on news space, while it spends dollars partying advertisers, or running big promotion ads for contests. It is a newspaper that gives the reader a comprehensive picture of what is going on— as comprehensive as it can make it.

Third, it's a *just* newspaper. It's a newspaper that doesn't pretend that everything it prints is bound to be 100 per cent accurate. It's a newspaper that isn't afraid to confess that it made a mistake; and one that does its best to rectify the error. It's a newspaper that gives equal prominence to the story of the man who has been cleared as it did to the story that he was accused.

Fourth, it's a *courageous* newspaper. Courage doesn't mean any constant flexing of editorial muscles. It means a newspaper that doesn't particularly go hunting fights, but which isn't afraid to get into one when it considers the fight important. It's a newspaper with some iron in its soul.

Fifth, it's a *clean* newspaper. And that doesn't mean being prudish. It means a newspaper that doesn't seek out cheap sex stories just to sell a few extra papers. It's a newspaper that has a sense of balance, a newspaper that doesn't have to apologize when it goes into the homes of its readers, a newspaper that tells what it has to tell with a sense of simple dignity.

Sixth, it's a *growing* newspaper. That doesn't mean growth in size particularly. It means growing in competence and in skill and in understanding. It's a newspaper that keeps on learning. It's a newspaper growing with its city.

Seventh, it's a *readable* newspaper. It is one that has a sense of knowing that a jumble of type makes it hard on the eyes. It's a newspaper that is trying to get away from the days of the old-fashioned disorder, the state of visual confusion. It is one that looks tidy and crisp. It takes pride in being neat.

Eighth, it's a newspaper that *leads,* not follows. It takes the high road of public service. It doesn't act as the organ of the chamber of commerce or the merchants, or the labor unions, or the country club, or the politicians. It leads in its editorial expressions, in the interests of *all* the people.

Ninth, it's a newspaper with *manners.* It is a newspaper courteous to its readers. Its reporters act like gentlemen. Be it a child on the telephone or a tramp in the office, the newspaper gives both a hearing.

And, tenth, and most important, it's a newspaper with a *conscience.* It's a newspaper dedicated to the service of the reader, of the community, of the state and of the nation. It has principles, ethics and morals. It believes in itself and in its mission. It is conscience that makes a newspaper different from every other industrial organism in society. It is conscience that gives a newspaper its individual character. It is conscience that makes a newspaper perform above and beyond the call of duty.

Given these ten attributes—or any substantial portion of them —and you have a good newspaper.

There are more than just a handful of such good newspapers in this land. And not all are big papers. William Allen White proved that they didn't have to be big to be good.

These good newspapers are respected ones. They produce reasonable profits for their owners. More important, they have made their owners distinguished and effective citizens.

Why aren't there more? Because newspapermen are human beings, like every other group in society. And human nature being what it is, newspapermen—like manufacturers, or doctors, or lawyers—are antagonistic to criticism.

We newspapermen seem to think we have a vested interest in the way newspapers are written, edited and printed.

We haven't. The only vested interest we have is in seeing to it that we try to do an honest job, that we try to report the truth, that our papers are fair and just. That's the vested interest: **Our** consciences.

What we need is what Mr. White called the "best American trait" some twenty-nine years ago. He was asked the question by the *New York Times.* He said the best American trait was "intelligent discontent."

That's what we need in this country and what we need in newspapers.

We need people in our newspapers who love newspapering with the same passion as did William Allen White.

We need people who seek no material riches. We need people who seek only the richness of usefulness to society. We need men and women who recognize the printed word to be the most powerful weapon in society and who seek to be its servants, not its masters; men and women willing to serve journalism as Schweitzer has served medicine. Men and women who realize instinctively that democracy will rise or fall on the quality and integrity of its journalism.

7

RESPONSIBILITY OF NEWSPAPERS

By ROY A. ROBERTS

What a flood of nostalgic memories arise as you turn back the tide of years on William Allen White of Kansas—Bill White, my friend.

Over the years, there has come to this campus and this school of journalism named in Mr. White's honor a distinguished line of newspapermen to discuss problems of the newspaper world. The William Allen White lectures have come to represent something significant in American journalism. My only excuse for accepting this valued invitation is not so much any contribution I might make to the thinking of today as the fact I knew Bill White, the man. Perhaps it is fitting on this, the twelfth anniversary of his death, that someone who really knew him should speak. William Allen White is fast becoming a legend, an inspiring one in American journalism. Those who really knew him personally are becoming scarce, indeed.

William Allen White had already left the *Kansas City Star* and taken up his work as a country editor, to which he brought distinction and honor, when I came to the *Star*, nearly 50 years ago out of this university. Even in the *Star* office then there were stories galore of Bill White, his scintillating wit, his devotion to good writing, his unswerving integrity. But Bill White's fame came not from the years on the *Star*, but as a country editor in a country town—Emporia. As a youngster in the newspaper field, I barely knew him, but over the decades our paths crossed so often the friendship with William Allen White became big in my life. I loved the man. More than that, he was a constant source of insipration, as well as joy. For Bill White lived the full life and to the end.

Thinking back on William Allen White, there are many, many lessons to be drawn from his career that are everlasting. They are just as sound today as when he was doing his delightful writing for the *Gazette*. The size of the newspaper has little to do with the writing thereof. Generalities are always dangerous. But, by and large, it's been my observation that the better writing in American newspapers through the years has been in the smaller cities, not in the great metropolitan newspapers. Possibly, this is because in the smaller cities, the publisher is his own editor and a working one. He may feel a greater freedom and put more personality and individuality into his work.

You don't have to be a metropolitan newspaper to emphasize style, good usage and display individuality and personality in writing. Bill White proved that. In the small country town of Emporia, he made the *Gazette* so brilliantly distinctive it was a constant joy to writers and literary folks everywhere. He became perhaps the best-known country editor of all time, the kindly, but penetrating philosopher and spokesman of small-town and rural life, certainly mid-America. To distinguished leaders from abroad, stopping off for a day's visit with the Sage of Emporia became almost as much a part of the grand American tour as looking at the Washington Monument or the Empire State Building. From New York to San Francisco there was a steady stream of interesting visitors to Emporia. It was my privilege to be invited down to small Bill White dinners on numerous occasions. Over fried chicken, as chicken should be fried, Miss Sallie's spoonbread—for Mrs. White always took this task to herself—and a salad, the making of which was almost a sacred rite to the genial host, there would flow the most stimulating conversation imaginable on books, governments, world affairs, human affairs. Well, all you had to do was sit back and receive an education in what civilized dinner-table conversation could be.

You can't all be Bill Whites, but the smallest, as well as the largest, newspaper can strive for better writing, better usage, more individuality and more personality. You can get away from the stereotyped. The newspaper of today can profit from a revival of better writing and less standardization. It's one field where the small city paper, I think, has a better chance than even the great metropolitan newspapers.

Youth was eternal and everlasting in William Allen White. The vivacious, youthful spirit of the man lived to the very end. Young at heart, life was a daily exciting adventure. He lived it to the fullest. Discouragement was never in Bill White's lexicon. Never cynical, although sometimes he could be devastating in his attack on some individual or cause or injustice. Two little snapshots of the man. I only wish I could give them in color. We "Bull Moosed" together and went to Armageddon in 1912. I can see Bill White today, tears streaming down his cheeks, his eyes gleaming with fervor as he envisioned the birth of a new political party, the Progressive party, that was to bring a new era to mankind. You might call it the New Deal several decades too early. Bill White believed. For effective writing you have to believe, right or wrong, not write with tongue in cheek, to put the feeling and force that he did in his writing. Whatever he wrote breathed sincerity, conviction. Just two years hence, the dream broke as the aforesaid political party passed into oblivion. But it was something, yes, something, to have dreamed and believed as Bill White did.

I recall again a decade after the conclusion of the Washington Armament conference, Bill White sitting over his typewriter, again tears upon his cheeks, his eyes aglow as he pounded out his sparkling prose. He had witnessed the dawn of the new day when there was to be no more war, the armament race was to end and mankind was to live in peace and happiness forever. A great sentimentalist, one of the most human beings who ever lived, was he. What mattered it that after we had sunk our great naval advantage in the waters of the Atlantic on the basis of promises and the new day dawned a nightmare instead, we only had two major wars and a world apparently headed through a cold war for generations. But you couldn't quench the fires of William Allen White to make the world better for mankind. He loved causes, sometimes, I thought, especially losing causes. But what a gallant warrior. The best reporter I ever knew over 50 years was one to whom every story he went out on was the greatest he ever covered. That's why readers could feel and experience his writing. Mr. White had some of that quality.

From these glimpses you might assume he was too much a sentimentalist. Bill White could be intensely practical. With all his lost causes, he never became cynical, discouraged. He was always ready for the next great adventure, whatever it might be. He did his best writing in his later years, especially in his last two books, the *Puritan in Babylon* and his own autobiography which he didn't get to finish. His *Emporia Gazette* sparkled and scintillated to the end. Youth, curiosity are eternally essential to a newspaper. When the deadly signs of age begin to show—look out!

Bill White hated injustice, oppression in any form with all his soul.

He didn't like for people to be pushed around. There wasn't even a taint of intolerance in his system. The only time he ever ran for public office was when he tossed his hat in the ring for Governor of Kansas in order to fight Ku-Klux control of the state. What a campaign it was! Bill White, slugging daily in his inimitable style in the Gazette and out every night on the hustings poking fun and ridiculing Kluxism. He ran as an Independent. He didn't desire to run at all. He had to be assured there wasn't a chance on earth of his being elected. Before the fight was over he was worried for fear he might accidentally win. That's the enthusiasm any candidate, novice or professional, always acquires when he hears the applause of the crowd too often day after day. This one race Mr. White lost.

But he likewise won. He had ridiculed the Ku Klux Klan out of the state. Never again did it lift its head. His attitude of a newspaperman in politics may be interesting. He supported fellow editors, campaign after campaign for governor or public office until it almost seemed you had to belong to the newspaper crowd to get elected. If others yearned for the accolade of office, that was all right with Bill. But for himself, he felt that being editor of the Gazette was a bigger job than anything he could be elected to. He was always intensely and keenly interested in politics. He felt every newspaperman should be. I might add he was probably one of the worst politicians that ever lived but how he enjoyed playing the game—the maneuvers, the conventions, the human frailties and vanities that campaigns and office-holding revealed.

There was always good humor through all his political ventures. Never will I forget that election night back in 1936 when we Kansans had gone to bat with Alf Landon and Old Susanna in a pitch against F.D.R. for the presidency. When the returns came in showing we had swept all of Maine and Vermont, I wired Bill down at Emporia: "How about taking the veil as political managers?" In ten minutes back came a message from Emporia: "Okeh, order two oversized veils from Kansas City Tent and Awning Company if they can make them large enough." I might explain that Bill weighed way up in his 200's then and I was cheating a bit under 300. He thrived on defeats and nothing ever soured him. I remember F.D.R. told me once: "Our good friend, Bill White, is the best supporter I have, three years and eleven months. But that last 30 days he's always back again in the Republican fold. I guess that's a fair average to expect, though, from a Kansan."

So you have a brief glimpse of what made William Allen White
tick as the greatest country editor of his time. The qualities, the
principles are just as enduring today in making a newspaper as
they were back in his decades. If every journalism school in the
land would have a short course in what made William Allen White
the great figure he was, it would turn out better-prepared acolytes
to carry on in journalism.

What would William Allen White think of the problems of American newspaperdom as of today? I don't know. I can't imagine anything more futile than trying to guess. Colonel Nelson, my great
first boss, has been dead now about 40 years. I still have folks come
into the office with some objective in mind, insisting that if Colonel
Nelson were still alive he would be doing thus or so. They never
saw or knew him. I did. Yet I don't pretend to know what he would
do as of today. Certain guiding principles and characteristics you
can absorb from the past. Today's problems, however, must be decided as of today. An effective newspaper simply can't be run by
the slide-rule pattern of past ownership.

This I believe firmly: Newspapers today are incomparably better, more useful than the newspapers of the past, even in that era
of great publishing giants which some think back to as the golden
days. It's all relative. The country, our mode of living our problems our horizon of interests have changed violently and newspapers have changed with them. They should. We have largely
passed from personal journalism to impersonal. We have become
more objective. We cover the world today as we used to cover our
community or even our state. Yet, curiously, newspapers do a good
job of selling everything but themselves. As press agents for newspapers, newspapers do a terrible job. By and large, newspapers
today are more responsive to their obligations to reader and community than ever before. Something of the glamour and personality
of the past may be lost as newspapers have become with the times
sizeable business operations. Just go back and read the newspapers
of 25 years ago. Then scan those of today. Draw your own judgment. There is only one answer. Our horizons of news coverage
now are global so the comparison itself may be unfair. The field of
entertainment is more varied, the appeal broader. If the same test
is applied 25 years hence, we of today will suffer in comparison.
That's progress. Newspapers have met the challenge of a growing,
changing world and still represent, in spite of rate increases, forced

by economic pressures, the greatest bargain that comes into the house. That, despite the amazing development of television.

Soul searching, self-criticism is always in order, even accepting the premise that newspapers are better today than ever before. To start with—the press services—and they are the backbone of bringing the world news, as well as national, to your home—have expanded not only in coverage but in intelligence in handling and interpreting what it is all about. You can't have real truth in news without such interpretation. Just mechanical transmission of barebone facts won't do the job. Accepting the principles of giving the background, as well as the barebone facts, is the greatest single advance in press services, even more than the miracle story of the expansion of wire service to the far nooks and corners of the globe.

I intend no invidious comparison with the other press services when I refer to the Associated Press. It's only because I sat so many years on the AP board and saw it function. The smallest complaint of one-sided presentation of the news from the smallest publisher receives almost incredible study and attention. With membership composed of every conceivable faith and thinking, political, economic and otherwise, the service has to be objective. Of course, there will be slips and mistakes. But how few! Right there you have a buffer against unfair presentation of the news. Consider what a percentage of columns each day originate with press services, especially on national coverage. That's just item one on why newspapers are better today because press services are better, more interpretative with background fill-in, with the entire world girded with wires and reporters.

Let's move to the editorial page. From personal to impersonal journalism, something was lost. But I believe we are coming out of the doldrums even there. Too often, editorial pages in the past were a catch-all for over-age writers you couldn't find any other place for. The trend today—and this goes even for smaller papers —is for building younger, better-informed editorial staffs, distinct from the news staff. The editorial pages are reflecting the opening of the doors of the ivory tower. The change is not universal, but it's coming. You sense, especially, too much of an inclination to abdicate editorial function to columnists and commentators. Let me make it clear I am not against columnists and commentators, per se. There are good and bad ones, as there are capable and wooden editors. Let me ask one question: Why should a publisher or an editor, large or small, apply different standards of resonsibility to a columnist or a commentator than he does to his own staff? We let the special writers carry on personal vendettas with each other, bounce the truth and fact about by innuendo, without applying the same tests of accuracy you insist on for your own staff and writers. The uneasy conscience reflected by the palliative explanation above a column that it "does not necessarily represent the views of the newspaper" is the most supine apology imaginable. To make it completely irresponsible you should add you are not vouching for its truth or accuracy.

In this day of increasing one-newspaper towns, the public is entitled not just to news, but diverse viewpoints of how it is evaluated. But, certainly, your own editorial policy ought to be vigorous enough so your readers won't be shocked and don't need to be told that you are printing something just to give the other side. Print it if you think it is fair comment or criticism, not scurrilous or irresponsible. You don't have to label it. There is one columnist—I won't mention his name—who has long been a good friend of mine. He comes up with something unusual every now or then. I have never let him in the *Star* and he knows why. He mangles English and good taste and good usage. That's his business and lots of folks like it. That's their business. But, I can't see making your own staff adhere strictly to principles of good writing and usage and letting an outsider, just because he has a name, chew up good writing. Instead of abdicating so much to the columnists and commentators, wouldn't it be healthier if more publishers wrote signed columns from time to time? Specifically, I have in mind such regular stints as Jack Knight turns out for the Knight newspapers. There are others, but too few. I have been on both sides, editorial and business. I know the problem of the publisher. I recognize he has his hands full, particularly lately in the complicated and costly years of operation. Ultimate responsibility, after all, rests in ownership. More publishers and owners should write powerful editorials, as well as powerful checks.

So the news staffs have changed and kept pace with the growing world. The day of the hardboiled, old-fashioned reporter out to get his scoop at any cost may be passing. Possibly, there may be too much reliance in some quarters on the ticker and the press agent or public relations releases, all of which makes for loss of initiative. By and large, the news staffs of today are better prepared for their job. That job is infinitely more difficult than it was decades ago—in the so-called good old days of old-fashioned reporters, old-fashioned at least to the extent of long hours and lots of glamour and mighty little pay. The good reporter of today has to have more technical training and background to do a good job. Staffs are evoluting into specialists along some line. It all makes for better written, more intelligent news presentation, more substance. Today's newspapers reflect the change.

So by the major tests the newspaper of today has met the challenge of the changing years. Yet, where do we stand today before our final judges, the public and our readers? As a profession we haven't done a good job of putting our own story over. We have sold everything else except the great contribution newspapers have made to national and local well-being. Newspapers have been too much on the defensive, too apologetic, if you please. You can hardly go to a newspaper meeting or hear a speech on newspapers without much of the oratory turning around the dangers of losing the cherished freedom. We convert each other, who don't need conversion, but we certainly haven't gotten over to the public what we're driving at or concerned about. Somehow, the notion prevails that newspapers are asking some special license or freedoms or privilege not accorded to anyone lese. Still lacking is full recognition that the right of the public to know is the very basis of a free democratic system.

It is my firm conviction freedom of the press will be preserved as long as newspapers deserve it—no longer.

Likewise freedom of the press encompasses responsibility of newspapers. The two are indivisible.

Clarify the atmosphere by stressing more our responsibility; dissipate the notion that newspapers seek to set themselves up as a special class licensed under the free speech and free press amendment guarantees, to some privilege not enjoyed by others.

If the public once understands it is its own right to know that is at stake, that the very foundations of a free democracy are involved, then there will be no question of the issue. Remember, a good newspaper doing its duty will never win a popularity contest. It may be respected. But popular, no.

There is another newspaper trend that makes responsibility of the newspaper a more impelling topic than ever. There is no good served in backing away from it. That is the continuing erosion in the newspaper field. The number of dailies, year by year, has diminished. The cities and towns with only one newspaper or a single newspaper ownership have steadily increased. My latest figures are for 1952. Only 110 cities and towns had competing mediums in all the breadth of this land, or barely a half the number a little more than a decade ago. Ninety-two per cent of the cities and towns had single ownership of newspapers. Whether it is healthy from a national standpoint or not, there it is. There it will be. Whether you like it or not, the sheer force of economic pressures is making it so. All the theorists on earth can't change such a picture except by reversal of the pressures that produced it. Costs—labor, distribution, sky-rocketing newsprint, once a cheap and plentiful commodity, and taxes—have been the big factors. Already in the average smaller town or even fair-sized city, competing newspapers are becoming as extinct as the Washington handpress. I am not passing judgment on the trend, just stating the fact.

I do say with conviction that by and large most newspapers have accepted the responsibilities that go along with a one-newspaper town or ownership. All is not to the bad. The medium-class city newspaper is incomparably better in every way than the papers used to be when two or three were struggling to make ends meet. In that field has been the greatest improvement in newspapers anywhere. Even in the larger cities, scan the lists of those cities with one newspaper and you find some of the best and strongest newspapers. It is curious, maybe, but often there you find more consecration and devotion to civic and community building than in the few remaining cities with fiercely competing papers, striving for circulation and supremacy. For the most part, the rule has been to give the reader more service, more coverage and a better package and certainly more objective presentation of the news. Whatever disadvantages of the one-newspaper town, the increased ability to serve is inescapable and beyond argument. Whether something in editorial vigor has been lost in the process might be questioned. The sheer responsibilities of a one-newspaper town generally have made for a more objective newspaper.

The most priceless asset a newspaper has is its integrity and reader confidence. This far outweighs monumental plants, high speed presses, distribution systems. So, not because of idealism or dedication necessarily, but just common sense, the publisher accepts the responsibility of single ownership and seeks to give more in service, not less. More effort toward objective news, not less. He is not going to jeopardize his position before the most important body of opinion of all—the reader and the community. After all, that's what counts.

Another trend I shall mention. Originally, I had expected to make it the central theme of my talk today. That is the proposed investigation or study under the auspices of a newspaper-based organization, Sigma Delta Chi, the research to be financed from some tax-free foundation, of irresponsible charges by self-serving politicians of a "one-party press." Just a year ago from this same forum, Norman Isaacs of the *Louisville Courier-Journal*—an editor whose opinion I respect and a newspaper I certainly regard as having the highest standards—launched the proposal for such a study covering the 1956 presidential campaign. I accord Mr. Isaacs full credit for sincerity of conviction that such a study would have been a service to American newspaperdom. The advocates of such a move are just as much entitled to their opinions as those to the contrary. Happily, and I use the word advisedly, for I feel strongly on the subject, the whole question has been disposed of. After a comprehensive poll of publishers, large and small, the verdict was adverse. The entire project has been completely dropped. There is no useful purpose served in kicking around or keeping alive the corpse of a dead issue.

I felt such a proposal was a disservice to American newspapers and expected to say so emphatically. My thinking was that it represented something utterly futile; would settle nothing; political demagogues would continue to make the same accusations whenever it served their purpose, as they have a perfect right to do, because this is free America. Responsibility in the premise is individual, not collective. All the resolutions and probes on earth wouldn't put integrity into a publisher and/or editor if it wasn't there basically. Just to measure the news content carried and not the editorial page or the columnists or the commentators would have made such a study without value. Yet otherwise you approach the danger line of control or an attempt to influence opinion in a probe outside the news columns. Other minor implications, such as appealing to a tax-free foundation for funds to conduct the study, didn't set well. But, prime and first responsibility must always be in the individual ownership of newspapers with the final judgment lodged with the readers. Fail in your obligation to them, it won't take you long to have something to worry about. You can't figure reporting in inches of space that each party got. The party or side that makes the most news will get the most news columns. This is inevitable. Editorial page? That's another thing. Comparisons were especially noticeable in 1948 when Mr. Truman with his whistle-stop campaign ran rings around the Republican nominee in making news. Even though a huge majority of newspapers were not supporting him, he got the news columns. On the editorial page, conviction and belief were the test — not news-worthiness.

The long-range aspects of free speech and of free press are not too happy. A totalitarian government moves first to circumvent the right of the people to know and the ability of the people to know by muzzling the press. The bigger government grows, the greater the threat. Social trends the world over all point to government getting bigger and bigger. So, it is well to be ever alert. Here in our own United States I have a sneaking feeling a return to hard-boiled reporting will kick open more doors to governmental secrecy than all the congressional probes or all the speeches of alarm that can be made. What is happening elsewhere justifies apprehension and fears.

There is one bright ray through the clouds of government suppression. Return of Doctor Paz to control and operation of *La Prensa,* down in Argentina, after making one of the most gallant and devoted fights against tyranny of an autocratic government— his great property was seized and he himself was chased out of the country—is one of the most significant and heartening chapters in the fight of the ages of man for freedom. Free men and a free world everywhere salute him and the outcome of his brave struggle.

Here at home I return to my original premise that newspapers will be more effective in their appeal to public opinion by stressing responsibility of the press as indivisible from freedom of speech and press. Reducing it down to simple terms, it means truth in the news. Truth in the news with every broad and full implication.

Truth in the news—but truth tempered with mercy, decency and humility.

Truth in the news—truth that means not being controlled or unduly influenced either by Big Business, Big Labor or Big Government. That last is becoming the more important.

Truth in the news—which encompasses telling fairly and intelligently what the news means, the background, not just parrot-like recording.

Truth in the news—truth which does not slavishly follow either a party line or an economic line or a cult. Too often you know just what a newspaper is going to say on an issue before you pick it up. Both liberal organs and conservatives fail to deviate often enough from their cult to be interesting. Nonconformity is more exciting at times, more useful.

Truth in the news—which can encompass hatred of intolerance and oppression or pushing folk around. Tell the facts.

Truth in the news—but truth dedicated to high ideals, community service, national service, with a first obligation the readers' right to know. That's our first and eternal job and responsibility.

That's what I mean by responsibility of the press.

This I believe.

8

THE EDITOR I WISH I WERE

By Irving Dilliard

I first heard the name William Allen White from my father, an avid newspaper reader who relished the style of writing that appeared on the *Emporia Gazette's* editorial page. That would have been when I was starting out in high school and had not yet decided on a newspaper career. When I was a sophomore I read the famous tribute to Mary White in an English course. I first met William Allen White when he stopped in St. Louis between trains and came to the *Post-Dispatch* to see Clark McAdams, editor of the editorial page. That was soon after I was admitted to the editorial page staff in 1930. He was the first eminent visiting editor I had the opportunity of meeting. I still glow at the thought of the experience which consisted of a friendly handclasp, a pat on the shoulder and a cheery smiling assurance that I was in a good spot for "a young fellow." I was then about twenty-six years old.

In 1934 when Brand Whitlock died, I wrote an editorial about that sterling citizen. I wrote, however, not about his heroic service as Ambassador to Belgium in World War I, but of his warm, human autobiography, *Forty Years Of It,* which told particularly of his experience as Mayor of Toledo, his association with Golden Rule Jones and a "city set on a hill" and his belief with Walt Whitman that "the song is to the singer and comes back most to him." I had found the book a joy as well as illumination and hoped to direct other readers to it. And I quoted from William Allen White's introduction which described Brand Whitlock's record of faith in the people to manage their own affairs as "an adventure in easy reading and high thinking." Quickly there came from Emporia a letter addressed in the long familiar purple typescript. William Allen White, busy man that he was, generously took time out to commend my editorial "about dear old Brand." He was, wrote William Allen White, "the salt of the earth."

When Sigma Delta Chi held its annual convention in Topeka

and Lawrence in 1937, the most memorable sesison to me was the
one held on this campus with William Allen White, Henry J.
Allen and Irving Brant discussing the then new American Newspaper Guild. Former Gov. Allen, who was publisher of the *Wichita
Beacon,* strongly opposed membership in the Guild. Irving Brant,
then editorial page editor of the *St. Louis Star-Times* and now
working on the sixth and final volume of his monumental life of
Madison, was equally strongly in favor of the Guild. For me at
least William Allen White tipped the scales for the Guild. Essentially what he said was that if he worked on some newspapers
in this country he would lose no time in applying for membership. But he did regret that certain greedy publishers had allowed
conditions to develop and continue which caused the Guild to
be formed.

I saw him also in the presidential elecion year of 1936 hard at
work in the press section at the Republican National Convention
in Cleveland which chose Alf M. Landon and again in Philadelphia
at the Democratic National Convention which re-nominated
Franklin D. Roosevelt. William Allen White was then almost
70 but maintaining a pace that kept him well ahead of many
of the younger Washington correspondents. That autumn, as the
campaign proper began, he published a book on the 1936 nominees
and issues entitled "What It's All About." I read it eagerly as
a veteran newspaperman's view of my first national political conventions.

I think of him too in 1938 for that was the year in which he
published his biography of President Calvin Coolidge entitled *A
Puritan in Babylon.* I wrote about the book for the *Post-Dispatch*
and called attention to William Allen White's use of previously
unpublished letters written by former President William Howard
Taft when he was Chief Justice. Many of these letters were
sharply critical of Taft's colleagues on the bench. They were critical
also of judicial decisions and activities. This was priority news
to me, and so I put it into my report on *A Puritan in Babylon.*
Again William Allen White, although a very busy man, took the
time to write me a friendly letter. He wrote that in his opinion
the Taft letters were a major part of the news in the book, and
he did not understand why the reviewers had not called attention to them.

I think of William Allen White two years later addressing the

Abraham Lincoln Association of Springfield, in my native state of Illinois. I remember him as he described the startling parallel between the 2,000,000 slaves of 1860 and the 10,000,000 jobless of 1940, "chained to public work which they must take or starve." It is not amiss to remind a new generation which did not go through the dreadful economic collapse of William Allen White's sober words on that occasion. He told his 1940 Illinois audience that he believed the "10,000,000 jobless men in our land present today a problem no less menacing than the problem of 2,000,000 slaves in Lincoln's time."

I have brought a printed release of that address with me today and am glad to take this opportunity to add it to the William Allen White Foundation collection of historical material.

I have two other recollections of William Allen White that I would like to mention. In 1939 he went to Harvard to visit with the first group of Nieman Fellows — the practicing newspapermen who take leave of their active work to study at Harvard — and to deliver the Godkin lectures, published later that year under the title, "The Changing West." Those were shining hours at Cambridge and we who shared them will always remember the kindly philosopher-editor at whose feet we sat. My concluding memory comes in 1942 less than two years before his death. In early summer I received at the *Post-Dispatch* the following telegram: "I will be in St. Louis Saturday morning from eight until nine ten. I shall be glad to buy breakfast for you and all your staff you care to bring at Union Depot."

Hardly do I need to tell you that I was there when his train came in, that I gladly carried his suitcase and that in the station dining room we were joined by several others from the *Post-Dispatch,* including Ferd Gottlieb, devoted Kansan and swearer by William Allen White. I tried to obtain the visitor's breakfast check but he would have none of it. He insisted on keeping the terms of his offer. When I entreated with him that we wanted him as our guest, he took a small white capsule from a box he carried in a vest pocket. "One word more about this," he said, "and I will drop this secret charge of high explosives onto the floor. That will be enough to set it off and blow this station to smithereens and everyone in it to Kingdom Come." His merry eyes lighted up so as to make me feel somehow that he was speaking the sober truth. Nothing more was said about the check for fear a large area of St. Louis would be destroyed by the Sage of Emporia, who presumably would be lost along with the rest of us. Certainly none of us wanted to be responsible for bringing on that catastrophe on a perfect June morning!

As some of you are participating in a William Allen White birthday observance for the first time, a word about the history of the foundation is in order. After the editor's death, Jan. 29, 1944, a group of his Kansas colleagues met in Topeka to consider a suitable memorial. His personal friend Henry Allen, who presided, suggested that a memorial foundation be set up to bear William Allen White's name. That was on May 13, 1944. At another meeting, June 8, Oscar S. Stauffer, publisher of the *Topeka State Journal* and the Stauffer newspapers proposed a series of annual lectures. The foundation itself was incorporated Nov. 20 — within 10 months of William Allen White's death.

The executive committee proceeded carefully in developing the William Allen White School of Journalism and Public Information and in planning the policies and services of the foundation. On July 31, 1948, Dean Burton Marvin came as director of the foundation and dean of the school, whereupon the program was launched.

The lecturers have been presented annually in February on or near William Allen White's birthday. Since this is the eighth you will be interested, I am sure, in a brief review of the lectureship. James B. Reston, chief of the Washington bureau of the *New York Times*, came first in 1950. Speaking on the subject, "Cops and Robbers in Foggy Bottom," he sounded "a call for responsible and aggressive reporting on foreign policy." He said that he believed that if William Allen White were to appear in Washington once more he would feel that there were not enough chips on enough correspondents' shoulders in covering the national capital.

The 1951 lecturer, Ernest K. Lindley, Washington editor of *Newsweek*, was twice an appropriate choice; first, for his eminence as an observer and commentator on national and world affairs, and second, because as Chancellor Lindley's son, he was once a student here. In his prophetic address, "The Years of Danger," he presented what he called "a consideration of facts, demagoguery and United States foreign policy." He noted that while "many of satellite peoples are unwilling prisoners," still "it is futile for them to try to shoot the jailer when they lack the power to break the lock on the prison door."

Erwin D. Canham came in 1952 from the editor's office of the *Christian Science Monitor* to deliver the third lecture and to join in dedicating the new Journalism building. His subject was "Newspapers and the Survival of Free Society" and he said that "everywhere in the world, in some way or other, freedom is in danger." He expressly included the freedom of the press and he made no exception for the United States.

The fourth lecturer was Palmer Hoyt, dynamic editor and publisher of the *Denver Post*, who spoke on "New Dimensions in the News" in 1953. Those were the days of "the mounting tide of McCarthyism," as Palmer Hoyt termed that social and political disease and he shared with his audience his office memorandum to his managing editor on how to handle the news about the wild claims made by the junior Republican Senator from Wisconsin. Stating the case against a prospective investigation of alleged Communism in education, Palmer Hoyt said the danger was that such an inquiry "would turn out to be a witch hunt in fact and the quarry would not be the red fox of Communism but the free flying eagle of American liberalism."

The late, much esteemed Grove Patterson, gave the fifth lecture in 1954. A contemporary of William Allen White, the editor-in-chief of the *Toledo Blade* compiled his basic principles for journalists in a lecture of reminiscenses covering nearly a half a century, entitled "Newspapering As It Seems To Me."

Two years ago the sixth lecturer was Norman Isaacs, managing editor of the *Louisville Times*, who spoke on "Conscience and the Editor." Last year at this time the seventh lecture was given by the president of the *Kansas City Star*, Roy A. Roberts, another longtime friend of William Allen White, whose theme was "Responsibility of Newspapers."

Taken together the Isaacs and Roberts lecturers presented two sides of the question of a study of newspaper coverage of the 1956 presidential campaign. Recalling the criticism of the press in 1952, Norman Isaacs, as chairman of the Sigma Delta Chi Committee on Ethics, strongly advocated a survey and described the ways and means to obtain it through foundation-supported university research groups. Roy Roberts, from this same rostrum, described the 1952 criticism as "irresponsible charges by self-serving politicians." He welcomed the fact that a majority of leading editors and publishers had come out against a 1956 survey and that "happily the whole question has been disposed of."

Now it is not my place on this occasion to referee the differences between my two most recent predecessors. But perhaps I may say two things briefly on this point. First, I believe that our press has nothing to fear, or perhaps, to put it more modestly, should have nothing to fear from honest self examination. Second, I think that I detected a substantial difference in the general news reporting of the 1952 and 1956 campaigns, and that this difference was on the side of greater fairness in the news, text and picture coverage in 1956. If this is true then I believe it altogether probable that the professional criticism of the 1952 coverage from such informed observers as Roscoe Drummond, plus the Sigma Delta Chi proposal for a 1956 survey, made editors conscious of their obligation to be reporters and not editorial writers in their news columns. Thus the criticism turned out to be constructive and brought its benefits after all.

This reminds me that I have just been reading the December, 1956, issue of UAW—AMMUNITION which describes itself as a documented report on how *Time, Life* and *Newsweek* "covered the campaign news." The attempt at analysis leaves a lot to be desired, but it does show that this is still a field for research and investigation, as the spot checking in the 1952 campaign had previously demonstrated.

These extracts do not do justice to my predecessors and their themes but they are enough to suggest the nature of what has gone before. Any newspaperman would be glad to be in such company. I am doubly grateful. For when I was first invited I could not come, and the foundatioin has bee nkind enough to allow me a second opportunity.

Now I cannot look back on a half century of newspapering as Grove Patterson could. I cannot speak against journalistic experience as varied as that of Roy Roberts. Nor can I inform you, as Scotty Reston, from an intensive study of the vital field of foreign relations. But it is my good fortune to have gone to work in 1927 — 30 years ago — for the newspaper that the first Joseph Pulitzer founded in 1878. Since then I have been happily associated with the second and third Joseph Pulitzers and for more than 26 years with that rare spirit and great artist, editorial cartoonist Daniel R. Fitzpatrick. I have learned a few things in that time and I have come to some conclusions. I do not put in the claim of originality. Neither do I presume to speak for others. Please hear as a preceding phrase to almost every observation I make the words "in my opinion" or "so I believe."

These lessons that I have learned and the aspirations that I entertain I purpose to cite briefly as notes toward a portrait of "The Editor I Wish I Were."

First of all the editor I wish I were knows his community intimately. Whether he lives and works in a small town or large city, he is always learning more about its people and their activities. He never grows content to go and come from his office by an unchanging route, as if in a groove. He knows that he can see for himself things that no one will think to tell him. He knows that the best of editors never cease to be a reporter of local news. He finds in many of the facts about his community encouragement to believe in its capacity for making contributions that reach far beyond its limits. The editor in Lawrence, for example, takes pride not only in knowing that Wilt Champerlain is currently a son of the community, but that the distinguished novelist, Dorothy Canfield Fisher, is a daughter of Lawrence, born here 78 years ago next Sunday.

The editor I wish I were knows his state. He knows not only the part in which he lives but the whole of his state. When he thinks of Atchison he thinks of Edgar Watson Howe and the *Globe,* and *Ed Howe's Monthly.* He thinks of how uninhibited an editor can be and how industrious. He thinks of a young man working all day on his paper and coming home to write bit by bit at night *The Story of a Country Town* and then, when no publisher was interested, setting it in type himself and printing it page at a time, also at night, to give the world a classic of prairie town realism acclaimed by Mark Twain and William Dean Howells a half century before Sinclair Lewis' *Main Street* and Sherwood Anderson's *Winesburg, Ohio.* When my editor thinks of Emporia, he thinks of the now almost legendary editor whose memory we keep today. But he thinks also of "Uncle Walt" Mason, who wrote headlines in rhyme on the *Gazette* and then, with William Allen White's help and encouragement, became perhaps the earliest and most successful of syndicated newspaper poets.

The editor I wish I were knows the history and politics of his state. He knows that the year 1957 is, among other things, the centennial year of the Lecompton Constitution and the attempt by proslavery forces to establish the legality of slave property in Kansas a hundred years ago. He knows from that struggle of 1857 how far the United States has come toward political equality for all its citizens regardless of race. He knows and is both saddened and heartened by the story of Edmund G. Ross, sent by Kansas to the United States Senate in 1866 at the height of the Reconstruction bitterness as an anti-Johnson Senator, who braved condemnation and calumny by voting against the conviction of the impeached President Andrew Johnson because, as Senator Ross himself said, he would not yield, no matter what the pressures, to "insufficient proofs and partisan considerations." The editor I wish I were knows in detail the rich fabric into which are woven the stories of Jerry Simpson and Carry A. Nation and of Mary E. Lease, who told the farmers of her day to "raise less corn and more Hell." He knows why the farm bloc of the '20s came into being and the role of a young editor-senator named Arthur Capper.

The editor I wish I were knows his nation. He knows the cities and the countryside, the wonders and the beauties in all forty-eight states and territories. He visits the national parks on vacation trips. He has stood atop Gay Head on Martha's Vineyard and looked west to the setting sun and he has watched it rise in the east from the height above Avalon on Santa Catalina Island. He knows the greatness, the diversity and the capacity of his nation from having seen it with his own eyes and walked about it on his own fee. When predatory interests seek to invade the national domain, as at Dinosaur National Monument, he rises up in righteous indignation against those who would trespass on ground that he himself owns.

The editor I wish I were has been around the world. He travels in distant as well as neighboring countries. He knows that he must write about faraway places and he must print news concerning them. And he knows that peoples overseas will seem less strange and their decisions and reactions to us less peculiar if he has met them in their home lands. He knows that travel helps him to understand and that understanding is fundamental to his work as an editor.

Let me say here to the students in the room that I hope none

of you will look regretfully to the time you may be required to
spend in military service as your contribution to the national defense. Your years with the Army or the Navy or some other
branch of the service may turn out to be a broadening and educational experience that you otherwise would be denied. Many
an American is a better informed citizen of the world because of
military service overseas. My editor, to adapt a phrase of John
Wesley, knows that "the world is his beat."

The editor I am describing reads his own paper thoroughly. That
goes without saying. But he also reads other papers. He may not
read all these at the same time but he rotates from a list that
includes, among others, the *Washington Post,* the *New York Times;*
the *New York Herald Tribune,* the *Christian Science Monitor* and
the *Wall Street Journal.* His list also includes the *Baltimore Sun,*
the *Providence Journal-Bulletin,* the *Milwaukee Journal,* the
Louisville Courier-Journal and Times, the *Chicago Tribune,* the
Kansas City Star and Times, the *Des Moines Register and Tribune*
and the *Atlanta Constitution.* From time to time he reads papers
from Denver and Detroit, Minneapolis and Sacramento, from
Richmond and Raleigh and Nashville, from Little Rock and
Watertown and Beaumont. He knows that editors such as William
T. Evjue of the *Madison Capital Times,* the gifts of the *York
Gazette and Daily,* William B. Johnstone of *Lewiston Morning
Tribune* and Charles A. Sprague of the Salem *Oregon Statesman*
regularly are far ahead of many large city editors in the exercise
of editorial leadership. Here I note that former Gov. Sprague is
another native son of whom Lawrence can be proud.

My editor receives from England the weekly air mail edition of
the *Manchester Guardian,* for he knows that in the dispatches
from Alistair Cooke in New York and Max Freedman in Washington he will read some of the keenest and most perceptive reporting to be found anywhere aout life and events in the United
States. He keeps in touch with the great tradition of Charles
Prestwich Scot, for a half century guiding genius of the *Guardian*
who once summarized his journalistic philosophy in a half dozen
words: "Opinion is free; facts are sacred."

To be as fair as possible my editor reads differing views on the
major issues of the day. He reads Thomas L. Stokes and George
Sokolsky. He sees what Marquis W. Childs has to say and also
David Lawrence. And he appreciates the opportunity he has

in following the informed, constructive editorial columns of Walter Lippmann, developed as they are against a 40 years' view of world affairs.

As William Allen White was, so is the editor I have in mind a man of books. I have mentioned several of William Allen White's books but there are many others in fiction as well as public affairs. Their very titles suggest the quality and range of the author's mind: *The Court of Boyville* (1899), *Strategems and Spoils* (1901), *God's Puppets* (1916), *In the Heart of a Fool* (1916), *Woodrow Wilson* (1924), *The Editor and His People* (1924), *and Masques in a Pageant* (1928). And of greatest interest for newspaper men are his *Autobiography* (1946) and the collection of his editorials *Forty Years on Main Street* (1937). There are books about him too and one outstanding is the biography written by Dr. Everett Rich, Chairman, Department of English, Kansas State Teachers College, Emporia. Another valuable book is *William Allen White's America* (1947) by Walter Johnson, professor of history at the University of Chicago.

The editor I am describing reads books because he knows, as William Allen White knew, that books are news, because they present ideas that newspaper readers soon will be acting on, because they explain the past and light the way of the future. He is familiar with the monumental publishing projects of his time in biography, in history, in the social sciences, in regional life, in the messages and papers of the great Americans—Franklin, Adams, Jefferson, Lincoln. He knows there is value for him as an editor in a novel such as John P. Marquand's *Point of No Return;* a biography such as Catherine Drinker Bowen's *Yankee From Olympus;* in poetry such as Stephen Vincent Benet's *John Brown's Body.* He knows the editorial worth in history such as Roger Butterfield's *The American Past;* in drama such as the Koestler-Kingsley *Darkness at Noon;* and a study of a current problem such as Corliss Lamont's *Freedom Is As Freedom Does.*

Here I regret to note the death of one of the truest friends our free press has ever known—Zechariah Chafee, Jr., professor in the Harvard University Law School. Thanks to Dean Moreau, Prof. Chafee came to the Kansas University campus in 1952 to deliver a series of lectures and Kansas can be grateful for that association with him. Prof. Chafee's book, *Freedom of Speech in the United States,* is a classic discussion of our greatest liberty.

The editor who takes it from his shelf from time to time drinks from freedom's very wellsprings. Chafee was a member of the Hutchins commision and made many valuable contributions to its pioneering study, *A Free and Responsible Press.* Every editor owes him a debt of deep gratitude.

My editor reads magazines. And not just *Life*, the *Saturday Evening Post*, *U.S. News & World Report*, *Business Week*, *Holiday*, *The New Yorker*, the weekly news magazines and *Fortune.* He keeps close track of *Harpers*, the *Atlantic*, the *Saturday Review*, the *New Republic* and the *Nation.* He is aware of the admirable studies of important issues that appear in the *Reporter*, and *Freedom & Union.* He recognizes among achievements of the *Progressive* its public revelation of a certain Senator in his real colors. He finds a case for the conservative side in politics in the new *National Review.* In *Frontier* he sees a mirror of the burgeoning life of the Pacific Coast and in *American Heritage*, for the first time, a publication that worthily reflects the greatness and wonder of the American story.

He knows that a religious week such as the *Christian Century* can have the rare editorial talents of the late Paul Hutchinson. He knows that insights and points of view that he otherwise would not share are provided by the *Commonweal* and *America*, by *Together*, the *Churchman* and the *Christian Register.* He is familiar with the contribution to our culture of the quarterlies —The *American Scholar*, *Foreign Affairs*, the *Yale Review* and the *Virginia Quarterly Review*—and of the "little magazines," published often by university groups.

My editor turns to the publications of the scholarly professions, such as the *American Historical Review*, the *American Political Science Review*, *Social Research* and the journals and reviews of the law schools. He keeps his eye on the *Bulletin of the Atomic Scientists*, and *Scientific American.* He does so in the knowledge that historians, economists, political scientists, sociologists and teachers of law, along with physical scientists are among his most significant news sources. For information about his own profession he reads not only *Editor & Publisher* and *Quill*, but *Nieman Reports*, *Public Opinion* and *Journalism Quarterly.* Yes, he reads many magazines, and because he does he knows the history of *Collier's* back to Norman Hapgood and the editorials of Louis D. Brandeis in the crusades of a half century ago. And knowing that, he knows what is lost when, for whatever reason, a *Collier's* prints its last issue and disappears.

The editor I am talking about may have scoffed at television. For some years he may have resisted having a set in his home. He does so no longer. He deplores what is cheap and trivial and bad on the air waves. He knows there is a lot that is good and he encourages it. He turns to TV to witness historic events, to follow "Meet the Press," to watch plays by Shakespeare and Sir James M. Barrie, by Eugene O'Neill, Robert E. Sherwood and Maxwell Anderson, to see a picturization as thrilling as that of the sinking of the Titanic, "A Night to Remember." He learns the story of how awareness first came to a blind and deaf girl named Helen Keller. He listens to Eric Sevareid, Edward R. Murrow and Edward P. Morgan whether on television or radio for he realizes that they have large followings and are worthy of them. He has come to appreciate the planning and effort that goes into a television program, as for example, Dave Garroway's "Wide, Wide World," which requires the services in one way or another of 4100 people each time it is presented.

My editor has heard the death knell sounded over the motion picture but he has not joined in repeating it. He knows that modern colored movies on their wide screens excel in ways that other mediums of expression have not yet challenged. He can cite, as an instance, from current films, the fascinating speculative story built around Anastasia, one of the daughters of the last Czar of Russia, with Ingrid Bergman, Yul Brynner and Helen Hayes in the leading roles. He remembers the delight of Audrey Hepburn in "Roman Holiday," the rare diversion of Humphrey Bogart and Katherine Hepburn in "The African Queen," the power of William Holden and the entire cast in "Stalag 17." He is busy but he finds time for some well selected movies. And as he can he keeps up with the theater for he knows that Julie Harris in "The Lark" belongs on a stage in the same room as the audience.

A few minutes ago I said that the editor I have in mind reads newspapers. I did not make an exception of the comic pages for he reads them, too. Not every comic panel and every adventure strip but his favorites and enough of the others to know in general what is going on in the world of Dick Tracy, Li'l Abner, Moon Mullins, Buz Sawyer, David Crane and Juliet Jones. And why does he read the comics? Because in Lichty's "Grin and Bear It"

is some of the richest of contemporary humor. Because the
Bumsteads and the Wallets picture the American family in a
way that no other presentation can do. Because mothers and
fathers keep in touch with the military life of their sons in part
through Beetle Bailey, Sarge, Cookie, Zero and Killer. Because
"Steve Canyon," a flawlessly drawn adventure story, backs an
adequate, well-supported defense as staunchly as any member
of Congress. Because the little people in Schulz's "Peanuts"—
Lucy who builds up a snowman and kicks it to pieces, then builds
it up again and kicks it down again, "torn between the desire
to create and the desire to destroy," her brother Linus finding
security in life in a towel, Schroeder devoted to Beethoven and
his piano, the hapless Charlie Brown and all their colleagues, including the dog Snoopy — go far in explaining thought and action
in mid-century America.

My editor knows that as Clare Brigg's "Days of Real Sport"
was a later version of Tom Sawyer and Huck Finn and Kin
Hubbard's "Abe Martin" successor to Josh Billings so is Walt
Kelly's "Pogo" our generation's "Br'er Rabbit" and "Popeye" its
combination of Paul Bunyan and Mike Fink. Although he has
read about World War II in the memoirs of the generals and in the
big, thick green volumes published officially in Washington, he
knows that an indispensable part of the history of the war was
written "Up Front" by Bill Mauldin's bearded infantrymen, Willie
and Joe. Yes, my editor has a few moments for what—for want
of a better name—is still called the comic page.

Now I want to note another group of characteristics of the
editor I am endeavoring to describe. He makes it a rule to be
courteous. The reader who telephones him or writes a letter does
not know that the editor receives countless demands on his time
and that if the editor yielded to even a small part of the requests
and invitations he could not do his work. My editor looks on
each contact with the public as an opportunity to create good will
for his newspaper. He always remembers that his newspaper owes
its continued existence to its readers. He does not bow to them
but he treats them as the individual human beings they are.

My editor is co-operative. He joins with his associates to produce the best newspaper possible. He knows that this process
has no place for wasteful jealousies and personalities. He makes
his decisions on the merits of the issues regardless of their origin

or support. He solicits and welcomes the suggestions of those who work with him. He does his part in creating on his newspaper an atmosphere of free and friendly interchange.

A strong characteristic of my editor is his curiosity. He wants to know the "why" of things and in a world that is full of new developments he is always asking about the "how." In his community, he may not learn everything first but he knows more new things than anyone else. In the words of that great Washington correspondent son of Kansas University, Raymond Clapper: He never overestimates the information of his readers and never underestimates their intelligence.

My editor has imagination. While he takes genuine satisfaction in believing that the press of the United States is the best press in the world, he is continuously aware that our press not only ought to be but could be infinitely better than it is. As he is able to see the need for improvements, so is he able to see the opportunities close at hand through which he can make his own contributions toward improving the press in appearance, in content, in service, in leadership.

The editor I am describing is a man of conscience. He recoils from the dishonest and he abhors the untrue. He believes, as did William Allen White, who said: "The only excuse an editor has for being is that his paper shall print the news. The question that comes to every man running a newspaper is: What is news? That he must settle for himself, and having found a rule, must stick as closely to it as possible. When an editor begins monkeying with his conscience, stretching his rule to shield his friends or to punish his enemies he is lost."

The editor who has the imagination to see what he ought to do and the conscience to know how to do it falls short unless he has the courage to be the editor he knows he should be. So my editor has courage that stands up to the test. Sometimes he needs courage in dealing with large numbers of people or strong group interests. Sometimes he needs courage in private consultations with his superior editor or publisher in situations about which only the two of them will know and for which his superior in the end may be truly grateful. But whatever the situation he finds himself in, courage he has and nothing else will take its place.

My editor has judgment and this ability to judge the circumstances tells him when his criticism, to be convincing, should he moderate, when it should be carefully argumentative, when it should be strongly condemnatory. He does not roll the heavy artillery into action if a spatter of birdshot will suffice. Neither does he rely on a rabbit gun when the blast of a howitzer is required. He is forthright and for a model of forthrightness he recalls what William Allen White said in the *Gazette* in 1925 on the death of Frank A. Munsey, a newspaper publisher who had buried many newspapers and magazines. He wrote:

"Frank Munsey, the great publisher, is dead.

"Frank Munsey contributed to the journalism of his day the talent of a meat packer, the morals of a money changer and the manners of an undertaker. He and his kind have about succeeded in transforming a once-noble profession into an eight per cent security.

"May he rest in trust."

The editorial on Frank Munsey shocked so many people that William Allen White took the time to explain it to Nicholas Murray Butler, president of Columbia University. He wrote:

"Probably I was a little rough on Frank Munsey but the whole tendency of the times in newspaper consolidation and standardization, I think, works badly. I would rather have the press as it was in John Milton's time, or Benjamin Franklin's time, when a man with the proverbial shirt tail full of type could express himself, air his views and get it off his chest, rather than to have the mass production of newspapers owned by investment bankers and filled full of stupid syndicate matter and conventional opinions. It is a bad thing for the newspaper business and it is a bad thing for the people. And Munsey and his kind are getting halos for doing a bad thing. I have no quarrel with Munsey, personally, but I had to say what I said for the craft I loved."

The editor whose portrait I am attempting to draw has his convictions but he respects the opposite opinions of others. In 1940 the great question in the United States was: What if anything should this nation do about the war which Hitler had unloosed in Europe? William Allen White was chairman of an organization known as the Committee to Defend the United States by Aiding the Allies. One of the readers of the *St. Louis Post-Dispatch* wrote to the editor at Emporia to express the view that this nation ought to avoid all involvement in the war situation. William Allen White wrote in answer as folows:

"There are, of course, two opinions held honestly by intelligent people in the United States. One is that to help the Allies keeps the war away from America by letting them fight the war in Europe rather than to wait until the Germans conquer Europe and turn their greedy eyes westward. The other opinion is your opinion and many fine, wise people hold it. There being two sides, perhaps the best thing each of us could do is to respect the honesty and integrity of each other's opinions and realize that there must be differences if there is progress in the world.

"All that you say I had considered before taking my position and felt that on the whole I was right, yet not without doubts as probably you have in holding yours."

I have brought the original of that letter and also gladly leave it for the historical center and collections over which Miss Jean McKnight so efficiently presides.

I am describing an editor who has informed himself on many things, one who knows that he can never know too much to do his work well. But let me make very clear that he also knows that he does not know it all and that he never will. He is continually aware of how much more he needs to learn every day from others to be accurate and fair in dealing with the ever more complex problems that arise in the news at all levels. He acts on the principle that guided the life of the late Justice Louis D. Brandeis, a principle that is particularly applicable to every newspaper man whatever the part he plays. It is this: "Your opinion is no better than your information."

My editor takes his work seriously and he is aware of the inescapable responsibiilty that is his when he uses the printed word—and also when he does not use it. He also can step outside himself and see how he looks to others. When I was in high school I read that Edgar A. Guest, the writer of newspaper verse, would make a talk in St. Louis. Eager to hear any newspaper man, and certainly one from far off Detroit, I skipped an afternoon of classes. The truancy was no mistake. For I will never forget a story the poet told. A newsboy rushed up to a man who came out of a building in a large city. "Paper, paper, mister," said the newsboy. "No," replied the sour-looking, gruff man, as he brushed the boy aside. "I don't want a paper. I'm the man who makes them!" The newsboy saw in a flash what was wrong and so he called after the departing editor: "No wonder I can't sell any!!"

Once I heard a colleague distinguish between two editors of the editorial page of the *Post-Dispatch*. He said that George S. Johns "loved justice" and that George Johns' successor, Clark McAdams, "hated injustice." The editor I am describing knows both emotions. He loves justice and he hates injustice.

My editor criticizes others every day. In turn he takes the criticism that is directed at him. He points out the failings and short-comings in others. When he is criticized he weighs with earnestness and humility the criticism for the truth that may be in it. And in fairness he frequently gives his critics their say in print. When he is wrong—and even the ideal editor I am describing ca nmake mistakes that call for correction—he prints an honest retraction to set the record straight.

I have spoken of some of this editor's characteristics. Independence is another. He is careful not to engage in activities that precious asset is gone. And so my editor is vigilant against the is sparing in his friendships because he knows that friendships outside his newspaper may at any time force the hard choice between personal kindness to a friend and devotion to duty as an editor. He knows that an editor seldom loses his independence in a sudden collapse of his position. The editor loses his independence rather by small concessions which follow one after another until that precious asset is gone. And so my editor is vigilant against the seemingly harmless yieldings that may set dangerous precedents.

As my editor cherishes his own independence, he does not ask conformity in others. He recognizes the right of people to be themselves in what they think, in how they live, in their likes and dislikes. He knows that William Allen White did not come from an assembly line, that the individuality which is the essence of American democracy is not produced by a mold.

This characteristic of individuality reminds me that I have been reading about a difference of opinion between some of the students at Kansas University, and certain of the university's officials. If I have read this news aright, the Kansan Board which governs the *Daily Kansan* decided that the editors of the student paper ought to have the authority to take sides in political campaigns. Their elders, however, took the position that such political comment would be unwise in that it would be misunderstood as seeming to speak for the university and that this would involve both the students and the university in unnecessary controversy.

Just how this matter stands now I do not know. There may have been developments that change the situation. It is not remotely my place as a guest to enter into differences, if any, that may remain. As a general proposition, I think we all can agree that basically students, faculty and administrative staff are here for the same reason. That is to help the oncoming generations grow into maturity the while developing the best possible intellectual means for coping with the complex problems that beset us all.

We can agree further, I believe, that one of the needs of our world is what William Allen White called "intelligent discontent." If we agree on that, then surely there is no better place to begin to learn it than in college, as William Allen White himself must have learned it on this very campus in the last century. I mention this because the editor I am describing seeks young recruits from the colleges trained in this "intelligent discontent" and he counts on the University of Kansas to produce its share.

And why does the editor seek students trained in "intelligent discontent"? Because he wants reporters who can see the things that need changing in his community. Because he wants editorial writers who appreciate, for example, the precious history of the Fifth Amendment with its guarantee not only that no man shall be required to testify against himself, but that life, liberty and property shall not be taken without due process of law. Because he wants writers who will not sit unmoved when demagogues dismiss with a reproachful sneer that vital part of our charter of liberties. Because he wants Washington correspondents who can tell when congressional contempt citations violate the Bill of Rights, who can foresee when punitive acts will be rejected as unconstitutional by the courts.

If there are still any law students in the room at this point, let me say especially for their benefit that my editor follows the work of the courts with as much concern as he follows the legislative and executive branches of our government. He knows that the United States Supreme Court can invalidate an act of Congress, that it can stay the President's hand. And so he applauds the appointment of qualified Justices and he deplores those who are chosen primarily because of political availability.

One of the characteristics that most marks my editor I have not yet mentioned. This is his enthusiasm. He has zest for life.

He communicates his enjoyment of his work to others. He finds too much to do ever to become cynical. And while his range of informational interests is wide, he makes of himself an authority recognized as such among his fellows on a subject worthy of his study and time. And he has learned the value of outside interests, whether some sport, hunting and fishing, gardening, collecting, making things with tools, engaging in music or art.

My editor's temple is his newspaper. He may be a member of a religious affiliation but he never allows church opinion to influence his judgment as an editor. He worships at the shrine of journalistic truth where no religious body holds a monopoly. He is a communicant with those who place the public good above all else.

There is one more characteristic of the editor I have been seeing in my mind's eye about which I must tell you before we bring this class hour to a close. I refer to his devotion to the improvement of the professional group to which he belongs. He has a long view of freedom of the press back to the stirring times of John Milton. He knows the stories of the colonial press heroes— Anthony Haswell, Matthew Lyon, John Peter Zenger. He measures himself against the sacrifice of Elijah Parish Lovejoy in defense of his printing press at the burning warehouse in Alton, Ill. He remembers the price Don Mellett paid in Canton, Ohio.

And remembering what these brave men did for his free press heritage, my editor works year after year to protect it and to improve it—in the American Society of Newspaper Editors, in the American Press Institute, in the National Conference of Editorial Writers, in the American Newspaper Guild, through the professional foundations and other groups that may be open to him. He encourages better training for careers in journalism and he welcomes research in the colleges and universities that will help him make the press beneficial to our democracy.

He is always on guard against those who violate the people's right to know. He is as quick to speak up when news is arbitrarily withheld in Washington as when it is suppressed in Argentina. He condemns a dictatorial Peron who tramples a great newspaper underfoot and he protests when an Attorney General, in charge of the Department of Justice, makes it a rule not to hold press conferences.

My editor does not keep silent when his government tells him that he cannot send reporters to a country with which we are not at war, as the Eisenhower Admnistration has now told our press with respect to reporting the news from China. He speaks up at once in defense of his right to go after the news and to tell his readers what it is. And he can speak up on a country weekly as well as on a city daily for if the metropolitan editor's freedom is trespassed by government so is the freedom of the rural or small town editor violated. My editor applauds the stand of Gardner Cowles, publisher of *Look* magazine, in calling on the State Department for an open hearing on the move to revoke the passport of Reporter Edmund Stevens, who had the will to defy our government's foolish ban on travel to China. My editor knows from the case of William Worthy of the Baltimore *Afro-American* that the United States can only harm itself in aping the restrictions that the Communists have imposed in the past. Here let me add as my opinion that if all the newspaper editors who supported President Eisenhower for re-election last November were now to hold him accountable as the responsible head of his administration this ban would be lifted in a hurry. John Foster Dulles may be Secretary of State, but Dwight D. Eisenhower is President and the ultimate responsibility for everything in his administration, bad as well as good, is his.

Above all else my editor knows talk is cheap and that only performance counts. He expects to be appraised not for what he professes but what he does. He knows that high-sounding resolutions and stirring speeches about the glories of a free press—yes, and lectures such as this one—are empty words unless they are practiced day by day, week to week, year after year in news columns and on editorial pages. My editor wakes up repeating the warning of the first Joseph Pulitzer: "Our Republic and its press will rise or fall together." He goes to bed at night asking himself what he has done this day to help his Republic and its press to rise.

The great American, Judge Learned Hand, once ventured a belief concerning a jurist about to pass on a question of constitutional law. He ought, said the wise Judge Hand, "to have at least a bowing acquaintance with Acton and Maitland, with Thucydides, Gibbon and Carlyle, with Homer, Dante, Shakespeare and Milton, with Machiavelli, Montaigne and Rabelais, with Plato, Bacon, Hume and Kant."

I am well aware that in describing "The Editor I Wish I Were"

I have set standards higher than those which Judge Hand established for the bench. And this is as it should be, even though you will say that no one man is or could be the editor whose portrait I have been drawing this afternoon.

With that I will agree and then say:

Why should our standards not be as high as we can envision them?

Why should we not be like the pole vaulter who keeps raising the bar and going up to the new height and over and raising the bar again and going up still higher and higher?

For freedom of the press—in William Allen White's America— amid a world as threatened as ours—who among us can do less than try and try and then try again?

9

THE INEXACT SCIENCE OF TRUTH-TELLING

By Jenkin Lloyd Jones

I believe that honest perplexity is just as much a part of the profession of journalism and education for journalism as honest conviction is. The strong, immature mind is a mind of many convictions. It is a mind that loves and hates, worships and abhors, admires and detests many things. It is youth that has recently discovered that his father doesn't know everything, and is now certain that his father doesn't know anything. It is youth whose political opinions and social observations are stretched or amputated to fit the Procrustean bed of his self-image. And that self-image is in his conception of himself as a fearless liberal who will drive away the shibboleths of an evil past, or as a staunch and clear-sighted conservative who will defend to the death the eternal verities.

I have no quarrel with such minds, although it is sometimes wearisome arguing with them. It is, indeed, the youth that has no strong convictions at all who is hopeless. But when a strong young mind begins to grow into a condition of maturity and balanced reasoning it suffers a series of distressing shocks, namely, the discovery that the copy book maxims are not always correct.

Love doesn't always laugh at locksmiths. Ask any convict.

There have been cases where the course of true love ran smooth as hell.

Murder does not always out.

Truth crushed to earth sometimes stays down for the count.

And, saddest of all, there seem to be times when honesty, if that means blurting out the unvarnished facts, is not always the best policy.

It is this latter circumstance which, this afternoon, I wish to relate to the problem of journalism.

We will not consider venal editors who lie for profit, or cowardly editors who are constantly trying to rationalize sins of omission because they fear a fight. This afternoon I want to talk about the perplexities that assail the vast majority of our editors today, men of decency and devotion, men who are not afraid of a righteous brawl, men who are trying to do a good job for their readers and their communities.

The editor who claims that his newspaper prints all the news all the time is either a liar or a fool. We often tell our readers only half-truths. We are constantly sweeping facts under the rugs.

Today we have gathered to commemorate a great forthright Kansas editor, a man who went at his job with such good-humored vigor that the whole world knew him.

As a young reporter I was with William Allen White one June day when he was to make a commencement address at a Kansas teachers college. It was a blazing noon and we had just left the college cafeteria when White discovered that he had forgotten his straw hat. He proposed to go back for it.

"Here," said the college president, "why don't you wear mine and I'll send back for yours later."

"No," said White, "I prefer mine. The acoustics are better!"

There was an honest editor. We all talk through our hats, occasionally.

The *New York Times* has a slogan — "All the News That's Fit to Print."

I believe nearly every editor will subscribe to that slogan. The argument starts when you get down to the last three words. What is "fit to print"?

Well, the old-time tabloids and the latter-day scandal magazines proceeded on the theory that anything was fit to print that didn't bring on a successful libel suit or an enthusiastic horsewhipping. The peddlers of scum and slime and smut even invented an elaborate system of innocent-sounding synonyms, which were adjudged libel-proof, but which didn't fool—and weren't supposed to fool—their evil-minded readers.

Happily, there has been a public revulsion against this garbage. At least in the field of daily newspapers those papers that had the lowest standards have, in general, had the greatest recent circulation difficulties, and those that have tried to do a good job with significant news have, in general, prospered most.

So my gorge rises every time I see a movie or a television program in which people are harassed as blackmailers who threaten to "spill it all to the papers." The fact is that the average newspaper in America today is not remotely interested in most of the stuff that makes for blackmail. Nor should it be.

No, ladies and gentlemen, there is a great deal about our communities that we do not tell. And we do not tell it because for a variety of reasons we consider it nobody's business, not even ours. Still, when editors get together in shop talk you will find a wide range of disagreement as to just where the line should be drawn.

We are, for example, often guilty of double standards. Here is a case. Think with me for a moment and tell me what you would do.

As in all cities, we, in Tulsa, have several celebrated bums. Our most eminent bum is a panhandler who makes whisky money by selling yellow jacket pills to other bums. These pills have often been seized and often analyzed, and always they have turned out to contain nothing but bicarbonate of soda. This is a brilliant and godly idea, for not only is bicarbonate of soda no transgressor of the law, but it soothes the lacerated stomach linings of the unsuspecting customers.

Anyway, our particular bum has only one glory in this life and that is his complete bumness. So, when we occasionally run a little story to the effect that he has crossed the 1,000 mark or the 1,200 mark in his arrests for drunkenness and vagrancy, he is consumed with pleasure and gratitude and offers to buy our police reporter a beer.

Now take the case of another drunk, this time a professional man of wide and favorable reputation, a pillar in his church and community, with a fine wife and intelligent children. On one evil night he took aboard one martini too many and crashed his car into a tree. Our boys saw him when they got him to the station. He was without doubt pie-eyed. Stricken with remorse, he was admitting it to everyone.

Of course, his friends hurried down and got the charge reduced to reckless driving, and he later paid a fine — all of which our newspaper recorded. But did we tell the real truth? We did not. No one was hurt. Damages were paid for the wounded tree. We never told on this man although his family knew it and so did his intimate circle. But his reputation as far as the general public is concerned remains unblemished. And he has never taken another drink.

Here is a double standard. The dereliction of the bum is published. The dereliction of the solid citizen is not. The first had no reputation to lose. The second could have been vastly injured.

Were we wrong to give the gentleman one more chance?

But here is another double standard:

When a local woman suffers a miscarriage the home town news-paper never mentions it. We consider it a private tragedy that will be known, anyway, to the family friends and that is of no particular concern to anyone else.

Yet when the same misfortune occurs to a movie actress like Marilyn Monroe or Elizabeth Taylor it goes on page 1. How can we justify this? Has the actress forfeited her right of privacy? Many of our readers find escape from their dull and hum-drum lives by peering into the personal affairs of celebrities. How far should we pander to this reader-interest?

I don't know. We used both the Monroe and the Taylor stories.

There is a sound axiom in journalism that when a man runs for public office his past becomes public property. The people have a right to know what type of men are seeking to do the people's busi-ness. Each election year we examine with great care the records of the candidates, and particularly of the candidates of the party to which we don't belong.

Yet for many years an ex-convict has been holding public office in my community. He doesn't belong to my party, but we never point to his penitentiary term. Why? Well, he does a good job. He has been re-elected time after time and has grown gray in public service. There has never been a suspicion of graft or malfeasance. So, although a few old-timers may know about his record, neither the newspapers nor, more strangely still, his political opponents ever mention it. Are we wrong?

One of our perpetual puzzles is whether to recall the criminal record of a dead citizen. Consider the vast difference in reader interest between these two apocryphal stories:

"Mr. Gerald Cantonwine, 68, house painter, of 2273 E. 38th St., died yesterday in a Tulsa hospital after a long illness. He was born in Danville, Ill. and came to Oklahoma in 1920. He is survived by his widow, Mrs. Mamie Cantonwine, prominent southside church worker."

Or:

"Death, which he had eluded in a dozen blazing gun battles, finally came yesterday to Jerry (The Gimp) Cantonwine, prom-ment early day bank robber. The once-celebrated thief and gun-man succumbed in a Tulsa hospital after a long illness. In 1922

Cantonwine, originally from Danville, Ill., was convicted of four bank robberies and a gold shipment theft. He served 15 years in McAlester penitentiary. On his release he married "Flaming Mamie" McGuire, his former look-out girl, and took up house-painting. The Cantonwines lived at 2273 E. 38th St. His widow is now the only survivor of a gang that once included Gaspipe Flynn, Brassnucks O'Toole and Nitro Burke. She is a member of the Altar Guild at All Saints Church."

Of the two, which story would you run? Personally, the story I would run would be much closer to the second than the first although it needn't be so cruel. But a prominent criminal record is a legitimate part of an obituary notice. A completed penitentiary sentence may, as we say, discharge a man's debt to society, but he cannot expect society to erase from its memory the crime that put him there.

Still, this is a very rubber standard on our newspaper. If a man's criminal record was long ago and not too remarkable, and if we can assume that the vast majority of his acquaintances are unaware of it we usually skip it on what, after all, is his final story.

This perplexity applies not only to obituaries. It can be a problem of marriages, too. For example:

A short time ago our boys heard that a girl figure in a prominent criminal case, who had done time in prison and subsequently been released, had quietly married a local man. As good reporters should they ran it down and confirmed it.

But the girl's mother appeared breathless at the office and begged me to kill it. I argued that there was nothing disgraceful about getting married. The distraught mother was not to be put off with any such sophistry.

"You are anxious for the story," she said, "only because my daughter had committed a crime. You want to interest readers and you know that readers love to gossip. My girl, as you know, has been under the care of a psychiatrist. He recommended the marriage. He said that if she can have a few months of happy quiet homelife right now it may change her whole life for the better. I don't have to tell you what the consequences may be if you choose this moment to start the tongues clacking and the neighbors gawking."

Well, she had me there. We certainly weren't after that wedding as a society item. Besides, I knew she spoke the truth when she mentioned the precarious emotional condition of the girl. So I killed the story.

Several days later our opposition woke up and did a big piece on the marriage. Everybody thought we had been scooped. Our managing editor and city editor have been looking at me with gentle scorn ever since. It's obvious they consider me less of a newspaperman than a patsy. I'm quite sure they're right. But I sleep wonderfully these nights.

Still, there is another side to this coin. Our obligation to protect the apparently repentant criminal is nothing compared to our obligation to protect the innocent public. Yet there are plenty of sentimentailsts who think that what a large part of the criminal element does is none of the public's business.

Consider the New York State youth court act which, if it isn't repealed, is scheduled to go into effect next April. The act would consider all offenders under the age of 21 as children. They would not be arrested — only apprehended. A man of 20 could have completed his military service. He could have had a long record of robberies, thefts and assaults. But his record could be buried in the super-secrecy of the youth courts. A suspicious prospective father-in-law couldn't find the truth. An unsuspecting employer is denied the right to protect himself.

Oxie Reichler, the editor of the *Yonkers Herald-Statesman*, is conducting a vigorous and so far unsuccessful battle to end this odd-ball notion that people of 20 are still children, and that if juvenile crime is wrapt up like a mummy it will somehow evaporate. How long must a human being remain a juvenile?

At the age of 12 English boys used to go to sea as midshipmen. At 16 Napoleon was a lieutenant in artillery and David Porter was commanding his first ship. At 17 Mohammed was proving an able camel trader and Mozart had completed his second opera. Juvenile delinquency is never much of a problem where children are allowed — even required — to assume responsibilities as soon as nature makes them ready for responsibilities.

But consider New York State, where the period of legal irresponsibility is already up to 18 and where the most elaborate legal blocks are thrown in the way of letting the press or the public know just who among youth is committing crimes. Does it work? We have the statement by New York City Police Commissioner Stephen Kennedy to the effect that in the five boroughs crime

among persons between 16 and 20 is going up at the rate of 12 per
cent a year, and crime among children under 16 is increasing 32
per cent a year.

Here is where dishonesty, based upon the same pseudo-psy-
chology that has reduced progressive education to an absurdity,
is apparently a long way from being the best policy.

The effort to twist laws to prevent the press from informing the
people is well advanced in many areas of government. Bureaucrats
are human, and human beings like to conceal their mistakes if possible. Who among us does not? So all kinds of flubs and bloopers
are hidden in sealed files marked confidential and secret. And in
departments in Washington where there is not the slightest question of leaking information of value to a potential enemy many
records are withheld from reporters under broad provisions of the
so-called "housekeeping" directives. These directives require employees to do what is necessary for the welfare of their departments.
Good Lord, there's a wooden horse, bigger than Troy, itself.

But here, again, perhaps I must perplex you. Many of my colleagues in the newspaper business have leaped to the conclusion
that all public affairs, not directly connected with national defense,
must be conducted in the open. Once again we hear the ghost of
Woodrow Wilson pleading for "open covenants openly arrived at!"

I disagree. I think that much of the important business in a
republican form of government will be carried on behind closed
doors. I see few dangers in that. I see many advantages. For it is
only behind closed doors, as William R. Mathews of The *Arizona
Star* has pointed out, that most politicians — yea, even statesmen
— honestly express their views and try to get at the meat of the
question. As soon as the doors are open, or as soon as these gentlemen arise in a congress or a legislature, they start speaking for
the gallery. Our slang word "bunk" arose from the days when a
backwoods North Carolina legislator kept making bombastic
speeches which he hoped would be published back in Buncombe
county.

I don't mean to imply that legislative voting should not be in
the open, nor that the public should be denied the right to appear
before all committees, nor that any legislator should be excused
from explaining why he voted as he did. But I do mean that in
every city hall, every courthouse, every state capitol and in the
National Capitol, the White House, and the various Washington

departments no sound policy is decided upon without frank exchange of views. And a frank exchange of views is rarely reached
with the public and the press looking over the shoulders of the
policy makers.

The government of ancient Athens was an absolute and complete
democracy, with all deliberations carried on in the goldfish bowl of
open debate. But Athens became smothered with oratory, para-
lyzed with demagoguery, and finally wound up with such an un-
stable mobocracy that nearly every able Athenian was banished
from the land.

Our struggle in America is to maintain a republican form of
government that can do three things: remain responsive to the
wishes of the people, provide a large measure of administrative
stability, and stay flexible enough to meet the immensely complex
problems of our age. If, in the pursuit of these aims, the boys
want to retire now and then for a private conference, I'm not going
to hurl myself against the door.

As you can see from these apparent contradictions I don't consider the business of truth-telling a simple one.

I have tried to point out to you that a newspaper that sought to
publish all the facts all the time would:

(1) lay itself open to ruinous libel suits, since many things that
are true and provable are not privileged,

(2) be an accessory to blackmail and stand guilty of bad taste,
since much that is privileged is also merely degrading,

(3) be responsible for many injustices since some truths which
are privileged and neither profane nor pornographic are cruel and
unnecessary, and

(4) paralyze our popular government by insisting on a level of
reporting so free that it would destroy deliberation.

On the other hand, I have pointed out that it is not only a right
but a duty of the press to hammer down those barriers to truth-
telling that are based upon many theories of social justice, or that
are raised to protect inept bureaucrats from the consequences of
their own stupidities, or that for any reason are designed to shroud
those things which can be included in, as Harold Cross has put it,
"The People's Right to Know."

The latter is a bitter, serious battle. At the moment we are not
even winning it. But America is lucky that men like Russ Wiggins
of the *Washington Post*, Jim Pope of the *Louisville Courier-Journal*,

Herbert Brucker of the *Hartford Courant,* and Congressman John Moss are waging an incessant fight for more light in dark places. Without the right to learn the truth the press is powerless to fulfill its obligations to the community. But, alas, it's time for another paradox:

The newspaper's obligation to the welfare of its community is so fundamental that there are even times when a newspaper must print a lie.

A few weeks ago Springfield, Missouri, was shocked when a robber stabbed two store proprietors to death and then escaped. After several days of searching the police discovered the murder knife hidden in a pipe a block from the scene. By agreement between police and reporters this discovery was concealed.

Instead, the *Springfield News and Leader* gave page 1 play to a phony story to the effect that the next day the police intended to make an inch-by-inch examination of the area in an effort to find the weapon. Shortly after midnight that night a furtive figure stole up to the pipe and began searching it anxiously. The police leaped from their ambush and had their man.

Is there anyone who can say that this fake news story was not fit to print? Happily that's a rare, rare case.

The inexact science of truth-telling involves essentially the difficult business of selecting facts. The proper selection of facts gives a reasonably accurate picture. The improper selection can give a false one.

I once had a personal lesson in this matter. Some years ago we had a police chief of whom I was very suspicious. We rode him editorially at all times. We reported with glee those occasions when the police department looked silly or when the chief put his foot in his mouth.

One day he stopped me. "Why are you giving me the business?" he asked.

I assumed an air of righteous innocence.

"Is there anything that we have said that isn't true?" I demanded.

He looked at me hard for a moment and then walked on.

A month or so later I was preparing to leave for one of those South American police states that require a certificate of good conduct before they will grant a visa. So I asked our police reporter to get me the usual form letter from the police department.

An hour later a motorcycle officer delivered a "To-Whom-it-May-Concern" letter over the chief's signature that read:

"An examination of our files fails to reveal any instance in which Mr. Jones has been convicted of a felony. However, our files are very incomplete."

And appended to it was a note in the chief's handwriting. "All this is true, too," it said.

How shall an editor select his facts? Is the primary purpose of a newspaper to uplift, to inform or to entertain its readers? We all like to think that we succeed in doing all three things, but we are constantly putting our thumbs on the scales.

One of the best-edited newspapers in America is the *Christian Science Monitor*. Its influence goes far beyond the boundaries of its church. In its early youth it tried to print nothing but good news, but it rose to greatness after it began printing quite a bit of bad news, but doing it in a constructive and hopeful manner.

The *Monitor's* test for the news that's fit to print seems to be this: Is it the kind of news a truth-seeking reader needs to know about or is it merely a distressing accident of no social significance?

So, two weeks ago, when the Nebraska gunman, Charles Starkweather, was busy murdering 11 people the *Monitor* looked the other way. Not a line did it print about a story that had the entire world looking on with gruesome fascination.

But the *Monitor* did print an item about a group of Chinese students who tried to kill Chou En-lai with a penknife. This leaves me confused. I'll take 11 home-grown murders any day over a botched assassination 9,000 miles away.

If you want to live by inflexible rules, stay out of the newspaper business.

If you like inexorable and unquestioned truths, go into engineering or accounting or chemistry. The laws of stress and compression are unchangeable. If properly done, the debits will always balance the credits. A given catalyst in a given compound will react tomorrow as it did today.

But not so the newspaper business. It is a business as variable as human beings. The editor is torn between that which is popular and that which is instructive. He must understand that uncompromising honesty carries cruelty in its saddlebags, and that too much gentleness will help evil thrive.

He is constantly wondering how to play the unaccountably-brilliant speech of the candidate he isn't supporting and the un-accountably-dull speech of the candidate he is. He perspires over profound editorials, knowing all the time that it is the picture of the fireman getting the cat out of the tree that will draw 100 per cent reader interest.

He hates to be maudlin and inconsequential, yet he is losing his grip if he doesn't realize that the tear-stained face of the baby abandoned in the bus station many carry a more powerful social lesson than reams of statistics on parental delinquency.

He tries to be consistent. He lays down rules for reporters and desk men. And then there's a midnight call from a frantic mother and the rules go blooey. And the next morning he detests himself. He snarls into breakfast and doesn't throw bacon to the dog.

The science of truth-telling remains inexact.

All day long the editor flies by the seat of his pants in a thick cloud layer, with the compass swinging and the artificial horizon turning circles. But somehow the paper gets out. Somehow the right guesses seem to balance off the boners.

And then a truly great truth dawns on him. How sterile are the routine professions. How dull the easy businesses! The thing that makes journalism one of the most challenging callings on earth is its very perplexity — its wide areas of error — the utter impossi-bility of doing it as well as it ought to be done.

The editor wouldn't have it any other way. He goes home to the supper table whistling.

And he feeds the dog.

10

SOME THOUGHTS ON MAGAZINE EDITING

By Ben Hibbs

One spring morning a good many years ago, I was standing on the Santa Fe station platform at Emporia. It was the day of the annual Kansas editorial meeting, and Bill White was playing host to his fellow Kansas editors. I had arrived an hour or so earlier and was waiting for a friend who was coming on the train from the eastern part of the state.

The guest of honor for the occasion was a notable newspaper editor from Chicago, and Mr. White, gracious as always, had driven down to the station to meet him. In due course the train arrived, and the Chicago editor stepped down from his Pullman, immaculate in spats and derby. Although Bill White was on a first-name basis with most of the great in this country, it happened that by some curious mischance he and his notable guest had not met, and the Chicago editor obviously had decided that this was the moment for a pretty speech. Probably he had been rehearsing it all the way from Kansas City.

"Ah," he said, "the one and only William Allen White." Then he added dramatically: "Mr. White, I think I'd rather meet you than my Creator."

"Well," said Bill White, a twinkle in his eye, "at least you'd be a damned sight safer."

It was this blessed sense of proportion, I think, more than anything else, which endeared William Allen White to all of us who knew him — and, for that matter, to the world. Fame did not rob him, as it does some men, of his deeply human qualities. He knew that a chuckle was often the most effective antidote for all manner of human ills, and for nearly a half century the sparkling stream of common sense which flowed from his littered office in the *Gazette* building was balm for what ailed us.

It was just thirty-five years ago this month that I finished my formal education here on this wonderful old hill and went to my first newspaper job in Kansas. (Somewhere along the way I had stayed out of school for a semester, to earn enough money to continue eating, and as a consequence I finished my course at Kansas University in February of 1924 rather than the previous June.) I went to my brand new job on the *Pratt Daily Tribune* with a sense of pride — as did all young fellows who cut their journalistic teeth in our commonwealth in those days — because Kansas had long been known as a state of remarkable small town newspapers. The Kansas newspaper tradition was a trust which we all felt obliged to maintain, and although we were not always successful, we put a lot of sweat into the trying.

Bill White, who even then was known wherever in this world the English language was spoken, was the bellwether of the flock — and our hero. I suppose most of us, unconsciously, tried to be like him, and we practically rolled over with happiness when our editorials were reprinted in the *Emporia Gazette*. It was characteristic of Bill White that he was kind to those of us who were trying to gain a foothold in the publishing field. Enormously busy though he was, he never failed to answer a letter from a young admirer seeking advice, and often he took the trouble to write a word of praise for a piece of work he regarded as good.

But above and beyond these little attentions was the simple, but dazzling fact that here among us, on our own green Kansas prairies, was the great William Allen White. His mouthpiece was no larger than most of ours, and yet he made himself heard around the world. He was living proof — and in this there was infinite hope for all of us — that it is not the size of the job, but the size of the man, that counts.

For the past seventeen years, I have edited a publication which reaches millions of people each week; yet now and then when I have a moment to take a look at myself and my job, I am still acutely aware, as I was in my Kansas newspaper days, that it is the size of the man, not the size of the job, that really counts.

Sometimes in that last calm half hour of a winter afternoon, when the last letter has been signed and the last fractious author has been seen and sent on his way, I stand at the window of my office for a few moments and watch the five o'clock shadows gather on the classic old clock tower of Independence Hall in Philadelphia. And I permit myself to dream a little about all the history that has passed this way — out there and up here. National history out there in that mellow colonial building across the square, publishing history up here — here in this office I now occupy for a little while.

And usually I come to with a sense of dismay and say to myself, with some degree of perplexity: What in the world has happened to the magazine publishing business?

For in those other days there were giants, and I don't say this facetiously. I think any honest magazine historian would tell you that the genuinely distinguished magazine editors — men who were public figures of some consequence, whose names were almost household words — are all dead and gone. Today the editor of a national magazine, to most of his readers, is a name at the top of a masthead, or, at best, a shadowy figure who makes the papers now and then when he is appointed, when he is fired, or when some controversial article pitches him, usually in a posture of defense, on to the front pages for a day or so.

Part of the reason, I suppose, is that the breed had more hair on its collective chest in those far-off days. But perhaps the more basic reason is that those were the days of personal journalism — in the magazine field as well as in newspapers. It was a kind of journalism we couldn't possibly practice, even if we wanted to, in an era when the volume of printed matter flowing from the presses has risen to a tidal wave. Magazine editing today has become a team job, simply because the volume of work is so vastly greater and also because no one man can even hope to possess a sufficiently all-embracing knowledge of this complex world to do the job alone.

The editing and publishing of magazines has become incredibly more complex than it was forty or fifty years ago. The reason for this has many components: the vast physical changes that have entered into publishing, such as the arrival and development of color printing and the coming to maturity of photography; the fact that the world rather than the nation is now our stage; changing tastes in reading matter, as in everything else; the fiercely competitive struggle for large and larger circulations; the rise of formidable new competitors in radio and television — and a host of other things. Yet I suppose that the broader, more dramatic answer is simply that the world itself has grown incredibly more complex.

In any event, the startling fact is that I now have about five times as many people on my resident editorial staff as did George Horace Lorimer during his long years as editor of the *Saturday Evening Post*. And there are no drones among us. Everyone works hard, and many of us carry home stuffed brief-cases almost every evening. It is simply that the work to be done has multiplied over and over and over again.

The company which I now serve produced two of the giants of whom I spoke a moment ago. George Horace Lorimer and Edward Bok certainly were among the greatest of the great editors, by any yardstick you care to apply. I live and work in the enduring shadows they left behind, and I have unlimited admiration for their brilliance and their really magnificent accomplishments. I suspect, however, that never again will the Curtis Publishing Company have another George Lorimer or Edward Bok — and I am sincerely saddened by the thought. Yet if by some chance such a man did come along, I wonder whether my company would know what to do with him. I suspect — and I say it humbly and with the utmost respect for all the great editors of the past — I *suspect* that he might not fit in. I am afraid the day of the one-man show in the editing business is forever gone. We live in a different world and a different publishing climate.

I hasten to add, however, that perhaps this change which has occurred cannot be written down as entirely a loss. For the simple fact is — although it is probably highly immodest of me to say so— that magazines, generally speaking, are a great deal better than they were a generation ago or two generations ago. They are more crisply written, more carefully edited, more informative, more entertaining and of course far handsomer. This despite the fact that there were giants in those days and there aren't any now. There are some undeniable advantages in the team method of editing.

Sometimes we magazine people are asked whether the magazines have a future. It is a question that has been asked rather often during these recent years of the rise of television. It was asked with particular persistence two years ago when the Crowell magazine empire — consisting of three once-great publications, *Collier's, Woman's Home Companion* and *The American* — vanished from the face of the earth. (I'll have something to say a bit later about that black chapter in magazine history.)

In any event, I'd like to answer the question as to whether magazines have a future with an emphatic Yes. But then I'd like to add, in the next breath, that those magaiznes which want a future must cleave to certain basic principles which have never been outmoded, and never will be, by all the volcanic changes which sweep through the publishing industry with each new generation.

There is a good deal of hard evidence that magazines will continue to be part of the American scene. For example, despite all the new forms of competition that have been thrown at us, aggregate magazine circulations today are growing faster than the population of this country — always a healthy sign. If I may be vulgarly boastful for a moment, I might mention that the circulation of the *Saturday Evening Post,* which was around 3,000,000 when I became editor seventeen years ago, reached the 5,900,000 mark this past fall, and I suspect we will pass 6,000,000 before the wild daisies bloom along the Kansas roadsides this spring. To nail down the point I am trying to make, I wish to add that the years of my editorship, the years of this growth, span precisely the period of the arrival and explosive growth of television.

Moreover, during the past ten years, while television has swept across the nation like a prairie fire, the readership figures on the content of magazines — as shown in the best readership studies we can produce — have remained fairly constant for most magazines. If you don't believe that people are reading the magazines these days, all you have to do is to sit where I sit, publish something controversial, something that stirs people up, and then watch the mailbags full of letters come in — and duck the brickbats.

I firmly believe that despite all the new diversions, despite all the demands on people's time, there will always be a large segment of our population which wants something informative and entertaining to read. I refuse to believe that we are about to become a nation of illiterates. There is too much evidence to the contrary. And so long as people want something to read, there will be a continuing place in their lives for the magazines — provided the magazines are honestly and intelligently edited.

It would be a bit silly, of course, to deny that television has had an impact on the magazines. Our new competitor has been taking an increasingly large bite of national advertising budgets, and of course some of this revenue has come right out of the hides of the magazines. However, I have noticed that surging changes of this sort have a way of leveling off, and this is what seems to be happening now in the national advertising field. In the end, I suspect, each medium will get a fair share of the take, and there will be enough for all. The long-range business outlook for the magazines is by no means as dismal as some of our electronic competitors would have you believe.

Obviously, since my whole life has been devoted to writing and editing, I am no authority on the business side of publishing, and I have no intention of going deeply into these problems this afternoon. I have taken this brief excursion into the competitive economics of the communications field for two reasons. In the first place, I think there is a widespread misconception about the effect of television on magazines. Television has not robbed us of readers or readership, as many people suppose; the threat has been on the advertising side. The second reason for taking this quick look at the financial skies is that there is no denying the importance of the balance sheet to the future of editing. One of the simplest and most inescapable facts of publishing life is that editorial independence is much easier to maintain, editorial courage is a lot easier to practice, when your publication is financially impregnable.

A moment ago I said that there are certain basic principles of editing which must be adhered to if magazines are to have a continuing place in the life of this country. Suppose we take a look at a few of them.

One of the current trends in the magazine field which we editors must watch, and deal with realistically, is the current race for larger and larger circulations and the impact that it is sure to have on the very structure of the magaiznes if we permit it to become the dominating motive in editing. I have already indicated that I am proud of my magazine's circulation performance in the face of severe competition. Yet I suspect that there are danger signs ahead for all of us.

If and when that rising curve of circulation becomes the primary objective of editing, we are in trouble — deep trouble. Every editor worth his salt knows that there are ways to reach farther and farther down the scale of human intelligence and emotions and pile in the readers. The temptation is always there. Yet in the end, if we go too far in this direction, we certainly will destroy the character of the publications we edit and betray the very people whom we really want as readers. And that, of course, would be the final disaster. We editors simply must not become so bemused by the numbers game that we forget our responsibilities to our fellow Americans.

Another part of this same problem was brought to my attention rather abruptly not too long ago by an intelligent friend of mine — a man who reads a lot and thinks about what he reads. He said to

me: "You know, a great many of the large magazines are getting
to be more and more alike." It brought me up short, because when
I stopped to think about it, I had to admit that the criticism was
at least partly justified. And again this is doubtless one of the results of the numbers game we are all playing. The picture magazines are using more text, the text magazines are using more picture stories, some of the women's magazines are trying to attract
the whole family, the general magazines are frantically pursuing
the female readers, as Harpo Marx used to pursue the blonde, and
we are all trying to pry the kids away from the television sets now
and then, with the hope that we'll have a few readers in 1975.

Perhaps some of this is good, even necessary, but I have a hunch
that we'd better watch it. If we try to be all things to all men, *and*
women, *and* children, we may destroy the priceless quality of dis-
tinctiveness that the American people have always liked in their
publications. Moreover, I can't help wondering how many of the
13- and 14-year-olds you can herd into the fold without losing the
35-year-olds.

One stinking hot day in the summer of 1957, my two top associates, Executive Editor Robert Fuoss and Managing Editor Robert
Sherrod, and I sat down to ponder some of these problems. All
three of us had an uneasy feeling that we were letting the magazine get a bit out of balance. Somehow we seemed to be drifting
over just a little more each year to the lighter side. We felt that
we were getting out a good magazine that was both informative
and entertaining, and we weren't publishing anything of which
we need be ashamed; yet we were considerably less than satisfied.
We had the unhapy feeling that in a world filled with the lack of
human understanding, with continuing crises both at home and
abroad, we were failing — to a degree, at least — in our function
as editors.

Now, it would have been a relatively easy thing to tip the balance back in the other direction simply by publishing a bit less
of certain types of material and a bit more of others — a mere
shift in the ratio of things we were already doing. I must confess
that I proposed we do just that. (I am told that as one grows older
the familiar rut looks more and more inviting.)

However, Bob Fuoss, who is younger than I am, who is often
frighteningly outspoken, and who is by all odds the best idea man
we have on the staff, promptly sat on my neck. If we were going

to nudge the *Post* a bit more over to the serious side, said he, then for heaven's sake let's not do it in the same old way. Let us devise something new in the mass-audience magazine field — something that would attract attention and resound to the glory and prestige of Benjamin Franklin's old magazine.

Well, said I, that sounds good, but specifically what? On that note the meeting broke up, and the three of us went away to think. Three days later, Fuoss slapped down on my desk a memo which became the blueprint for our enormously successful new feature, "Adventures of the Mind."

Briefly, the basic idea was that there existed in this country a vast chasm between the great thinkers and scholars in almost all fields of knowledge and the common, garden variety of citizen who sells automobiles, runs a bank, prospects for oil or raises cattle and wheat. In other words, the intellectuals weren't communicating with us ordinary folks. The scholars conversed with one another through their erudite journals and in their rarified meetings, and most of the rest of us simply lumped all such people together under the general heading of "eggheads" and made no effort to understand what they were saying.

We convinced ourselves that it was important to establish a bridge between the first-rate brains of this earth and the rest of us people. We thought that perhaps a mass-circulation magazine such as the Post, reaching a large and diverse audience, could provide one such bridge, and we decided to make the attempt. We decided to spend $100,000 to get the thing launched, and we decided if we ran into adverse winds, not to give up in a hurry, but to give the idea a real run for its money. We told ourselves that we could be satisfied if the new feature scored a readership of one-third to one-half the average of other features in the magazine.

So we detached one of our ablest staff men from his regular work and brought in another man from the outside — a highly successful free-lance writer with an intellectual turn of mind. With Fuoss riding herd, these two men went to work. They dug into the scholarly literature of this and other lands, compiled lists of possible contributions and, in due course, began hopping around the landscape seeing these people and proposing that they write on subjects of their own choosing — for the *Saturday Evening Post*. They were assured that they would be permitted to speak in their own scholarly way, that they would not be forced into the journalistic mold

and that they could say what they believed even ·if the editors
disagreed wholly or in part. They were offered a tempting price for
their contributions.

The project got under way slowly. This was something quite
different from assigning an article to a nimble, professional writer
and having him turn in a readable manuscript a few weeks later.
This took a lot of pulling and hauling. And so it was not until ten
months after the idea was born that we were able to launch our
new series. By that time we had a safe backlog of excellent and
thoughtful essays by some of the leading people of this country in
the sciences and arts and letters.

We started the series, with appropriate fanfare, in the late spring
of 1958, and the response was immediate, large and highly favorable. Approving letters flowed in, not only from college professors
and other intellectuals, but from the filling station proprietor and
the housewife. Newspaper publicity was enormous and continues
so to this day. Presently our readership studies began to come in,
and we found to our delight that the figures were approximately
twice as high as we had anticipated. "Adventures of the Mind"
appeared on an every-three-week basis through the summer months,
but by the time autumn came the feature was proving so successful that we stepped up the schedule to every two weeks.

We have now published twenty of these "Adventure" essays and
have touched upon a whole range of intellectual subjects such as
art, architecture, anthropology, biology, nuclear physics, electronics in medicine, history, poetry, religion, the theater, international
relations — and so on. The topics which fit into this frame seem
to be endless, and now that the feature is established we find that
it is much easier to persuade the scholars we want to participate.

Sixteen book publishing houses in New York have been competing for the privilege of bringing out the first eighteen or twenty
of these pieces in the form of an anthology. The contract has just
been awarded to Alfred Knopf, and the book will appear next fall.
We now expect to continue the feature indefinitely, and we think
it may well become as much of a fixture in the magazine as Tug-
boat Annie or Alexander Botts. We hope that eventually there will
be a whole row of anthologies derived from this material.

I have recounted this epiosde in editing in some detail because
I think it has a rather important meaning. I think there has been
a lamentable tendency on the part of editors to underestimate the

intelligence, and the latent thirst for knowledge, of a considerable segment of the mass audience. And if we magazine editors have been guilty of this sin — then, *brother*, what about television? (Forgive me, please. I couldn't resist that wicked little aside.)

There is another basic principle of editing which I feel is sometimes apt to be neglected in the current scramble for circulation and for public favor. If a magazine is to be vital, I think it must deal rather frequently with dangerous material — material which may bring in a wave of subscription cancellations or even result in troublesome and expensive law suits. You simply cannot avoid problems of this sort if you are to reflect the American scene honestly — the bad along with the good.

Last fall, for example, we published a four-part series about an obnoxious little character in Los Angeles named Mickey Cohen. Mickey had been for many years one of the kingpins in the rackets on the West Coast, until finally he was sent to prison on a Federal income tax rap. After he was released, he set himself up in Los Angeles in a luxurious apartment and lived off the fat of the land, meanwhile still owing Uncle Sam a large sum of money in back taxes, which he said he couldn't pay because he had no income. Hollywood society took him to its bosom, and school kids sought his autograph just as they do from movie stars. We thought the false social standards which can produce such a disgusting phenomenon needed airing.

So we assigned an able free-lance writer, Dean Jennings, to dig in and get the story. Cohen soon became aware, of course, that we were preparing a series, and he enlisted the services of a Philadelphia attorney, who came to see me and in an amiable but firm way made the remarkable suggestion that Mickey ought to have the right to see and edit the manuscript before it was published. I commented, with equal mildness, that if we were doing a piece about the president of General Motors, he wouldn't have the privilege of editing the manuscript.

We showed the Jennings manuscript to our attorneys, of course, and they told us, as they often do in such cases, that it was a calculated risk. We might well get sued, but if we did they felt they could defend us successfully. So we published the series, and Mickey came to Philadelphia and, flanked by a Los Angeles lawyer and a Philadelphia lawyer, filed suit against the *Saturday Evening Post* for one million dollars — with appropriate front page publicity.

It seemed that our series of articles had prevented this fine fellow from regaining a good reputation in the eyes of his fellow men. The story made a nice tid-bit for the papers for a couple of months, and then on the day that a preliminary deposition was to be taken from Mickey by our lawyers, the suit was withdrawn. We hadn't lost too much sleep over the suit, but we had gone through an expensive period of preparation for the trial — for one never knows whether such threats are a publicity gesture or the plaintiff really means business. Anyway, it's all part of the cost of doing business in the rough-and-tumble world of editing.

Incidentally, the Internal Revenue Service is now once again digging into Mickey Cohen's improbable finances, and it could be that in the end he will have to pay his taxes — just as we less favored citizens do.

The other category of dangerous material — and it is perhaps even more important and more troublesome than the kind that invites libel suits — is the sort of thing that brings down upon the editors' heads the wrath of a considerable segment of otherwise loyal subscribers. Some three months hence, we will publish a series of articles by Virgil Blossom, the recently deposed superintendent of schools in Little Rock, Arkansas. The series is approaching completion by Mr. Blossom and a collaborator, and we have seen most of the copy. It is a meaningful and tragic story, and, editorially speaking, it is loaded with dynamite.

Mr. Blossom is no rabid integrationist; indeed, he felt that the Supreme Court decision was premature. But he is a conscientious and law-abiding citizen, and he and his school board worked out a plan for the gradual integration of the secondary schools in Little Rock. His plan was received with genuine acclaim by the people of his city — so much so that only a few months before the trouble started Virgil Blossom was named Little Rock's man of the year.

But then the extremists on both sides of the issue got into the act, demagoguery had its day, and we all know what happened on a public level. What the public doesn't know is the incredible inside story of what happened to an honest and sincere man who tried to do what he thought was right. Blossom tells that story in our series, clearly and with forceful restraint. When we publish it, we will be subjected to violent criticism by the extremists and also by a good many decent people whose minds have been pre-condi-

tioned over the generations—and we'll get some cancellations from
an area where the *Post* has long been strong in circulation. Again,
I say these things are an inevitable part of the cost of doing
business.

On previous occasions when I have spoken about this phase of
editing, I have mentioned that I come of Quaker ancestry and by
nature I shrink from a fight. But, the Lord knows, I get into plenty
of them. Maybe it's because I decided a long time ago that any
publication worth the paper it's printed on must stand up on its
hind legs now and then and speak its piece. More probably, however, it's because some of my associates are forever egging me on
into these indiscretions.

Having declaimed at length here today about the serious, often
troublesome and perhaps more virtuous side of editing, I wish to
say that there is another side which cannot be neglected by a mass
circulation magazine if it is to perform its entire function. We,
along with most other publications in the multi-million circulation
category, are also in the business of entertaining. I defend that
function of the magazines.

It is a pretty grim world we live in these days, and those publications which deal with the current scene must, inescapably, mirror some of that grimness. Yet, after all, the world is not entirely
composed, even in 1959, of hydrogen bombs, juvenile delinquency,
race riots, mental institutions, heart disease and cancer. These and
a host of other defects in our civilization must be dealt with. Yet
I can remember the time when people thought *it was fun to read.*
Some of them still do, and we must convince more of them, particularly the rising generation, that this is a fact.

Incidentally, I am not advocating froth, nor am I talking about
the sweetness-and-light, everything's hunky-dory type of nonsense
which pervades some of the writing that gets into the magazines
these days. I am talking about good, wholesome entertainment.
Why shouldn't we provide our readers with a bit of "escape" — to
use a dirty word — from the cares of daily life, through the ve-
hicle of a buoyant human interest article or an absorbing story?
It is one of our functions, and a highly worthwhile function, I
think. I can't help remembering that President Wilson, the most
intellectual of American presidents in the twentieth century, thoroughly enjoyed who-dun-its. There is nothing incompatible in in-
tellectuality and love of entertainment — in a man or in a maga-

zine. The principle of balance of which I spoke a while back works both ways.

And so, if you should pick up a copy of the *Saturday Evening Post* that went on sale today and notice that the lead article, the first of a series, begins the story of Arthur Murray, the famous dance master, as told by his wife, Kathryn Murray, I hope you won't feel a bit cynical about some of my high-minded remarks in this lecture. Why are we running the Murray story? Because it is a gay and lively human document, full of the fun of living. It's readable; it's good entertainment. That is its only purpose.

And now finally, before I bring this interminable paper to a close, I want to say just a few words about that cornerstone of all editing — editorial independence. Earlier in this lecture, I mentioned the collapse of the Crowell magazines two years ago, and I referred to it as a black chapter in the history of magazine publishing. It was precisely that. It was a blow to the pride and the welfare of the entire magazine industry.

Why did it happen? Well . . . you can get a variety of explanations, depending on whom you are talking to. The advertising boys have one explanation, the financial people another, the circulation men another and so on. I'm an editor, and I'll give you the editorial explanation, and I think it is the right one, the basic one.

Briefly put, editorial independence to a large extent went down the drain at the house of Crowell long years before the final collapse of the publications themselves. During the last ten years of their existence, as financial troubles deepened, the editors were given less and less freedom of action. Someone from the business office was always looking over their shoulders. Things often were done editorially solely to attract advertising — always a vain procedure and in the end usually a fatal mistake.

During the fifteen years from the day I became editor of the *Post* until the death of *Collier's*, that once great magazine had six editors-in-chief. I knew all of them except the last one. There were at least two of them who were able men and who probably could have made a go of it if they had been given the right to do their best, without interference from the business office. They weren't. The business office ruled, and change after change was made in policy and personnel — too often for business reasons alone. It didn't work.

I am fully aware that it is bad taste to speak critically about the dear departed, but in this case I don't apologize. It is one of the tragic stories of publishing, and it should be known. The cornerstone of editorial independence is just as important as it has always been.

11

THE FIGHT FOR FREEDOM IN LATIN AMERICA

By Jules Dubois

If William Allen White were alive today I am certain he would have many opinions to record on the editorial pages of the *Emporia Gazette* about current events in Latin America, especially Cuba.

Here in the heart of the United States, William Allen White viewed the Latin American scene with a foresight of friendship and hope. Thirty-three years ago our relations with the United States of Mexico were as strained as they are today with Cuba. The Mexican Revolution was overrunning American property and interests.

Then President Calvin Coolidge chose Dwight Morrow as his ambassador to Mexico City, and on February 4, 1927, William Allen White wrote the following letter:

"Dear Mr. Morrow:

"I wish I could take our dearly beloved President and persuade him that the friendship of the Latin nations is on the whole and in the long run vastly of more cash value to America than the money that he would make in forcing our view of the Mexican situation upon Mexico at this time without arbitration. If he would only go to the World Court, or the Hague, with our case and let it rest there America would make billions in that imponderable thing that produces capital known as good will. Pardon this outburst from an anxious heart."

Three years later President Herbert Hoover appointed William Allen White as a member of a commission to investigate the occuation of Haiti by the United States Marines and to submit appropriate recommendations. Naturally, he and the other members of the commission recommended the termination of our occupation of that sovereign nation.

William Allen White was long an advocate of the Good Neighbor Policy, which President Herbert Hoover founded and to which President Franklin Delano Roosevelt gave a name and impetus.

The Sage of Emporia envisaged a Western Hemisphere free and friendly from pole to pole and, I am sure, he would be one of the most rugged pillars of the Inter American Press Association were he with us today.

Yes, he would be in the front line, raising his vigorous voice against the excesses of dictators and would-be tyrants of the right or left who silence the independent press and confiscate newspapers. And, there is not the slightest doubt, he would also be in the forefront, condemning the machinations of the communist conspiracy, which has been boring into all mass media of communications in Latin American and which is attempting to supplant freedom of expression with controlled and directed news and opinion as part of a methodical and studied plan to consolidate totalitarian tyranny.

Our government has acquired global headaches in assuming the political, economic and military responsibility in the struggle against the menace of Communism. Latin America no longer possesses any formidable barriers to communication between the republics because of the air age. The speed and frequency of air travel has helped to develop isolated areas and at the same time has created new problems in its wake, all of which you as newspapermen will have the responsibility to report and comment on.

European powers maintain colonies, some of them disputed by Latin American nations, in the Western Hemisphere. These include the islands of the West Indies, most of which are British, French and Dutch possessions, the Falkland Islands in the South Atlantic and the colonies on the mainland of Central and South America. Argentina claims the Falkland Islands. Claims to British Honduras are voiced by the neighbors, Guatemala and Mexico. There is no pending territorial dispute over British Guiana, to the south of Venezuela; not to Surinam or Dutch Guiana to the south of the latter and the same holds true for French Guiana which borders both Brazil and Dutch Guiana.

The twenty independent republics to the south of the United States are collectively referred to as "Latin America." The official language in each of the republics is of Latin origin. In Brazil, the largest, Portuguese is spoken. In Haiti, the smallest, French and a Creole patios are spoken. In the other eighteen, Spanish is the official language.

Puerto Rico, the easternmost island of the Caribbean Sea, whose shores are also caressed by the breakers of the Atlantic Ocean, is an Associated Free State, or Commonwealth, of the United States where Spanish is the official language. In any report of Latin America and its role in United States strategy, Puerto Rico, Cuba and Panama must inexorably be included these days.

The eighteen Spanish-speaking nations obtained their independence from Spain. These are Argentina, Bolivia, Chile, Colombia, Venezuela, Uruguay, Paraguay, Ecuador, Peru, Costa Rica, El Salvador, Honduras, Guatemala, Mexico, Dominican Republic, Nicaragua, Cuba and Panama. The latter, the baby of the republics, after having joined Colombia in the 19th century, seceded from it in 1903. Cuba won its independence in the Spanish-American war with the help of the United States and the valiant sacrifice of the lives of hundreds of Americans.

Today the Communists and their tools have been endeavoring to drive that irrefutable truth from the minds and hearts of the Cuban people in the most devastating, ceaseless and concentrated "Hate America" brainwashing operation in contemporary history.

Brazil obtained its independence as an empire when it broke away from Portugal and, before the end of the last century, it became a republic.

Haiti severed its relations with France.

The twenty republics have one thing in common: the Roman Catholic religion is dominant in most of them. In many it is included in the constitution as the official religion of the country and in some the president is required by the constitution to be a Roman Catholic.

The European maritime powers, searching for a short route to the fabled wealth of the Indies, discovered and colonized North and South America in the fifteenth and sixteenth centuries. The initial colonization progressed rapidly and seventy-eight years before the Pilgrims landed on Plymouth Rock, there were settlements of Portuguese in Brazil and Spaniards in Mexico, Central America, and most of South America.

The impact of the philosophy of the rights of man, inspired by the ideals of the French revolution, the successful American Revolutionary War, Spanish colonial maladministration and oppression, and concern over the Napoleonic Wars in Europe set the stage for a series of revolutions in Latin America to liberate these colonies from Spain.

It has been a most difficult task for the people of the Latin American nations to shake themselves loose from the Old World colonial heritage in which the military played a predominant role under the Captain-Generalcies. Consequently, dictatorships were the rule rather than the exception for many years.

Most of the nations in Latin America have adopted our system of democratic representation and separation of powers as their form of government. Many constitutions are patterned after ours. As the nations of Latin America have been achieving more and more physical integration, and as a rising middle class has been replacing the extremely disparate rich-poor social structure, there has been an increasing trend towards demand for permanent respect of democratic processes and with it stability of government.

The stability of any government is dependent primarily on the loyalty of the armed forces and linked with this is economic prosperity. Latin Americans have long ago tired of the farce of the so-called "constitutional" dictatorships. There is alive and burning in most countries a fervent spirit for the realization of democratic ideals which, if properly cultivated and encouraged by competent and honest leaders, is the best antidote in the fight against Communism or any form of totalitarianism.

The instability and violent overthrow of governments has been the product of a variety of forces, notably ruthlessness of dictators, graft and corruption, ambitions of army officers either through their own independent action or encouraged by equally ambitious politicians or a combination of both, incompetency of politicians and flouting of constitutional processes by attempting to extend the lucrative presidential tenure, and, with increased intensity since World War II, the agitation and subversion of the communist conspiracy in the global master plan of the Kremlin for world domination.

The Communists and political demagogues who are either allied with them or use their dialectic have made Latin America a fertile field for class warfare and with it ultimately oppress the people and stifle liberty. The economy of those countries has long been dominated by the landed aristocrats and industrialists who are branded as oligarchs by the extremists of the right and left.

The landless peons are easy bait for the rabble rousers, chauvinists and communist agitators because they are told that they, as the human product, are exploited on the large estates and plantation, especially should the operation be owned by an American corporation. Since the slow, but steady, advent of a middle class, especially in the cities where the universities and industries have been established, labor leaders, many of whom are Communist-trained, sound the Kremlin klaxon against private investment capital with all the emphasis of their barrage directed against the Americans.

All this is germane to our subject because every demagogic dictator who whips up class hatred among the masses and attempts to destroy the system of private enterprise strikes out first against freedom of the press.

The same procedure is pursued by chiefs of state who wish to hide from the public knowledge any exposure by a vigilant press of their arbitrary acts against personal and political liberties, their personal enrichment through illicit as well as reprehensible means and any comment that might be critical of their regimes.

Hardly a year passes that we do not read of a new martyr of the press somewhere in Latin America because an editor or writer may have had sufficient courage to ignore the threats and intimidations of a ruler.

The United States had its John Peter Zenger in 1734 but near the end of the 18th Century Colombia had its counter part in Antonio Narino who was tried and imprisoned by the colonial authorities for editing a tract entitled "Declaration of the Rights of Man." Narino emerged from his incarceration to become one of the precursors of Colombia's independence from Spain.

The pungent pen of Florencia Varela produced the first martyr of the Argentine press. In 1839 he joined the illustrious Domingo Faustino Sarmiento on the staff of the newspaper *El Zonda* of San Juan, a city at the foothills of the majestic Andes in the north-western section of the country. With Sarmiento and others like Bartolome Mitre and Alberdi, the valiant Varela was persecuted by the Dictator Juan Manuel Rosas.

Varela moved to Buenos Aires to write in *El Comercio del Plata* and his critical bombardment of the dictatorship angered the tyrant so that an assassin was hired to stab the editor to death. This was accomplished in 1848. The mere 400 copies of Varela's newspear, an infinitely small circulation, it will be admitted, were of sufficient power to provoke the criminal act of desperation that was ordered by the target of his criticism.

A century later another dictator was to commit the same mistakes as Rosas and persecute the press of Argentina, refusing to learn the lesson of history. But there were martyrs in other countries . . . real heroes of the fight for freedom who refused to bow to the will of the tyrants and preferred to see recorded in the columns of their newspapers the dialogue of democracy rather than the monologue of dictatorship. Hence, they lost their printing plants or found them arbitrarily sacked, closed and/or destroyed and had to flee into exile for some years to live in safety abroad until they could return to a restored freedom at home.

This was the case of Julio de Mesquita, the editor and publisher of *O Estado de Sao Paulo,* of Sao Paulo, Brazil, when Getulio Vargas ruled as dictator in that great country in the thirties. Had the Inter American Press Association existed at that time, the Mesquita case and the odyssey of *O Estado de Sao Paulo* would have become better known throughout the Americas.

With the exit of Vargas from power in 1945, Julio de Mesquita returned to his native city, reopened his newspaper and contributed to guide that nation back to the road of freedom. A few years ago the courts of Brazil decided in his favor and ordered the nation to indemnify him for damages suffered because of the closure of his newspaper.

But can such a decision, which speaks highly of the independence and honesty of the courts of Brazil, ever fully indemnify Julio de Mesquita and his family or others who have suffered similar fates?

The same holds true with regard to events in Argentina in the last dozen years when a now thoroughly discredited dictator plundered the great newspaper *La Prensa* of Buenos Aires, closed more than 100 others, threatened and intimidated those who had sufficient courage to try to survive or absorbed most of the publications that were left to convert them into dull organs of prefabricated propaganda.

I was a witness to the plunder of *La Prensa.* Unable to silence the publication of news or comment that he considered dangerous to the permanence of his dictatorial rule, Peron resorted to the subterfuge of a strike by the servile bosses of the news vendor union who obeyed his every will. I watched the loyal employees of *La Prensa* petition the government and solicit protection to enable them to return to work and saw that same government ignore their repeated pleas.

And I stood on a balcony in the patio inside the *La Prensa* building one February afternoon, exactly nine years ago, as more than one thousand employees of *La Prensa* gathered there to vote on whether or not they would attempt to resume publication of the newspaper without guarantees.

With patriotic emotion those loyal workers sang the Argentine national anthem which ends with the words LIBERTAD! LIBERTAD! LIBERTAD! (Liberty! Liberty! Liberty!) From among that crowd a voice exclaimed with determined fervor: "We are disposed to give our lives to defend our country. Now we are ready to give our lives to defend freedom of the press!"

Little did he know that within thirty minutes his words were to be prophetic. The employees left the building to march to a building less than a mile away where the printing plant was located. I accompanied them. But Peron and his goon squads were ready for them. Before they could reach the plant they were attacked by goons and I saw them shoot down and club some of those employees. One of them, a linotypist named Roberto Nunez, was fatally shot, fourteen others were wounded.

Undaunted, the employees entered the plant and began to set type and make up pages. But, with them and *La Prensa*, Peron was not yet done. His federal police raided the plant, asserting they were searching for weapons that were used by the employees in the street battle. As always happens in totalitarian countries, the police "discovered" two pistols, one in a trash can and one in an employee's locker.

The police left the plant but before midnight they returned and arrested the 400 employees, shut the plant and hauled the workers away for questioning before a federal judge. *La Prensa*, which had last published on January 25, 1951, was not again to publish under its rightful owners until February 3, 1956. Before that could happen an aroused Argentine people had to overthrow Peron and force him to flee into exile.

On the morning of April 12, 1951, an obedient and equally servile congress by a vote of 103 to 16 approved a Peron bill to expropriate *La Prensa*. The 16 votes were from the helpless opposition bench. One of the opposition congressmen was Arturo Frondizi, today President of the great Argentine nation.

"My party," Frondizi said in the debate, "is defending the right
of all newspapers in the country to speak the truth and to express
their opinions with freedom. But there is no freedom of the press
as far as Peronism is concerned. What Peron wants is a press at
the service of Peronism and not a free press."

That night the all-Peron senate unanimously consummated the
plunder of *La Prensa* by a vote of 23 to 0. As soon as the vote was
announced the entire facade of the *La Prensa* building on Avenida
de Mayo was lighted to celebrate the occasion, for two weeks
earlier it had been seized by a congressional committee.

Under the brilliance of tiers of allegoric lights shone twenty-nine
color-tinted photographs of Peron and his wife Eva Peron. These
had been plastered on to its columns, on the windows and on the
iron doors of the building facing the avenue. There were only four
pictures of General Jose de San Martin, father of Argentina's independence. Forty-nine blue and white Argentine flags fluttered
in the chilly autumn breeze. Atop of the building the dome light
held by the Lady of Liberty, which was extinguished when the
Peron congressmen seized the newspaper, was lit. The light sym-
bolized, under the rightful owners of the newspaper, truth illuminating the world through a free and independent press. At the base
of the statue of the Lady of Liberty the plunderers of *La Prensa*
placed a large placard which read: "Now, it is Argentine!"

Even the handpicked labor bosses of Argentina to whom Peron
delivered *La Prensa* had no stomach for the Lady of Liberty, and
much less for a free press. They promptly dismantled the beautiful
damsel and, fortunately, stored her in a safe place where she was
discovered after Peron's flight and now shines once again in majestic glory over a free Argentina.

There is one little known anecdote of the *La Prensa* story which
deserves mention. It underscores the fact that freedom can be re-
gained if there are people with sufficient courage to fight for it,
and one of the most valiant fighters during the Peron dictatorship
was Mrs. Zelmira Paz Gainza-Anchorena, mother of Dr. Alberto
Gainza Paz. From her home in Buenos Aires she would telephone
the *La Prensa* of Peron almost daily throughout 1954 and 1955
and ask "When are you going to return my newspaper to me?" or
"When is Dr. Alberto Gainza Paz returning?" This constant need-
ling from the Grand Lady of the Free Press of the Americas, who
is now 85 years old, required courage under the dictatorship that

had frozen all her bank accounts and confiscated most of her property.

The drama of *La Prensa* electrified the people of the United States and of the rest of the free world. But there have been other equally vile acts committed against freedom of the press in various countries in Latin America. In 1952 in the name of a leftist revolution the government of Bolivia closed the newspaper *La Razon*, of La Paz, and it has been closed ever since. The next year officials of the same government directed the destruction of the newspaper *Los Tiempos*, of Cochabamba, only a few days after Communist delegations invaded the plant and demanded that the editor cease his criticism of their party and their activities. The editor and publisher, Dr. Demetrio Canelas, would have been executed by a firing squad if it had not been for the Inter American Press Association, to quote his own words of appreciation over the fact that he is still alive today. But he never has been indemnified for the loss of his property.

In 1953 an irate president closed two newspapers in the city of Guayaquil, Ecuador, and imprisoned a protesting editor of *El Comercio*, of Quito, Jorge Mantilla. After the Guayaquil newspapers were allowed to republish the same president closed *El Comercio* and that newspaper remained closed for some weeks before it was allowed to resume operations.

The list of heroes and martyrs is long and it is impossible to mention them all here. David Michel Torino, editor and publisher of *El Intransigente*, Salta, Argentina, spent three years in one of Peron's jails after the dictator closed his newspaper and confiscated his properties. For this he was awarded the first "Hero of the Freedom of the Press" medal of the I.A.P.A.

To Pedro G. Beltran, who today is Prime Minister of Peru, must go the credit for the fact that his country can be proudly listed among the free nations of the Americas. Four years ago, on February 17, 1956, he published in his newspaper *La Prensa*, of Lima, full reports of an army uprising in the Amazon city of Iquitos in Peru. The government attempted to censor the news and he refused to submit to censorship. With 51 editors and loyal employees he was arrested after the police invaded his plant and blasted them out with tear gas. He spent three weeks in an island prison before the dictator repented and released him and allowed his newspaper to republish without censorship in a country where the constitution proscribes censorship of the press even if civil rights should be suspended.

For this Senor Beltran was rightfully awarded the second "Hero of the Freedom of the Press" medal of the I.A.P.A.

One of the most lamentable situations confronted the people and press of Colombia for seven of the ten years of the last decade. Another great newspaper *El Tiempo,* of Bogota, was closed by a now thoroughly discredited dictator, General Gustavo Rojas Pinilla, and other newspapers in Bogota and in the provinces also suffered from the high-handedness of a man who sought to subjugate every one to his will while he enriched himself in office. When he was ousted by his own generals after a nationwide general strike on May 10, 1957, one of the first acts of the provisional government was to restore freedom of the press.

Today, Colombia is governed by a former distinguished editor and now eminent statesman Dr. Alberto Lleras-Camargo.

The press of Venezuela was under firm dictatorial control during the regime of General Marcos Perez-Jimenez and played a major role in his overthrow on January 23, 1958. Editors and publishers were imprisoned and in protest all the newspapers, except for two or three owned by friends of the dictator, halted publication. When Perez-Jimenez was shipped out of the country those newspapers resumed their operations.

Now we come to the present day situation in Cuba, which, of course, is of primary interest today. During the dictatorship of Fulgencio Batista most newspapers continued a practice that had existed for many years to accept what we would consider as subsidies from the government. This in no way inhibited some of them from publishing all the news about terroristic and counter-terrorist activities during the civil war led by Fidel Castro. It may have inhibited some from expressing forthright editorial opinions.

Several independent editors and publishers as well as reporters were targets for assassination by Batista's repressive forces. An Ecuadoran journalist was killed by one of Batista's agents shortly after he returned to Havana from the Sierra Maestra where he had interviewed Castro.

Castro's victory brought an end to the subsidies but the advent of a system that every day bears more and more identification with that employed by Peron in Argentina to end press liberty. Peron amassed for himself a publishing and radio empire the like of which no Latin American ruler had ever acquired on a proportionate scale except Trujillo in the Dominican Republic. Included in Peron's empire was a Latin American news agency which he founded and then had to abolish in 1955.

Castro's revolution has seized every newspaper in the provinces of Cuba as well as most of them in Havana. There are still a handful of independent newspapers in Havana but those, too, may soon find themselves additional victims of Castro's dictatorship of the working class.

It takes indomitable courage to criticize the Castro regime and his Communist advisers these days, and editors like Jose Ignacio Rivero of *Diario de la Marina* and Jorge Zayas of *Avance* have refused, together with the Carbos and Humberto Medrano of *Prensa Libre*, all of Havana, to join the maleficent monologue of praise and servile adulation which would ultimately destroy every vestige of liberty in that country.

The fate of Zayas and his newspaper is still fresh in our minds. He is in exile in this country and as Gainza Paz did in 1951 he elected to flee to safety to keep the flame of the torch of liberty burning for a free press through his writings and pronouncements from this land.

Now Zayas' newspaper has been taken over by the Castro revolution, and the first act of the new owners . . . the workers to whom it was given by the government just as in the case of *La Prensa* . . . was to call on the President of Cuba and thank him for the "gift" and convey to him their expressions of loyalty and defense of the revolution.

What was the basis for the Zayas conflict? The same as always. News stories, criticisms, commentaries published in *Avance* irritated and angered Fidel Castro, a man who had promised the Cuban people unrestricted freedom of the press. But let a translation which I have made of an editorial in *La Prensa* of Buenos Aires on last January 23 put this case in perspective. I quote:

"Very little time has sufficed in order to define the true scope of the hostility against the free press that the Cuban dictatorship has unchained. The editor of *Avance*, one of the organs most offended by the proclamations of Fidel Castro, has had to seek refuge in a foreign embassy, and the personnel of his newspaper, voluntarily or compulsorily at the service of the government, has taken charge of its publication, of course without risk that their editorials and news stories appear with a contradictory footnote as occurs in the non-subjugated newspapers.

"The operation, as we see it, is technically perfect. The government affirms that it has no complaints against the editor of *Avance*, and that it will give him all kinds of guarantees in order to leave the country. Nothing more logical, of course, for what is sought is to prevent that he continue acting freely as a newspaperman. The pretense is to show that what happened is a case of voluntary resignation of the exercise of journalism and even of the property of the newspaper. It will not be possible to fool anybody who knows the non-perplexing procedures of the governments of force.

"An imaginary labor conflict served as a pretext to the dictator who fled from Buenos Aires in 1955 to plunder *La Prensa* and all of its properties. Here we know the methods used to distort the truth and legitimize the most audacious usurpations. The dictators believe in the skill of such dissimulation, because they have limitless confidence in the popular ignorance. But they are wrong.

"The imagined procedure in Cuba consists in disposing of space of newspapers belonging to someone else — in other words of private property — in order to attack the orientation and conduct of their owners on the grounds that the unions also have the right to exercise freedom of the press. They have that, undoubtedly: more so when they do it in newspapers that belong to them.

"To maintain that they can use the columns of any newspaper in order to say what they want and attack its editors is something so irresponsibly absurd that it is painful to comment upon it as an expression of government opinion.

"The editor of *Avance* refused this right; but he could not prevent the abuse from continuing and understood that his attitude carried for him grave consequences. Because of that, he asked for diplomatic asylum to leave the country. His newspaper has remained in the hands of the revolutionary shock groups. This is what was sought from the first moment and what would have been clearer to have arrived at directly, without so many subterfuges, clevernesses and adulterations, which in final analysis only unmask the rule of force. The new preaching of the plundered newspaper was not of much service to the Cuban dictatorship. On the other hand, its example will remain as conclusive proof that in Cuba today there neither exists freedom of the press nor guarantees for legitimate property."

The fact that the Newspaperman's Union of Havana and the Graphic Arts Union are dominated by Communists helps, in addition to other obvious reasons, to explain the predicament of the press of that country. The totalitarian concept of freedom of the press has been and is being invoked and the fact that the remaining independent newspapers have not yet been confiscated need stir no ray of hope.

Neither need any one suspect that those unions have been acting entirely with independence and without the full concurrence of Fidel Castro, for he himself confirmed that in a radio broadcast only last month.

You will be interested in the footnote which the unions attach to any story or commentary which is critical of the Castro government. I quote:

"CLARIFICATION: This cable is published by the will of this newspaper company in legitimate use of existing freedom of the press in Cuba, but the reporters and printers of this center of work also express in use of a legitimate right, that its contents are tendentious and form part of the conspiracy against our country."

The most laughable feature of that is the fact that the unions have designated their own "Committee of Freedom of the Press" to execute the surveillance and application of the absurd footnote.

Some editors have elected the course of least resistance and do not publish any dispatches or commentaries that might bring the footnote. One newspaper, *Informacion,* has decided to test its constitutionality in the courts, a forlorn hope in a country where laws are being made at the whim, and to further the designs, of one man.

Contributing to this unhapy situation in Cuba is the heavy dose of Castro-oil which is being administered to the people — and, mind you, many of them swallow it with delight — by the bearded premier in the most concerted and concentrated brainwashing operation in contemporary Latin American history. This is done by television, by radio and in the captive press.

Although the subsidies and "botellas" have been abolished by decree, Castro has found other ways and means to control the "friendly" press while threatening to kill the independent ones through economic strangulation.

A noted Cuban once said, and I quote: "It hurts at times to see how certain newspapers court the mob. They please their likes, they sacrifice their own culture, they try to please the vulgar and the brutal ones: they perform in the hope of receiving a gratuity, using servile trappings and the painful smile of the lackeys."

The man who said that was Jose Marti, the George Washington of Cuba and the man who is most quoted by Fidel Castro to try to justify the road along which he is leading that country.

The pattern that is being followed by Fidel Castro is not unlike that of Peron. He, too, has formed a Latin American news agency, the primary mission of which appears to be to promote Castro's revolution and friendship with the Communist bloc of nations and to attempt to undermine the prestige of the United States.

Neither is it a strange coincidence that the executives, personnel and correspondents of Castro's news agency are mostly Peronists, Communists and red fellow travelers.

There is room for a legitimate, objective news agency in Latin America, operated by natives of those nations. Perhaps some day it might be born and become a reality.

If William Allen White were with us today and were examining the Cuban scene he would probably repeat what he wrote to Dwight Morrow in 1927. But at the same time, I am certain, he would raise his respected voice and warn the people of our country of the pincer movement that is being directed from Moscow in alliance with Peiping to attempt to destroy our way of life and the liberties of the people of Latin America.

The first goal of the Communists or dictators of the right is to gain control of all mass media of communications. Once in their hands, the mesmerizing process and brainwashing are used to establish thought control. The Committee on Freedom of the Press of the Inter American Press Association took cognizance of this at the Fourteenth Annual Meeting held in Buenos Aires in October 1958 as follows:

"There was concern expressed in the deliberations by your committee over the increasing militancy of the communist organizations to propagate the destruction of the independent press through penetration and propaganda in the field of mass media communications. The question was asked whether or not the independent press is alert to this problem as well as to the danger of similar action by other totalitarian organizations and whether enough is being done to counteract the termite tactics that are being employed to undermine liberty.

"We should not forget that dictatorships are the breeding ground for communism. Yet how often do we hear the praises sung of dictators by themselves and their adulators and ingenuous public officials of democratic countries, who are described as champions in the fight against the advent of communist tyranny.

"The Inter American Press Association has no remedy for fear. Yet, unless the independent press of the Americas assumes its vigorous role of vigilance, through the printed word, to counteract the increasing penetration of communist and other totalitarian opinion in the field of mass communications, the day may not be far away when that penetration will blossom into an explosion that will destroy freedom of expression and all the freedoms which we cherish.

"The free press of the Americas has a grave mission. Freedom must go in hand with responsibility. Democracy can never be any stronger than the ethics, practices and eternal vigilance of those who have the responsibility to preserve it."

An appropriate resolution was adopted at the I.A.P.A. convention in Buenos Aires which read:

"WHEREAS:

"1) Totalitarian regimes and their agents undertake systematic propaganda against free journalistic enterpries and in favor of state owned newspapers that can be controlled by Government.

"2) Supporters of this campaign assert that freedom of the press can only be achieved by state newspapers which would represent the 'common interest'; and

"3) This campaign tends to confuse even governments that consider themselves democratic which may decide to establish and maintain state newspapers, or to favor the expropriation or confiscation of existing independently owned publications;

"THE I.A.P.A. RESOLVES:

"1) To warn Governments that a systematic attack on freedom of the press is a totalitarian practice intended for the purpose of bringing into disrepute real freedom of the press which exists when people are not obstructed in the free expression of their ideas in writing;

"2) To point out, at the same time, that publication of state owned newspapers and laws enacted for the expropriation of newspapers and their delivery to collectivized or state exploitation is contrary to the Charter of the Inter American Press and is an affront to the free spirit of democracy, which communism or any other totalitarianism seeks to destroy."

William Allen White would undoubtedly have subscribed to that. The issue of liberty or enslavement in Latin America has been joined, and the fight for freedom there will be a paramount interest for all of us in the days and years that lie ahead.

No people of any country in Latin America have for so long a time been subjected to so complete a blackout of news of what happens within their frontiers as the terror-stricken inhabitants of the Dominican Republic. Recent events there should serve as a lesson that even the blackout of the news will not prevent a people subjugated for thirty years from arising against a dictator, for the word-of-mouth telegraph can be as devastating as what appears in print.

William Allen White always believed that courage and integrity are the highest ideals of the newspaper profession and that freedom is something that is always worth fighting for. That is what made him a great man and that is why his memory will always be revered.

12

THE EDITOR AS A CITIZEN

By HODDING CARTER

I must relate a story and then challenge its conclusions. The story has to do with a little male monkey on that spectral day— not, pray God, an inevitable day—when the world turned to its ultimate weapons in the insanity of self-destruction. As the radio-active smoke and dust began to clear away, the monkey found himself, apparently alone, huddled in the shadow of a great molten pile which once had been a city. He was frightened out of his wits. He was shivering with shock. He was also hungry. And so, he began moaning over and over: "I'm hungry! I'm hungry!" Suddenly, out of nowhere, came the voice of another little monkey, a girl monkey. The voice said soothingly, "Have an apple! Have an apple! Have an apple!" The little male monkey forgot his hunger and fear. He rose to his hind feet and screamed his answer.

"What do you want to do? Start this damn mess all over again?"

Unlike that monkey, I would like to live all over again each of the years that lie behind; the doghouse years of a dissident newspaperman that have been a compound of frustration and satisfaction, of contentment with discontent.

It is only fair to tell you that the topic of this talk was determined upon through a process of elimination and by a helpful coincidence. The coincidence indirectly involves a noted son of Kansas who was a recent recipient of the William Allen White Citation. He is also the editor of a magazine which has helped me pay off the mortgages for nearly 16 years. You have only one guess as to who he is.

But first, the process of elimination.

A few years ago I might have talked about the problems of the small town editor and publisher. Nowadays, however, I've sort of lost touch with those problems because we—my wife and I— have turned most of them over to our oldest son. For a year and a half, he has been solving them with techniques learned in his post-college service as a Marine platoon leader. His decision to come home as a newspaperman gave me another moment of great professional elation.

Having thus discarded the subject of newspaper problems I considered next a "Whither Are We Drifting" approach. But as a Kennedy Democrat, I decided that not only have we stopped drifting but that we ought to give the new pilot at least a hundred days at the helm before dropping him over the side—even though two-thirds of our Southern Congressmen appear unwilling to wait that long.

Next I thought of dragging out another tried and true favorite, "The New South." But that one went out the window for two reasons. One is that some 80 years ago, Henry W. Grady, Georgia's greatest editor until Ralph McGill came along, described it, prophetically, and much better than has anyone else since. The other is that sometimes I tend to wonder how new, in an economic or democratic sense, are those areas of the New South where a man's right to vote is still challenged because of his color, and where unwarranted wage differentials too often provide a principal and near-irresistible lure for Yankee industry.

Then, of course, racial problems appeared on the horizon. But I live in Mississippi, and anyone who lives in Mississippi knows that there wouldn't be any racial problems if it hadn't been for John Brown, Mrs. Roosevelt, the Supreme Court and the NAACP; and that besides, if they'd just leave us alone, we'd settle them for good. I'm not sure whether that word "them" refers to the problems, or to the Negroes. The Citizens Councils won't tell me.

Finally, as a Civil War buff, I toyed with the idea of a backward glancing oration to be titled "One Hundred Years Ago—Why Did It Start?" But then it occurred to me that too many of our deep Southern politicians haven't discovered it ever stopped.

So, in despair, I almost telegraphed the Foundation that I must regretfully decline this great honor.

And, then, through Bill Breisky, associate editor of the *Saturday Evening Post,* who directs the Keeping Posted department, came salvation. It arrived in the form of a photostat of a letter I had written the Keeping Posted department, by request, nearly 16 years ago, after I had sold an article to the *Post* for the first time. As Bill said in an accompanying note, my letter had been a little long. He added that this was usual with first-time contributors who have been asked to tell something of themselves. He was gracious. The letter was overlong, self-consciously autobiographical and not a little fatuous. Its central theme was our newspaper and how we ran it.

The re-reading of that letter after all these years prompted what I will say today about the editor as citizen. In the summer of 1945, I had written only of the editor as the community's chronicler, commentator, and general hell-raiser. I have learned since then—and I may have suspected in 1945—that such a role, however stimulating or worthwhile, is an incomplete one. The editor should be equally the citizen, participating to the fullest in the life and aspirations of his town.

A clear division exists among newspapermen as to this concept of the editor's role as citizen. The cleavage is most apparent between metropolitan and small city daily editors. But it also cuts across each of these principal sectors of the American press. In opposition to my thoughts on the matter stand many newspapermen, on small as well as large newspapers, who are convinced that the editor should stay clear of what might be described as local entanglements, of which there can be many.

The argument for such detachment is reasonable. If the editor becomes actively identified with any organization or group which is likely to indulge in or be a subject of civic controversy or civic pressures, he cannot approach the issues thus created with the requisite Olympian detachment. Therefore, he should stand to one side, holding a mirror before his community, reporting what he sees in it, and, if he thinks editorial comment is required, make it from the vantage point of non-involvement.

We have pursued, especially during the last 15 years, precisely the opposite course. As a result our news columns may have reflected the civic, economic, political, social, and perhaps spiritual biases I have acquired through being a participant in a variety of community activities. It may be that our editorials have been similarly affected. I suspect they have. I also suspect that every newspaper reflects, in one way or another, the biases of the editor or the publisher, whether or not the said editor or publisher is a joiner. And it should be remembered that *bias* is not necessarily a dirty word.

Perhaps what I'm trying to say is that the editor can contribute more to the community's well-being if he thinks of himself

first as a citizen of his town, who by good fortune happens to be
a newspaper editor in that town, rather than as a newspaper editor
who happens to be a citizen, permanently or in passing, of some
particular town. Fortunate—though not yet rare—is the newspaperman who, in a day of newspaper monopolies, absentee and
chain ownership and the dramatic, inevitable reduction in the
number of daily and weekly newspapers, can make the choice of
his own free will. I am thankful to be one of the lucky ones who
can freely make a choice.

Now let me offer some illustrations taken from the experiences
of a very much involved editor to explain what I mean by all-
out civic identification, and why I believe such identification can
be alike beneficial to the editor, newspaper and the community.
Call it a case history of near-perpetual motion. It fits many of us.

This editor's first serious involvement in civic affairs came soon
after his return from military service in World War II. The local
school board and the community were alike divided on two issues.
One had to do with the qualifications and policies of the superintendent of schools. The other concerned the admission to the
white public schools of children from what is the second largest con-
centration of Chinese-Americans in the South. The resignation of
an undecided member of the five-man board had created a 2-2 dead-
lock on both issues. The city council asked the editor if he would
accept an appointment to the vacancy. He accepted. Subsequently
he supported, at board meetings and on the editorial page, the
superintendent of schools. The superintendent's critics had argued
that he was unacceptable because he advocated a mildly progressive system of education and because, as an alumnus of The
Teachers College of Columbia University, he almost certainly was
subversive. The editor also supported, in similar manner, the admission of the Chinese children although the state constitution
barred from white classrooms all who were not of Caucasian de-
scent.

The end results were something of a draw. The superintendent
eventually went out—but also up. He became dean of the state
university's Graduate School of Education without missing a day's
pay. The editor also went out. The city council did not reappoint
him to a full term. But the Chinese kids went in. Their younger
brothers and sisters are in the previously all-white schools today.

Two or three years later, a perhaps forgetful city council appointed a new library board. Among the members selected was the editor. The board was told to modernize the library to the extent of weeding out the almanacs and old mystery novels that filled most of the shelves, to eliminate also the pathetically underpaid, over-age, and untrained librarian, and to buy some books. The board followed orders. It pensioned off the ancient librarian. It bought new books, some of which were, in due course, considered by some citizens to be radical or indelicate. The editor personally selected and removed the worn old volumes thought suitable for the ash-heap. Almost everyone appeared satisfied with the changes. Then, success went to the editor's head. He proposed at a board meeting that Negroes be permitted to use the library at certain hours since no adequate branch library service was available to them. Out went the editor. In time, however, up went a Negro branch library which can call upon the main library for any books not found on its shelves.

Here ended the editor's direct affiliations with the city's officials. He turned next to the Chamber of Commerce, with some of whose prevailing policies—notably its attitude toward organized labor—he disagreed. In the years that have followed he has served variously as a director; a member of the executive committee; a member of the industrial committee whose purpose is to kidnap industries from other regions; and, almost continuously, as chairman of the publicity committee. At times during the unceasing search for new plants his newspaper resembled the official publication of the East Toonerville Booster's Club. During a sucessful campaign for community approval of a bond issue to build the nation's largest carpet-making plant, one reader said that every time he read the newspaper he spit wool. The editor himself spent almost as many hours in C. of C. meetings or out of town on the trail of industrial prospects as he did writing editorials. In between times he argued with his fellow directors and committee members, in meetings and in print, as to the propriety of the C. of C. serving as an outpost for the Democrat or Republican Far Right or as a buffer between low-wage-scale employers and labor organizers. He doesn't feel that the time away from his desk was wasted, nor the industrial publicity useless. Today the town has six more industries of creditable size than it could count ten years years ago. More than 2,000 people work in them!

As time passed, the editor rediscovered his church. Perhaps it was just because he was getting older. At any rate, to the amazement of his wife, his sons and his felllow parishioners, he began to attend church with some regularity, to share in the teaching of the adult Bible class, to turn up now and then as a delegate to state, regional and national assemblies of the church, and lately, to serve as the senior warden of the parish. As is not uncommon among religious bodies, the church was split over the merits of the rector. The editor found himself placed in the position of peacemaker — an unfamiliar role for most newspapermen—in the middle of a church fight, which, next to civil war can be the most bitterly divisive of conflicts. He also found more peace of mind than he had known for a long time.

Along the way, he somehow became involved in a variety of other civic affairs, all having, to his way of thinking, a common denominator. He has been a member of the Boy Scout Area Council, and a sponsor of a Sea Scout ship whose crew is mostly made up of youngsters from low-income families. He has taught night classes for the State University's Extension division. He has served as president of the state's historical society, if only because some rebellious college and university professors saw, in supporting his election, a way to irritate the politicians. For a long time he has been ringmaster and publicity man for the Cypress Saddle Club which began as a neighborhood organization of very young riders and today presents, twice a year, creditable, well-attended horseshows. He is an unpaid deputy sheriff, by appointment of a sheriff whom he supported and who has kept a campaign promise to clean up the county. He has been a member of two military-related local committees which might fairly be described as pressure groups. The purpose of one has been to keep the nearby Air Force installation open in some capacity until every last guided missile is in place. The continuing objective of the other has been to obtain city, county, state and federal funds for the enlargement, modernization and eventual rebuilding of the National Guard Armory. He has maintained memberships in two other pressure groups, some of the members of which have not always been pleased with his editorials—the American Legion and the Veterans of Foreign Wars. And he has remained for nine years a director of an organization which has been subjected to more pressures of a different kind and vilification than has any other of Southern origin and exclusively Southern membership. It is the Southern Regional Council, the only southwide, inter-racial body. Its single concern is racial justice; but its activities have earned for its staff and board members the epithets of Communists, fellow travelers, and nigger lovers. His membership has won for the editor the special distinction of being identified with Communist front organizations by broad innuendo of a state legislative committee.

During these post-war years the community in which the editor lives has prospered. Its population has doubled. Its business and industrial enterprises have been trebled and diversified. This happy situation has been achieved in considerable part by local citizens who have jointly invested in new business and small industries, not always with satisfactory results. It may be that the editor should have stuck to his knitting, using any available funds to enlarge or better equip his plant or to look for other newspapers which might come within his means. Instead he became involved in an assortment of local ventures which, in addition to the profit motive, have been undertaken because of community needs or goals or hopes. He has lost a sizable piece of his shirttail in a pleasure-boat building enterprise and another piece in a locally financed wildcat oil well drilled in the country. He is a director and stockholder in a million-dollar downtown hotel-motel, now a building with funds subscribed by more than 500 fellow-citizens in amounts from $100 to $25,000. The principal motive in this undertaking was the rejuvenation of the downtown shopping area which, like many another, has suffered blight because of the growth of neighborhood and suburban shopping centers. He is a director and stockholder in an industrial supply company, designed to meet the assorted needs of the new industries which continue to locate in the community and in the smaller towns nearby. The jobs and business and hoped-for profits would otherwise go, in considerable part, to distant metropolitan firms.

He is a stockholder in one of his town's banks which (by local sale of stock) raised additional capital to expand its loan facilities so as to help meet a growing community's banking needs. He is a stockholder in a relatively new insurance company, wholly owned by citizens of a state where most life insurance premiums are paid to companies far removed from their policy holders. He is a partner in a poultry raising company which produces some 400,000 broilers a year. A dozen or more of his fellow citizens have also gone into the chicken business. The compelling reason is that the community would otherwise lose a broiler processing plant, employing some 150 workers, because the plant was having to bring in live chickens from too far away for profitable operation. Until these townsmen went into broiler production, none of them even knew chickens could catch colds. They now know they can. He is also a partner in a projected long-range agricultural experiment, an interlocking pecan and peach orchard located on land ill-suited for standard crops. This is one of several diversification schemes recommended by federal and state agronomists for an agricultural area which must find new uses for land.

It may be argued that a man cannot serve two masters and that, accordingly, the danger of conflict of interest is too great; that the editor's chair is likely to be vacant too often if he is overly active in civic affairs; and that the concept of such partic-ipation is in itself provincial. Each of these criticisms may have validity. But I do not think them valid enough.

As for the threat of conflicting interests, it seems to me that the opportunity for good outweighs the likelihood that the editor might be improperly influenced by his participation in the diverse affairs of his town; and that if a newspaperman seriously doubts that he can be any less impartial or factual when dealing, as a newspaperman, with affairs with which he is closely identified as a citizen, he shouldn't be in the profession in the first place.

Concerning absences from the job, it must be admitted that were the newspaper under discussion much smaller, the editor could not have the freedom of movement which he now enjoys. But there are relatively few daily newspapers which are much smaller than this one. Besides, except for trips out of town on industrial missions, most of the time devoted to civic affairs is off-duty time.

I would like to discuss the matter of provincialism at greater length. *Provincial* is a word too loosely and too derisively applied to behavior and folkways associated with the American hinter-lands which that brilliant old debunker, the late H. L. Mencken, once populated exclusively with his Booboisie. Provincialism should not be so glibly categorized. You can find hicks in New York City—a great many hicks—in terms of their awareness of the nation and the world in which they live. You can find world citizens in Lawrence, or Emporia, or Greenville. In numbers, if not in total combined circulation, a majority of our dailies and almost all of our weeklies are provincial in purpose, outlook and achievement. There is nothing wrong about that. Provincialism is a healthy counterweight to concentrated urbanism. Politically, the small city newspapers have only limited influence. Their editorials may contribute to the election of a mayor, a councilman, a state representative, even a Congressman, but beyond that they cannot aspire. They cannot help a federal administration reach a decision or influence social change save to the extent that they report or reflect the thinking of the areas that they serve. Most certainly, they contribute nothing to the formulation of foreign policies. But their usefulness is great. Their local news columns give a sense of individual existence and individual worth to millions of Americans. In this century of faceless man, their editorial comments concern mainly, and give identification and sometimes direction to, the communities in which these millions live. Their editors, whatever their personal preferences, cannot live in ivory towers or in anonymity.

The small dailies have other similarities which combine to make it proper and sensible for the editor to be first of all a citizen. Here are the principal ones:

(1) Most of them are monopolies.

(2) Many of them have editorial policies which may seem too vigorous or advanced for the essentially conservative character of the American small city.

(3) All of them compete for circulation with the metropolitan newspapers nearest to them and with other mass media.

(4) The communities they serve are in unending competition with established metropolitan industrial and trade centers and with each other.

The *Delta Democrat-Times* embodies each of these likenesses. Our circulation is small and our range of influence is narrow. Our political and other comments are effective only within a limited area. Our editorials are almost always parochial. We emphasize local and regional events and achievements at the expense of global or even national reporting. We now enjoy a monopoly. I hope we always will. Our town is in active competition with our sister communities throughout the South which, like Greenville, must adjust to a society in which agriculture now plays second fiddle to industry. Our newspaper must compete for readership with two large city dailies. We are considered by many of those who read our paper, and by almost everyone in Mississippi who doesn't, to be out of step with most of our fellow citizens. Incidentally, this suspicion apparently exists because we take the Constitution and all of its amendments seriously; because we believe our public schools should be kept open under any circumstances; and because we do not believe that the justices of the United States Supreme Court are Reds in black robes.

Under these far from unique circumstances, I do not see why I should refuse or how I could refuse to identify myself actively with those who seek to meet those challenges. I have no right to be the town scold without taking part in the town's life. I could have no better defense against our critics than to prove that I am as such a citizen of Greenville as is any other person who dwells there. If only as a practical matter, I could take out no surer insurance against competition than to make our newspaper the community's spokesman and its editor an active practitioner of the civic effort that the newspaper preaches. Again, if only from selfish motives, I should make whatever personal contribution of time and money I can to the material welfare of Greenville. Every new citizen means a potential new subscriber. Every new job he fills means new business. New business means more advertising for our newspaper. More advertising makes possible a better newspaper, a larger and more competent staff. The larger and more competent the staff, the more time the editor has to join in the extra-curricular activities that build his town. Which brings us around full circle.

But practical, material or selfish motives do not suffice. At the core of my interpretation of the editor's role lies what may be a too sentimental concept of the relationship of a man to his town. Some of us live where we live because it is a place where we can make a living. Some of us are citizens of our towns by inheritance; some because we cannot get away; some for other and assorted reasons: health, status achieved, living costs, scenery, climate and so on. All of these reasons are understandable. None of this is bad. Not a few of them contribute to our liking where we live.

But there is another reason why we prefer Greenville above all places we know, and why, so preferring, are impelled to make its every cause our own. Nearly 25 years ago Greenville accepted two young strangers from Louisiana who came in the depths of the depression to establish a competitive daily newspaper. Its citizens largely have stood beside us, whether in agreement or not, in these all but hysterical days of Southern trial.

This is not a happenstance. Our town's personality, its spiritual expression, is an amalgam of ordeals—of trials by flood, and yellow fever, by the destruction of a long-ago war, by a later struggle, waged against the Ku Klux Klan, in which the good in men triumphed over the evil. Out of it all has been forged a rare community tolerance for the dissimilar and the dissenter. Out of it has also come a community compulsion to close ranks when the chips are down. This spirit may not be as strong as it was when our town was smaller, and counted fewer citizens who, like ourselves 25 years ago, were newcomers. But the spirit is strong still and it must wax stronger. Our job on the *Democrat-Times* is to respond to every challenge which bigotry, social and economic evaluation and the shrill demand for conformity make to that spirit.

Most of what I have said today I have said before, though not at one time. Harry Ashmore, that all but Faubused newspaper-man-turned-Encyclopaedia Britannica-intellectual, once introduced me to the members of the Arkansas Press Association thusly: "Our speaker gets more mileage out of one subject than any newspaper-man in history." But Harry was wrong. I have another theme which can be stated briefly:

I would rather be a small city newspaper editor and publisher than anything I know.

13

THE AMERICAN NEWSPAPER — A CHANGING IMAGE

By BERNARD KILGORE

While William Allen White was a unique personality on the American newspaper scene and the exact duplication of his energy and his talent seems most improbable, we could use today in the editorial offices of this nation a dozen—yes, a hundred— William Allen Whites.

To begin with a note of cheer that seems unusual in most discussions of the press these days, I firmly believe that we are even now beginning to develop better opportunities for such men to occupy such places.

That is the conclusion, or part of the conclusion, that I hope you will reach with me in the course of this brief discussion.

The general subject which I propose to discuss is this: The America newspaper—a changing image. We hear a good deal about images these days—the corporate image, the product image, the national image and, perhaps our own personal image. I must apologize for introducing a word that is being overworked. But it happens to fit better than anything else that comes readily to mind, for I think we are, in fact, dealing with an image when we undertake to discuss the press of America in relation to its critics and with respect to its future improvement.

This will become a little clearer to you, I hope, as our consideration of the matter proceeds.

We have to begin by reconstructing or bringing back into sharper focus the image that is now fading. (Parenthetically—I think it truly is an image that has been fading and not the American newspaper itself. To this extent, I tend to disagree with the emphasis in the title of a recent book on the subject by Carl E. Lindstrom—*The Fading American Newspaper*.)

What is this image? Briefly, it is the image of a metropolitan newspaper—the big city sheet. It is the image of the mass-minded metropolitan newspaper—a paper for the "common man" as the politicians put it. It is a newspaper dominated by showmen and promoters, and the key figure on the scene is the publisher, not the editor. The publisher, furthermore, is journalistically eccentric.

This last statement should not be taken, by the way, as a slap at any particular publisher or any group of publishers, living or dead. A man can be journalistically eccentric and quite normal in every other respect—even admirable. But I would define journalistic eccentricity as covering not only such things as William Allen White would have considered odd or ridiculous, but also more fundamental elements such as the fact that the publisher in our image of the American newspaper got rich doing something else, that he has a vast range of other interests that cover not only publishing but industry or banking or storekeeping or politics, and that he may do and often does a good deal of buying and selling.

As for the product itself—the newspaper in our image, that is —it tends towards sensationalism in the treatment of news, and this involves not only selection but emphasis; it has a reputation for irresponsibility; it relies heavily on pretty light entertainment and cheap features. If I may toss in a few fringes, just for fun, the editor is primarily a hired hand, the copydesk men wear green eye shades and the reporters wear hats indoors and trench coats outside.

You will, I'm sure, recognize this image. You have seen it on the movie screen, the television tube and you have read about it in novels, short stories and critical articles and serious books. All these things have come to pass because, for half a century or more, this image of the American newspaper has been the image in the minds of many, if not almost all, of our intellectuals. More damaging than anything else, perhaps, it has been the image in the minds of our teachers—and it has helped steer bright young men and women away from careers in journalism.

Hasn't anybody quarreled with this image? Of course they have. It is far too simple. It leaves out entirely what many of us regard as the best in American journalism these past fifty or sixty years. And to repeat what I said a few minutes ago, it is a fading image.

But I don't think we ought to say that we are unable to understand how it came about, or why, or that it lasted as long as it did. For if we just look back over newspaper history the past fifty or seventy-five years and if we hit the high spots, as even historians must do, we find the newspaper scene dominated by men and events that have produced the image I have been describing for you. There is, I regret to say, a real basis for the image—if, of course, we disregard the exceptions to it.

I am not going to try to deliver a lecture here and now on newspaper history—particularly in the presence of individuals who know it far better than I do. But it doesn't take much to outline the story. I suppose that what you might call the intellectual leaders of our country and quite a few newspapermen themselves fully expected a golden age of journalism would dawn in America with the birth of the twentieth century. New tools of the trade were available—the telegraph, the high-speed press, the photo-engraved plate, the typesetting machines and many other things. Great enterprise in news-gathering had been demonstrated during and after the Civil War. A number of outstanding editors had won positions of influence and authority with their pens.

But journalistically it turned out to be a gilded age at best, rather than a golden one. The color was there all right, but somebody called it yellow journalism—and the name stuck. Joseph Pultitzer showed how big city circulation could be built up in New York and William Randolph Hearst observed this and decided to make it his career—or one of his careers.

Between the yellow journalism of the early nineteen hundreds (when the *Christian Science Monitor* was launched as a protest) and the roaring tabloids of the roaring twenties, the casual student of newspaper history will find names and events that made William Allen White shudder and, on some occasions, he expressed his opinions in no uncertain terms.

What William Allen White would have called decent, dedicated American journalists were not proud of what appeared to be the leadership in American journalism. They tried to disassociate themselves from the prevailing image. And let me say quite plainly at this point that there were many such journalists and many newspaper publishers who were exceptions to the dominating big-city pattern.

I believe, in fact, that the exceptions have now finally prevailed. There was a turn in the tide and if I had to put a date and place on it, it was the failure of those who tried to outdo the *New York Daily News*. It did not work. There has been a big city downtrend of one sort or another ever since.

The newspaper picture has been changing these past twenty years and the prevailing image is finally beginning to change, too. Of course, the basic situation is what controls the image in the long run but the reason I am talking about images today is that they affect the thinking of so many people and the image lags behind. We have heard, up until quite recently, so many critical assaults on the old image that we haven't paid enough attention to what has really been going on.

I am not surprised, for instance, that so many big city newspapers have disappeared. I am surprised, actually, that so many have survived. I suspect the secret of their survival in some instances at least is the fact that they have become to such an important extent, Sunday newspapers. The Sunday newspaper—to the extent that it becomes really a weekly newspaper—is quite different from the daily.

At any rate, the big brassy metropolitan newspaper has all but come to the end of its era. It was hit first by the competition of the moving pictures as the primary entertainment medium, but this didn't hurt much. Radio hit the big newspaper with flash news plus entertainment. Television made both the news and entertainment more compelling.

Meantime, great changes in our social structure have been taking place. Levels of education, on the average, are vastly higher. There is no massive, half-literate population available in every big city to buy a cheap newspaper. Employment and income statistics have changed remarkably—the working man these days is more likely to be dressed in a white collar than a pair of overalls. His interests and his tastes in reading material have changed as much as his clothing.

Along with everything else, and in certain respects above everything else, our great population movement from the farm to the cities has become a movement into a suburban organization. The big cities have been breaking up. They have been fractionating into sub-cities and sub-towns and sub-neighborhoods. These sub-communities have interests of their own, shopping centers of their own, newspapers of their own, and churches of their own.

Newspapers have to fit the community they serve. They have to fit it editorially and they have to fit it as an advertising medium.

So what we have in reality today in America is a very complex journalistic picture, more so than we had in the past. We have a broad spectrum of informational and news media. This includes, to put it very briefly, the radio, the television, the metropolitan or regional daily, the local or community daily, the weekly newspaper and the weekly newsmagazine, plus a host of special publications which are primarily concerned with news in a specialized sort of way. These special publications may be daily, weekly and in a few instances even monthly.

The complexities of the journalistic scene make it unlikely that as our image of the old, dominating, American newspaper fades out, a simple image of a new newspaper will take its place. Our new image is certainly going to be harder to describe in simple language. Furthermore, it hasn't even developed in many of its details as yet.

But I would suggest that the newspaper image of the future will be the lively, local community newspaper which performs, first of all, the service of pulling its own community together with information about itself and takes a position of editorial leadership in the affairs of that community. Such a newspaper will do well in covering state and regional news and will bring in the best report on national and international affairs that it can afford. It will comment on world affairs because its readers will expect their editor to have opinions and ideas.

But it will not, I suggest, try to do everything everyday that the weekly publications can do better on a weekly schedule; it will not try to duplicate *The Wall Street Journal;* nor will it undertake to compete with *The Saturday Review, Business Week* or *The Scientific American.* I don't believe, furthermore, that a good community newspaper, putting first things first, should be scolded because it does not try to meet these national publications head on. And as for entertainment, the radio and television people have us beat all hollow in everything except things that are just fun to read.

I believe that as this new image of the American newspaper becomes somewhat clearer, it will be increasingly attractive as life work to those young men and young women who have special talents to offer in this field. I believe newspaper editors will become more important people in their communities and in the broader world of intellectual effort and leadership. I think, in this newer image, editors may again begin to outrank publishers and newspapers will again be regarded more as local institutions rather than properties that can be bought, sold or traded about.

And no one, I'm sure, would have been more pleased to see all this come to pass than the man whose memory we honor here today, William Allen White.

14

INSIDE A NEWSPAPER GROUP

By Paul Miller

I speak as one who knew William Allen White and who subscribed to his newspaper; hence as one personally aware of the privilege of lecturing in his name. Everybody sensed, away back there in the twenties, the very great contribution he was making to American newspapering. I was editor of the *Okemah* (Okla.) *Daily Leader* when I subscribed to the *Emporia Gazette* principally to study the editorials. Thanks to the glowing example of Mr. White's career, hundreds of young newspapermen were able to observe that the small daily newspaper offers major journalistic rewards along with careers of great service and occasional fame.

It is not my purpose, however, to attempt to evaluate the contributions of William Allen White to American journalism, although before I have finished I hope that we shall have agreed that various torches lighted by Mr. White are still flaming brightly today.

Emporia is not too far from Missouri, where I was born, or from Oklahoma, where I was reared. I met Mr. White when I was Night News Editor of the Kansas City Associated Press bureau in 1934. And I believe it was in that year that there was a minor earthquake in this region—one, by the way, not caused by William Allen White. At my suggestion, Mr. White generously wrote a byliner for the Associated Press night wires describing the dish-rattling, lamp-swinging but hardly very damaging 'quake as it affected Emporia.

Roy Roberts was my mentor in those days, and I got to know Oscar Stauffer and Jack Harris and Fred Brinkerhoff. Dolph Simons became one of my close friends on the Associated Press board in the 1950's.

These happy recollections are included here not to trade on mutual associations but to allay any suspicion that newspapermen in New York State, say, differ in any basic respect from those in

Kansas, Oklahoma or Missouri. The professional tenets of William Allen White are by and large the foundation stones on which successful newspapers are built in New York, as elsewhere.

Yet, Mr. White gave none of us a secret formula for instant publishing success. Rather, he proved that success in newspaper work need not be measured solely in circulation figures, or market size, or column inches of news and advertising. He showed how one individual of idealism and genius can add luster to an already distinguished field. He lived to illustrate the truth that the paths of public service have not all been discovered, much less charted. The search for such paths continues to this day. And I believe it is appropriate for me to say that participants in the search include newspaper groups, or "chains" as they are more often called.

Gannett Co., Inc. embraces such a group. It consists of 17 newspapers, three radio staions and two television stations in four states—New York, New Jersey, Connecticut and Illinois. Our smallest newspaper has a circulation of about 6,000; the three largest, about 130,000 each. Our aim traditionally has been to keep them, in the dated but still meaningful words of a founder, "as local as the town pump." All are of a size and homeyness with which William Allen White would have felt strong bonds.

But would he approve of such newspapers? Would he feel that "chain" newspapers are having good effects or bad on American journalism? Could he have reached world eminence as an editor of a so-called "group newspaper"?

My answers to all three of these questions are optimistic and affirmative. Indeed, I see the great majority of American newspapers tending toward still greater service and value, whether locally owned or otherwise. Poor, unenlightened management can ruin any newspaper. And diligent, high principled management can, given a sound market, produce a worthy newspaper.

Currently, according to *Editor & Publisher,* there are 118 groups or chains publishing a combined total of 579 daily newspapers in the United States. These groups range in size from two or three papers in different cities, to several of the larger ones with a dozen or more newspapers each.

You are familiar with some of the fine newspapers being published by Kansas groups, such as Stauffer Publications, the Jack Harris newspapers and the Seaton group.

I am going to tell you how one group is operated—at least, how we try to operate it. But before going further I want to say this:

When we talk about a free and responsible press as basic to the preservation of America, we must include radio and television. These newer media, for all their growing pains, have taken their place in the front ranks of journalism. They are becoming increasingly important contributors to knowledge and understanding.

Now and then we hear voices raised against joint ownership of newspapers and broadcasting stations. These are the same voices that call for even better handling of news and comment on radio and television. Logically, then, why shouldn't they be urging that more newspapers get into radio and TV? For even the critics concede that newspapers bring to broadcasting a time-tested concept of objectivity, of responsibility, and of public service. But newscasting in general is getting better all the time.

Now back to newspapers. First, a little background.

The Gannett Company is not publicly owned. Its outstanding voting common stock is owned 100 per cent by the Frank E. Gannett Newspaper Foundation, Inc. Its preferred stocks are owned almost entirely by directors, officers and employes.

The Foundation is a non-stock corporation organized in 1935 as a philanthropic and charitable agency through which the Gannett Group might be perpetuated. Its charter stipulates that at least seven of its eleven directors must be newspapermen. It derives its income from dividends paid on the common stock of Gannett Co., Inc. It has no other source of revenue. Up to now it has given away $2,921,500 in communities we serve.

But let's get to operations: to the business of building better newspapers and making the money, if you please, as distinct from gving it away.

The Gannett Company encourages local autonomy and it exercises a relatively loose general control over its member newspapers. We believe that local autonomy is good journalism and good business, too. A competent local management is more likely to operate successfully under a minimum of outside control or interference.

In recent years, we have relinquished some properties and added some. The *Camden* (N.J.) *Courier-Post* is the latest newspaper addition. We are now, subject to FCC approval, purchasing television station WREX at Rockford, Ill. I believe we will continue to grow in strength as long as we deserve to.

Let us take up a few questions asked by outsiders about our operations; they ask most frequently about our editorial and news policies.

There is no overall editorial policy. The Central News and Editorial Office expects to be advised, or consulted, on any major operating problem or a sharply controversial issue in which a member newspaper becomes involved. But final decision rests with that newspaper's own executives. Editorial positions on major local questions are determined by the local editors and publishers or general managers, in consultation.

Logically, then, another question is frequently asked: "What responsibility does the Gannett Company itself assume for the public-interest operation of its affiliates?"

We believe and preach and, I hope, practice the old-fashioned doctrine that each individual newspaper should "stand for something." A newspaper should stand for everything that is best for its community and vigorously oppose the bad, as the local management sees it. It should not duck local or other issues.

Yet, as I've said repeatedly, in all its activities a newspaper should be fair and unbiased in its columns, no matter how strong the opinions on its editorial page. And, even on the editorial page, a newspaper should bend over backward to see that a hearing is given those with contrary views. In many cases, I believe, contrary views should be solicited; especially in a single-ownership or one-newspaper city such as some of ours.

I hasten to emphasize that this is elementary for most newspapers nowadays, group or non-group.

Strongly partisan newspapers have declined in number and in influence. Most of the professionals who manage America's successful groups today avoid personal participation in partisan politics. More and more publishing companies are employe-managed. The professional manager usually feels less disposed than his owner-predecessors to make his weight felt politically on a strictly partisan basis. With all due respect, I suggest that what we have lost in color, in individuality, has been offset by a gain in responsibility and in public confidence. Newspapers no longer snarl, and rarely thunder, but when they speak out on some big issue, in reasonable language, with an air of quiet authority, they are more influential than ever.

In any given state or national election, our newspapers may be all over the editorial lot. The *Hartford* (Conn.) *Times,* for example, is traditionally Democratic, although it is tied to no political party. It supported most of the Democratic state ticket in 1962, and it endorsed Kennedy in 1960 — yet it had supported Eisenhower in 1952 (even before he was nominated) and again in 1956. Most of our newspapers formally list themselves as "independent"; a few proclaim their leanings under the label "Independent-Republican," and only one (the smallest) is "Republican."

I have often seen group membership supply telling support and encouragement for local editorial independence and editorial vigor. Let me give you a personal illustration. While our Utica newspapers were fighting elements which had gained control of certain municipal affairs, I prepared statements making it clear that the Utica newspapers had both editorial autonomy and ownership support. These statements were published as front-page editorials under my byline in Utica. This put a stop to efforts in some quarters to go over the heads of the Utica editors.

The *Utica Observer-Dispatch* and the *Utica Daily Press* later were rewarded with a Pulitzer public service prize for their efforts in cleaning up that community.

Of course, autonomy never was intended to be an umbrella for poor performance locally. General management at Rochester must see to that. We aim to lead, not operate — the best local management is the one the Central Office is impelled to bother least. Each individual newspaper is expected to live up to the highest standards. Broadly, this means that each should strive to be the best of its class, taking into account the circulation and advertising potential of the area and the special needs of the community.

Autonomy also means that each newspaper is expected to stand on its own feet financially. By agreement between the company and holders of its $6 preferred stock the Gannett Company may not guarantee the debts of any subsidiary. In practice, this means that when Gannett Co., Inc. acquires a newspaper or a broadcasting station we ordinarily invest about one-third of the purchase price. The new property then is expected to pay off the borrowed remainder out of earnings.

Each Gannett Newspaper does its own hiring. However the Central Office is increasingly active in recruiting, training and placement at all levels. Some centralized recruiting is done with the help of executives from the newspaper nearest the campus or city where the recruiting takes place. If no opening exists for a likely prospect at one newspaper, he may be recommended to another. But local executives are not required to hire any specific recruits.

With rare exceptions, no comics, columns or other features are bought on a group contract basis.

We expect our local managements to participate personally in community affairs, to support local drives and fund campaigns with dollars as well as with space. Often this has meant that, after joining The Gannett Group, a newspaper has been found contributing more in hard cash to community causes than it had done before.

The same can be true of rewards to the individual employe. Some papers now in our organization would never have dreamed of a pension plan for employes while outside the Group. And never has membership in our Group reduced or eliminated existing retirement programs for employes. Whenever we have added a newspaper or a broadcasting station, we have continued whatever benefit program has been in operation, with the aim in view to keep it in effect until the property is paid for and can come under our own broader Gannett program.

Likewise with employe profit-sharing. Since 1936, when a general plan was instituted, some $10,000,000 has been distributed.

So far, I have been speaking almost exclusively about my own organization. But I believe that much of what I have said applies also to other large newspaper groups. Some do better than we do in some respects, perhaps not as well in others, and so on. Certainly, for example, our policy of local autonomy is by no means unique.

Now a few more observations:

Many a newspaper has staggered along, or run down, because it had to support too many owners. Group ownership, which does not depend solely upon any one property, can forego dividends while one newspaper buys new machinery, or as in so many cases in our group, expands its plant or builds a brand new one.

Know-how is shared among newspapers and stations, and the services of specialists, which few individual concerns could afford, are available to all.

A group offers extraordinary opportunities for promotions within the organization. A majority of our top executives and more than half of the general management grew up on Gannett newspapers.

But we have not hesitated to bring in talent from outside.

Chains and groups help lead in furthering the education and training of practicing newspapermen, not only through their own programs, but particularly through strong support of the American Press Institute at Columbia University.

Few single-ownership small dailies can afford independent news bureaus in state and national capitals. Actually, few of our newspapers could afford them individually. But the Gannett Group, *as a group,* has such bureaus and good ones. This is true of many other groups. In fact, most independent reporters who cover Washington are in bureaus operated by groups or chains. Many who travel on foreign assignments can afford this only because they cover for several newspapers.

Thus far, I have failed to answer one important question implicit at the start of my remarks:

Granted — if it is — that group-operation is efficient and public-service minded, could a new William Allen White reach maximum effectiveness in a group?

My answer is "yes." I could cite a long list of names to back up that answer. So could you. Indeed, many of the most respected editors today — and among the most individualistic and independent — are editors of group newspapers.

Newspaper groups, like alert individually-owned newspapers, are looking twelve months a year, every year, for young men and women who view newspapering as Mr. White did. But getting good prospects is only a first step in a program of finding, hiring, training — and rewarding.

And this leads me to Mr. White's warning that "a once-noble profession (journalism) could be transformed into an eight percent security." (Many a hard-pressed publisher today might grimly ask, "What's wrong with eight percent?") But Mr. White was making a point. Such a possibility as he feared is remote indeed, but to guard against such a danger, if it does exist, I know of no better defense than high-principled instructors in universities such as this — and high principled leadership in individual newspapers and in newspaper groups.

Well, I have told you some of the good — the great — things about newspapering, and about the part of it that I know best.

What about the tidal wave of criticism directed toward newspapers that seems to become more menacing every year? There's no use protesting that this shouldn't happen to dedicated people. It is happening and most newspapers are doing something about it.

They are continuing the effort to wipe out every reason for legitimate criticism—sloppy reporting, mealy-mouthed commentary, cheap gossip, questionable advertising . . .

More and more newspapers are being dressed so that they look as good as they are. There is growing agreement that there's no excuse for small body type, messy makeup, or smudged pictures. Newspapers are emulating daily some of the orderly presentation for which magazines can take a week.

Then, more publishers and editors are meeting critics head-on. It amazes me how often a sweeping charge still goes unanswered, or a mistake in reporting or judgment is left uncorrected.

Publisher Barry Bingham of Louisville provided an example of how to meet attack in a panel discussion of mass media in New York City on Jan. 22, 1963. There had been the usual criticism of newspaper monopoly situations with the usual implications and wit hthe usual failure to identify the causes. Mr. Bingham said:

"We are up against a law of economics here. The critics of the press mislead the public when they portray monopoly as the chief villaino Monopoly is less a threat to press excellence than monotony."

Amen.

We have a continuing job of education and selling to do — and starting, if I may say so here, with the schools and colleges, as well as with our own readers and advertisers. We must get even closer to them.

If anything good is coming out of the tragic strikes in New York and Cleveland, it is the public realization of how closely related those newspapers are to the needs of their communities. The world now sees that nothing — not even good out-of-town newspapers, and certainly not newscasts however comprehensive or expertly-done — can take their place.

Summing up — and at the risk of being corny in Kansas — we must everlastingly keep making sure, first that we are doing the best job possible (and that's not easy these days), then go out and sell it.

In our Group, we may not come up with products that are necessarily superior to the *Emporia Gazette* under William Allen White! But ours and other groups and chains today often are among those at the forefront in experimenting, as he did; in improving, as he did; in setting a high mark for other newspapers to shoot at — as he did.

As William Allen White well knew, newspapers require sound financing — yet dollars themselves cannot make newspapers great or respected. Only newspapermen and newspaperwomen who have purpose, resourcefulness and high resolve can give to their publications the touch of greatness.

We are looking for such. When any of the caliber of William Allen White come along, and I pray that they may, I hope that some of you will be around to steer them our way! Then, as now, I'll say — I thank you.

15

LIFE LINE OF DEMOCRACY

By Clark R. Mollenhoff

The future of the American democracy is contingent upon the performance of the American press. If the newsmen of today and tomorrow are diligent workers and balanced thinkers on problems of governing our society, then I have no doubt that the American democracy will survive and flourish as a symbol to the whole world.

If the press fails in its responsibility — if it flounders in a quagmire of superficiality, partisanship, laziness and incompetence — then our great experiment in democracy will fail. In 150, 100, 50 years — or even sooner — it will be replaced by a more efficient authoritarian form of government, and will be remembered as an interesting but impractical system.

Communication is the life line of democracy. It is a noble goal to seek to be an effective part of that communications system. It is little short of treason to knowingly contaminate that life line with political partisanship, propaganda or clever but superficial commentary.

It would be pleasant and reassuring if we could simply assume that our form of government has some divine blessing that will guarantee its survival and steady improvement. However, this is not the case. Travel in more than 40 countries has demonstrated to me how precious our democracy is. In the midst of revolution and threatened revolution in Africa and the Middle East, I observed the relatively short step from our freedom to the oppression of authoritarian rule.

Democracy is contingent upon an informed public with the means to learn what the government is doing, the right to criticize what the government is doing, and the mechanism for effectively expressing opposition by voting to oust our highest officials from office.

It would be impossible to overemphasize the importance of the newsman's role in a democracy, for the public depends upon newsmen for both the facts upon which opinions are based and the balanced reporting of the criticism of government programs, policies and personnel.

I stress these points at this time because the press of the nation is failing in its responsibilities, and because there are disturbing signs that the press does not recognize its failures. There are many spectacular examples to demonstrate the press does not understand many stories of major importance. There is a growing accumulation of evidence indicating the press even fails to understand itself and its own self interest.

It is unfortunate, but there are only a handful of reporters and editors who comprehend the fine work the Government Operations Subcommittee (headed by Congressman John Moss) has been doing for the press. There are only a few with enough historic perspective and balance to really appreciate the significance of the freedom of information work done by the American Society of Newspaper Editors, the Associated Press Managing Editors or Sigma Delta Chi.

There is press resentment when Senator Wayne Morse presents a justified indictment of the journalists who are "the parrots of the 'line' from the executive branch" and who are "largely ignorant of the American system of government and the role of Congress in that system." There will be too little attention to the warnings by James McCartney in *Nieman Reports* of the distortions and propaganda that flow from "The Vested Interests of the (Beat) Reporter."

The press is proud — usually too proud to accept criticism. There is an understandable pride in newspaper improvement in recent years — much needed mechanical developments and better educated personnel. But, it is folly to be so dazzled by such improvements that there is a blindness to failures of substance. Mechanical improvements are important, but only if enlightened people use them to make government problems more understandable and our democracy more effective. That is our real reason for being.

All expense is futile if it fails to develop a press that is independent and aggressive in serving as a watchdog over government.

It is not my intention to view with alarm the deterioration of the press since the days of William Allen White. I do not believe there has been a deterioration. I do question whether the press has improved enough to meet the responsibility of a job that becomes more difficult each year. Despite the fact that there are hundreds of well-qualified reporters and editors, the performance is often mediocre or poor in Washington.

I think, strongly think, we need more tough self-criticism in regard to our most vital function — the coverage of federal government.

There *are* areas in which press performance *is* equal to or even superior to what it was 30 to 60 years ago.

There are works of highest merit, including the depth reporting jobs of the *Wall Street Journal*, and the periodic brilliant local investigative reporting in Chicago, St. Louis, Cleveland, Des Moines, Atlanta, Nashville and dozens of other places. The great financial resources of the news magazines result in consistent fine depth work by *U.S. News and World Report* and periodic flashes of greatness by *Time* and *Newsweek*.

But even the wealthiest news organization can become bogged down in the complexity of national and international problems that face us today.

William Allen White had limited financial resources and manpower, but he used them to capacity in seeking to understand the local, state, federal and international problems of his day. He judged and occasionally misjudged as all of us do from time to time, but he was independent of his friends as well as his enemies.

Most certainly, the governmental structures of the town of Emporia and the State of Kansas were more simple and more manageable than our national and international problems today. But it can require as much ability and a great deal more courage to report on local issues and local people than it does to ponder over outrages in Zanzibar or Leopoldville.

In the days when William Allen White was making his mark the federal government was small. The entire budget was less than a billion dollars until 1917. With the exception of 1918 and 1919, the federal spending did not exceed $10 billion until 1941.

The major press problems of today can be linked directly to the size and complexity of the $100 billion-a-year federal operation. Bright reporters and editors can still find ways to understand and police most city, county and state operations. But too often they are frustrated and then overwhelmed by the seemingly impossible job of serving as a watchdog on federal spending and policies.

There is some awareness of the problem, but no one really comes to grips with it. There has been a floundering by a press that has become more and more dependent upon handouts in Washington. Trapped in its own superficiality, the press is an easy victim of the Big Lie. Lacking understanding, the press follows the fads of the best Madison Avenue sloganeers.

Steps to deal with the problem of bigness have resulted in some unhealthy developments. Specialists have been assigned to governmental agencies to provide more knowledgeable coverage. In too many cases these specialists have been converted into propagandists for the agencies they cover — a type of kept press. The TFX story is an illustration of how many "watchdogs of democracy" were transformed into lap dogs of the Pentagon political appointees.

Certainly we need specialization, but there needs to be constant examination to assure that the specialists are not seduced by their sources. How much objectivity can one expect from a Pentagon reporter who shows up to cover a hearing accompanied by his wife and the wife of the Defense official who is under a critical investigation. Some social contact with high public figures is inevitable, but reporters and editors have an obligation to ask themselves if they have sacrificed independence for a White House dinner or a scuba diving party with the Secretary of Defense.

The press would have protested violently at the suggestion of creation of a federal propaganda office. Yet, the government press specialists in many agencies have become propaganda officers. Instead of serving as a press contact for a quick guide to information about an agency, many of these men have become propaganda officers, seeking to build the image of political figures by policing and controlling press contacts with all agency personnel.

Not content with central information control in an agency and some departments, there are continuing periodic efforts to establish more coordinated information operations between the agencies. The explanation is always that it is for more efficiency and to avoid confusion or conflicting stories. If effective, the result would be creation of a federal propaganda office.

A few weeks ago, I received an irate call from a government press officer who objected to my direct call to a cabinet officer for an appointment. I was told it was improper for me to by-pass the press office.

In the following conversation, I informed him I had no obligation to make contact through a public relations office. I told him

I would make my contacts without consulting him, and that when I wanted help I would let him know. He bristled when I referred to him as "a public relations man" for the department, and he insisted he is a "professional newsman" with the duty of giving the public a truthful and objective picture.

I have no doubts he regards himself as an objective newsman, and I am also certain that in most cases he tries to give reporters a balanced picture of activities in his department.

However, he is hired by a Democratic administration to serve one of its cabinet officers. I am certain he would be somewhat less aggressive than an independent reporter in penetrating the excuses and half-truths that are so often tossed out to explain away mistakes, mismanagement and corruption.

While most reporters do not accept the tight policing and discipline that some press officers would impose, there are a good many who find it more convenient and even essential to retain a cooperative working relationship with the agencies' propaganda centers.

A Defense Department order to police press contacts at the Pentagon is a clear example of a formal effort to control press activity. The order by Assistant Defense Secretary Arthur Sylvester was signed on October 27, 1962. It has the backing of Defense Secretary Robert S. McNamara and remains in force despite complaints by the press that it amounts to a "gestapo" directive to discourage circulation of the views of persons who dissent from "the departmental line."

The order states that all Pentagon personnel — military and civilian — must make a report of all conversations with reporters before the end of the business day. Sylvester justifies it as necessary to keep defense secrets from leaking. He also says it is to keep him abreast of all information made available, so he can make the same information available to other reporters in an orderly manner. He doesn't mention that it would also spot the sources of stories indicating disagreement with the McNamara line, which it is unlikely Sylvester would distribute widely.

The Sylvester order still stands. The press, after a few cries of rage, has accepted the chains with only a whimper. It remains as a precedent for other departments to follow if they feel too many dissenting opinions are being peddled by governmental subordinates.

Fortunately, some officials disregard Sylvester's directive and some reporters are enterprising enough to evade it. This should not make the existence of the directive any more acceptable.

Add to this, the McNamara "economy" move toward a single press office for the $50 billion-a-year Defense Department.

Also, examine the indications that the Johnson Administration may curtail the presidential press conference. There are indications he will depend mainly on those little spur-of-the-moment meetings with the regular White House reporters. These gatherings present a minimum danger of the tough question that often needs to be asked. Johnson has indicated he might supplement this with some informal television chats with a few reporters, who I will wager will be hand-picked.

If that is to be the news press conference format, then I'm against it. I would hardly accept the logic of one editorial writer who suggested that if Johnson feels the open press conferences of the past do not "fit his personality" then he should be allowed to change.

In the light of that type of editorial thinking, we can only hope that democracy fits President Johnson's personality.

The national television networks can, and do, serve as a great force in informing the public on important issues. However, television seldom serves as a leader in exploring bad government — seldom operates in a watchdog role. Television, with all of its money and manpower, usually waits until the daily press has done all the spadework on an issue.

It is unrealistic to expect more of television. The industry operates on government licenses, and under constant threat of more government control. This certainly limits its independence. But even without direct government control there are factors that tend to make our three big networks "soft" on an incumbent administration without regard to profits.

The networks put great stock in exclusive interviews with high government officials, and it is obvious that they pay a price by limiting their independence. The price may be an unspoken assurance that the cooperative official will face friendly reporters, and will be treated in a kindly fashion. Official reluctance or refusal to cooperate with an aggressive television team can often be an effective way of destroying independence. It is not necessary to be angry at newspapers or television reporters or commentators who fawn over public officials with a simpering sweetness. Only feel sorry for them.

Examine these problems in context with a presidential directive to authorize a nation-wide government news service to be made available free to newspapers, radio and television. At the same time, there is a trend toward much higher costs for wire service for the independent press agencies — AP and UPI.

In addition to direct and subtle government controls many newspapers have been putting themselves in strait jackets of conformity by copying the story play and the editorial positions of some large East Coast newspapers. This tends to destroy the independent thinking and diversity William Allen White believed to be the strength of the press. It is particularly destructive when the editorial policies copied come from newspapers that have been demonstrably wrong on policies on Cuba, Ghana, Viet Nam and other areas.

Individually or collectively these developments cause me great concern. I believe they should cause great concern in the entire newspaper profession.

Over a period of 13 years, I have had the occasion to be critical of information policies of the Truman Administration, the Eisenhower Administration and the Kennedy Administration. I have tried to make that criticism tough and objective.

There is no need to apologize for the past criticism, for some high officials in each of these administrations engaged in unjustified secrecy policies that seriously interfered with the public's right to know about government. Each used a wide range of public relations techniques, distortions and outright lies to deceive the public.

The public offiicals deserved a lambasting for their arrogance in hiding or distorting the facts, but the press was also responsible.

It is true that high officials of any administration may fool any of us on a few issues for a short period of time despite diligent work. But if it becomes apparent that any large segment of the press is being fooled for any extended period of time, then the press just isn't doing its job.

Under the Truman Administration there were efforts to hide the tax scandals, the R.F.C. scandals and a good many other bits of "influence peddling" and "favoritism." However, there was aggressive independent reporting that cut through the Truman Administration's claim that there was no wrong-doing. The press did its job, and the public finally understood.

Under President Eisenhower, there were other unjustified efforts to hide the record. This time the press was slow to move. However, there were enough pockets of press aggressiveness and sufficient push behind two or three congressional committees to force exposure of the "conflicts of interest" in the Dixon-Yates case, and the illegal improper activities at some of the regulatory agencies.

In the 1960 campaign, John F. Kennedy spoke of the importance of open government information policies. He indicated he would not permit use of "Executive Privilege" to hide records from the Congress and the public. In his State of the Union address he told us that healthy dissent would not only be tolerated, but encouraged.

However, for some reason it didn't work out quite that way. Kennedy authorized use of "Executive Privilege" to bar Congressional committees from information about government operations, and there were a large number of efforts to curb dissent and stifle criticism. Unfortunately, unknowing and short-sighted elements in the press were patsies for the Kennedy Administration. They even helped justify barriers to curb dissent and to curtail the flow of information.

Two major stories of the last year — the TFX case and the Otepka case — can serve to demonstrate how many Washington reporters and columnists failed in their role as watchdogs. They failed on important stories, and became propagandists for two political appointees. They failed despite the documented record and the fine guidelines available in the excellent balanced reporting of Cecil Holland in the *Washington Star* and the columns of Hanson Baldwin in the *New York Times*.

The TFX story involved the integrity of the spending practices in the Defense Department, and the judgment of Defense Secretary McNamara. McNamara over-ruled the top-level Pentagon Source Selection Board that had favored the Boeing firm for a large plane contract. Testimony before the McClelland committee shows McNamara will waste more than $400,000,000 by an arbitrary decision to hand the $6.5 billion TFX program to Texas-based General Dynamics Corporation.

A few hero worshiping reporters and columnists, feeding on Pentagon press office distortions, have been giving the public the line that McNamara's decision will somehow save the taxpayers a billion dollars. They have taken and repeated factually inaccurate smears against the McClelland Subcommittee from anonymous Defense Department spokesmen. They have disregarded or rationalized the evidence of "conflicts of interest" that should have caused two of McNamara's top aides to disqualify themselves from having anything to do with the TFX decision.

McNamara over-ruled the unanimous recommendation that favored the Boeing version on the basis of a "superior performance" as well as a price that would be lower by $100,000,000 to $415,000,-000.

It was possible that McNamara could have been right, but certainly the burden of proof was on him to establish he was right since he overruled his subordinates to give the contract to General Dynamics. He signed a five-page memorandum of "justification" on November 21, 1962, that was loaded with errors, according to the McClelland committee record. One of the errors was "a little slip-up" on the entire performance rating of the General Dynamics plane. The performance rating was generally inflated. Also, McNamara had a little error of $77,000,000, a little error of $32,000,-000, and a little error of $29,000,000.

To justify his decision, McNamara made a claim that General Dynamics had greater "commonality" of parts in its Navy and Air Force versions that would result in great savings on maintenance, repair, spare parts and training. The experts — civilian and military — testifying on engineering and military matters, have stated that the General Dynamics plane has little or no advantage over the Boeing plane in this area. One experienced aeronautical engineer declared that the idea of any substantial savings because of "commonality" was "poppycock."

McNamara stated he could disregard the low bid by Boeing because Boeing cost figures lacked "realism." Boeing officials stated they submitted detailed cost figures to the Defense Department, and had "backup material" available to demonstrate the realism on every figure in their bid. Boeing officials said the Defense Department never challenged their figures, but had arbitrarily tossed out their low bid. The McClelland committee proved the only Defense cost figures available had some rather dramatic errors — $291,000,000 and $340,000,000. McNamara could not have been right if he relied upon these figures, which he now admits were in error. What figures did McNamara have before him when he decided that Boeing lacked "cost realism" in making the low bid? When the auditors of the General Accounting Office questioned McNamara about his decision, he admitted he had no other cost study available. He said he made "a rough judgment" from his experience as an official at Ford Motor Company.

McNamara told the GAO he got the figures "out of my head." Comptroller General Joseph Campbell expressed his "surprise" that McNamara had no cost figures for such an important decision, and stated that the GAO feels there must be written documents to support multi-billion dollar decisions. But this wasn't all.

McNamara downgraded a modern braking device — the thrust reverser — in the Boeing plane as being a risky engineering venture. The General Dynamics plane had a conventional drive brake that some say will make the plane obsolete before it is in production. The Navy and Air Force wanted the "thrust reverser" in the General Dynamics plane because of its superiority. Experts have testified it will cost $446,000,000 more to equip the General Dynamics plane with the "thrust reverser" at this stage.

McNamara contended that Boeing's use of titanium in the wing structure was also "risky." On this point, the McClelland Subcommittee has produced expert testimony of metallurgists, including specialists in titanium, who disagreed with McNamara. The experts testified there was no unusual risk involved in the use of titanium in the wing structures, and that the use proposed by Boeing was conventional.

General Curtis LeMay and Admiral George Anderson, then Chief of Naval Operations, approved the Boeing plane. They have told McNamara that they had reservations about the General Dynamics plane, and called it a "wrong decision."

Granted, this was a complicated and technical subject, but it was not impossible and the press, generally, failed to get to the heart of the matter.

There were only about a dozen reporters who read the whole record of the TFX investigation, and a few who read enough to be familiar with the weakness of McNamara's position — that he was wrong on facts. However, there were dozens of apologists for McNamara who have written authoritatively without benefit of reading the record. They have written from Pentagon handouts and from confidential "inside information" straight from McNamara, Assistant Secretary Arthur Sylvester, former Deputy Defense Secretary Roswell Gilpatric or former Navy Secretary Fred Korth.

Why would Defense Secretary McNamara over-rule a unanimous recommendation to make what experts regard as a "wrong" decision to pay the highest price for the second-best plane?

He had help on this case from Gilpatric, the former lawyer for General Dynamics, and from Fred Korth, whose Continental National Bank of Fort Worth had General Dynamics for one of its best customers.

It should be no surprise that both Gilpatric and Korth recommended that the contract should go to General Dynamics, rather than Boeing. Chairman McClelland and others have given the opinion that neither Korth nor Gilpatric should have had any role in the TFX contract in the light of their prior associations with General Dynamics. But many reporters and editorial writers — ignorant, gullible or lopsidedly partisan — could see no "conflict of interest" problem in the role of Gilpatric or Korth.

Reporters I had worked with, and I might say agreed with, on the "conflict of interest" in the Dixon-Yates case in the Eisenhower Administration, had no interest in going into the details of the role of Gilpatric or Korth. Others who had been aggressive in pointing up the role of Adolphe Wenzell in the Dixon-Yates case wrote only apologies for Gilpatric and Korth.

In some cases, it was ignorance of the facts. In some cases it was laziness in dealing with a complex record. I am afraid that in a few cases it was a foul political partisanship.

I believe that the press has an obligation to aggressively pursue any evidence that high officials have lied under oath about government operations. There is an additional obligation to ferret out all evidence that others were engaged in subornation of perjury or in condoning false statements or illegal wire taps. This would seem basic. However, in the words of Senator Morse, many uninformed reporters were "the parrots of the 'line' from the executive branch . . . (and) care nothing of the merits of the case made . . . in Congress."

Otto F. Otepka, the chief security evaluator at the State Department, became a State Department employee in 1953 shortly after the Eisenhower Administration came to power. Some reporters found this fact alone to be grounds for being hostile to Otepka, and they characterized him as the last vestige of McCarthyism at the State Department.

They did not know, or at least did not report, that Otepka was a career civil servant with no political ties who had been transferred from the Civil Service Commission to the State Department because of his experience as a lawyer and security evaluator. Otepka believed in a strict security operation, but he was not an irrational man who saw a Red under every bed. In fact, it was Otepka who had recommended clearance of Wolf Ladejinsky in 1954 when some more zealous persons sought to label the career Agricultural Attache a "security risk."

He served with such distinction as a security evaluator that in 1958, Secretary of State Dulles awarded him the department distinguished service award. Early in the Kennedy Administration, Deputy Under Secretary of State for Administration Roger W. Jones commended Otepka as a skilled and balanced security evaluator. That was before direct conflicts of testimony developed involving Otepka and his superiors.

Otepka delivered three State Department documents to the Senate Internal Security Subcommittee to prove he was telling the truth about the handling of a security problem. One of Otepka's superiors charged this was "insubordination" and violation of rules. To some reporters the delivery of documents to a Senate Subcommittee was justification for firing.

They did not know, or at least did not report, that Otepka delivered the documents to prove that he was telling the truth with regard to the handling of a security matter. His testimony had been in conflict with the testimony of one of his superiors, and he produced the records to prove he was truthful.

Otepka delivered documents that also proved his superiors were wrong. To some State Department-oriented reporters and editorial writers, this was "McCarthyism."

There are veteran reporters and editorial writers who do not understand the vital function of Congress in checking the administration and operations of the Executive Branch. Many can't tell the difference between a responsible investigation as conducted by the late Senator Kefauver, Senator McClellan, or Representative Blatnik, and one of the late Senator Joe McCarthy's free-swinging extravaganzas. Many didn't try to tell the difference. They are automatically against any investigations, and automatically mouth the Executive Branch line without regard for its inconsistency or provable fallacy.

In their eagerness to oust Otepka, two State Department officials — John F. Reilly and Elmer Dewey Hill — took part in attaching a listening device to Otepka's telephone. A third official — David Belisle — knew about it.

All three testified under oath that they had no knowledge that any wire-tap, "bug," or listening device had been attached to Otepka's telephone. Not until after a Senate floor speech warned of perjury, did these three high State Department officials write letters to the Senate Committee admitting the use of listening devices on Otepka's telephone. However, in admitting the use of the listening device, the three high officials explained that there was no listening on the wire and no interception of Otepka's calls. Since then, these letters — prepared in the State Department legal office and approved by Rusk — have been established as being inaccurate.

Electronics expert Hill has testified that he actually recorded more than a dozen conversations on Otepka's wire as part of a plan to try to get evidence to serve as a basis for ousting the security evaluator. He testified that Reilly knew of the recordings and had a special interest in one of them.

The documented record shows what is characterized by Senator Dodd as "perjury," "falsification" and "lying" by three high level officials who were trying to "get" Otto Otepka. Yet some newspapers have ignored this story. Others have continued to take the State Department line that the proof of "false" testimony on the wire-taps is not connected with efforts to get Otepka.

Although Reilly and Hill have resigned, they have not been criticized by Secretary of State Rusk. Rusk allowed Belisle to remain in the State Department for weeks after becoming aware of the "untruthful" statements in the transcript. Secretary Rusk and his top aides continue ahead with the Reilly-initiated charges to oust Otepka for cooperating with Congress.

The activities of the State Department have been an outrageous, cynical and brutal effort to crush a dissenter for telling Congress the truth. In many ways, it is as bad as anything Joseph McCarthy did in his most irresponsible moments.

But more outrageous than the State Department's action has been the press performance. Some newsmen accepted the State Department philosophy that dissenters like Otepka should be squelched, and Congress barred from the facts.

The Otepka case involves the effectiveness of the whole Department security program. It involves the question of the integrity of many high level officials in a Department that is entrusted with vital foreign policy decisions. Yet, with only a few exceptions, the press has ignored this major investigation or has given it coverage warped by State Department distortions.

Fortuantely, most reporting has been better than the reporting on the TFX investigation and the Otepka case. Most stories are less complicated, and take less concentrated study.

The comments on the weaknesses of the press and the problems of the press should not discourage the young reporter. Where the job is being done poorly, there is great opportunity for those who will study and work on the complex jobs. There are always many reporters willing to cover the easy story — the story that takes only a small amount of background study and guarantees good play in the paper. There are always too few on the stories that take weeks of work, that have an uncertain future, make sources angry, and may be buried with the want ads.

For this reason, there will always be plenty of room for reporters and editors who will tackle the tough story.

Last October and November [1963], the press demonstrated in the Bobby Baker case that it has the courage and the great capacity for a dee pinvestigation when it has the will to do the job. In a few short weeks the press had a hundred or more reporters probing nearly every political, social or business deal that Baker had touched.

Unfortunately, I must report that the interest of many others did not arise until after the appearance of a story about a German party girl who had been on the fringe of some of the Baker social action. She had also cavorted with some important political figures. Prior to this story there were only a handful of us doing any more than casual work on the subject. They included Julian Morrison of the *Washington Daily News,* and Larry Stern and Jack Landau of the *Washington Post.* It is amazing how a little sex angle stimulated editorial interest in good government.

I have been fortunate to work for publishers and editors who understand important stories about government without the necessity of being stimulated by a sex angle, a vicuna coat, a mink coat or a crude pay-off. It isn't that they are uninterested in sex, but simply that they don't need it to be interested in "conflicts of interest" and the more subtle forms of bad government.

Our editors understood when Senator John J. Williams said the integrity of the Senate was involved in the Baker probe.

They understood that the evidence of an arbitrary decision on a $6.5 billion TFX contract was important, even though complicated and lacking a flashy angle.

They understood that evidence of laxity in the State Department security division was vital, and that allegations of falsification by high officials was a grave matter.

If we are to have effective reporting of complicated issues of government, it is vital to have editors who understand what they are doing. William Allen White knew what he was doing, or he tried to find out the facts. He understood the folly and failures of the press of his day, and he made no claim to personal infallibility. He worked hard and constantly re-examined his position.

The William Allen White attitude exists today, although it is not as prevalent as it should be. It exists here in the Middle West in many places. I know it exists in the work and attitudes of Editor Kenneth MacDonald, Managing Editor Frank Eyerly and News Editor Charles Reynolds of the *Des Moines Register*. I know because I have had the closest association with these men over a period of about 20 years. Intelligent and balanced independence is the quality they have in common with William Allen White.

I know that some of the same inquisitiveness, independence and dedication exists among other editors in the Cowles organization and on other newspapers far removed from Washington and New York. The independent editors seek to avoid being simple mirrors of the writings in a few Eastern newspapers. The editors with real common sense can distinguish between informed and independent Washington commentary and the comments of a few journalistic prostitutes who simply parrot the shallow (but often sophisticated sounding) views of a few high-positioned political frauds.

I am elated when editors and reporters demonstrate aggressive independence as in the Bobby Baker investigation. We are all hurt when independence is destroyed or given away as it has been in much of the coverage and comment on the Otepka and TFX investigations.

Newspapering is a profession that gives us the opportunity to be in day-to-day touch with the great people and the great moments of our time. It also brings us in contact with some worshipers of good and bad alike. It is a disservice to our profession if we mislead our readers about the crooks and the clever charlatans who often win public office.

Ours is a profession that gives us the opportunity to be a strong voice and a strong force for good government. We can mold good public officials into better public officials by demanding top performance. We can make bad public officials toe the line or risk exposure and ouster.

It is in the power of each reporter and each editor to make his own choice. He can take the easy way and be a patsy for those in political power, but knowing in the end that he was a weak-kneed hero worshiper who bent to any political wind of strength. Or he can be a force for good and serve as a real check on government.

This is a business I love. I am submerged in it. If I am critical, it is because I know it can do so much more and can be so much more effective than it is. It has improved, but it needs more improvement. It needs people who will work in the face of the frustration of long and difficult tasks. It needs people of courage who will not flinch when the job requires risking the disfavor of the mighty or the popular view of the moment.

The press needs, and always will need, the independence characterized by William Allen White. The least we can do for his memory is to constantly remind ourselves of the many ways that a free and independent press can be weakened or even destroyed. It is our responsibility to aggressively oppose anything that may contaminate the life line of democracy.

16

THE REALITIES OF WORLD NEWS EDITING

By Earl J. Johnson

One of the most important developments in journalism in my time has been the emergence of two highly responsible and intensely competitive worldwide news services — the Associated Press and the United Press International. I should like to talk about how these services grew and matured, how they operate and how they differ from other news media. It is my conviction that their toe-to-toe competition and the balance of power that exists now in this area of news communicating have become the public's best guarantee of being accurately and promptly informed about world and national events. This is the theme of the lecture.

Aside from what's occurred in my own field in my time there have been other important developments in journalism which are more familiar t oyou. I'll mention only those which relate to my own work.

We have seen in the last 40 years a gradual shift in the newspaper's primary role. William Allen White's *Emporia Gazette* was famous, in the main, for its editor's provocative opinions and brilliant style. Mr. White was bigger than his newspaper. Today the best newspapers and the most successful ones are those which tell their readers the most about what is going on in the nation and the world and provide the most lucid explanations of what these events mean. In most cases the newspaper is now bigger than its owner.

In the first 18 years after he gained national recognition with his editorial, "What's the Matter with Kansas," Mr. White's *Gazette* could give its readers only a small window on the outside world. The window was a skeletonized news report by Western Union from the AP in Topeka. This could be expanded by the Gazette into about a column and a half of copy. In 1914 the service became a telephone "pony" service of 45 minutes a day. And not until 1922, four years after the end of World War I, did a leased wire bring the *Gazette* a continuous flow of telegraph news during its publishing hours. This was in no way exceptional at that time.

For example: In his recently published professional autobiography, Raymond Swing recalls working in the Berlin bureau of the *Chicago Daily News*. He says that not until after the first world war began would his publisher, Victor Lawson, permit him or his counterparts in London and Paris to send anything by cable, not a word, except the names of Chicago travelers who that day had registered at the European bureaus of the Chicago paper. There was no hurry about news. It could be sent by rail and steamer.

These references to Emporia and Chicago show how and approximately when the newspapers of the midlands began taking up the burden of catering to widening interests. The first two decades of the century were a time of newspaper expansion, especially afternoon newspapers. It was then that the wire services began to move too.

Humanizing the news by telling it in terms of people, the use of bylines and the staged interview were innovations of the United Press from its organization in 1907.

And under a new management which took over in 1925, the AP began adopting similar practices with great success.

However, it would be a mistake to assume that this expansion and improvement was due entirely to a growing public hunger for news. That was *part* of the story. But business initiative, merchandising and salesmanship played important roles too. New papers were started and editors began opening wider windows on the world and *enticing* readers with a new breadth of coverage.

The United Press sent American-trained reporters to foreign capitals before the first world war. It pioneered in breaking through the barriers of a world cartel which consisted of official agencies abroad and the AP in the United States. In the middle 30's the AP pulled out of this cartel, but already had begun sending its own staffers abroad and depending less on newspaper members for its coverage in this country.

The 20's and 30's were days of opportunity for the UP. AP memberships were limited. Where there were two newspapers in a field, one subscribed to UP and the other to AP.

Then because the UP was exploring new ways of reporting and writing, and because it offered exclusivity to no one, some of the AP papers began adding the UP wire. They then had everything their opposition had and more too. Today any newspaper may subscribe to either or both services, but it took a Supreme Court ruling to make that possible. Between 30 and 40 per cent of the dailies now use wires of both agencies.

So man's growing curiosity about his neighbors near and far plus imagination and enterprise in the news business brought about a widening of news horizons for all of us.

Then came radio, depending on the wire services for basic news, and experimenting before large audiences with new techniques of presenting it. Today there are twice as many radio stations in the country as daily newspapers. UPI serves more than 2,000 radio stations with news written for the ear rather than the eye. I don't know how many the AP serves, but it must be in that neighborhood. There are fewer two-service radio stations than newspapers, but still the large independents and the networks subscribe to both services to have the best of each.

The weekly news magazines are another relatively new development. They are not as directly dependent on the wire services as newspapers and radio are, but they have access to the newspapers all week, and their lure is not so much in having something new as in their slants and treatment of previously known facts.

Time magazine was the first thing really new in journalism in several generations. It devised an entirely new approach and writing style and has been a stunning success.

If we find that *Time* lives in a higher-keyed, wittier and more brightly colored world than the one most of us inhabit, nevertheless the popularity of its innovations has affected other news media, including our own.

Thus, the two primary news services are the main reliance of the printed and electronic news media. No other two organizations have as large an audience for news. The public's understanding of events in Moscow, Washington, Cape Kennedy, at the United Nations and Topeka, and the public's opinions about those events, are largely conditioned by what it reads and hears about them under the logotypes of UPI and AP. Should I say that for better or worse this is the case?

I think I should say *for better* because the central fact here is that the two services now compete on almost equal terms, and this competition contributes to the quality of each. They provide in a general way similar types of services — spot news in the main stream of man's curiosity about his world neighbors — financial news, sports wires, newspictures, features, interpretive news — and additionally UPI provides news film for television and audio reports for radio. Each service spends between 40 and 45 million dollars a year covering the news. Each serves between 6,000 and 7,000 publications and broadcast stations. Their manpower is approximately the same with variations from region to region.

But these physical facilities are not the full measure of their importance. The quality of their performance is what counts, and here again I return to the competitive posture which underwrites their quality.

The public's best hope of knowing promptly and comprehensively about events in Washington, where we all have such a large stake, lies in the fact that the AP and UPI maintain there aggressive staffs of approximately a hundred men and women each. The constant goad of competition, the competitive reporter's ceaseless search to detect the first sign of a new policy trend, his insatiable probing curiosity and his pride in being first to know, in being first with the answer that exposes the political maneuver — those are the public's safeguards (yours and mine) against lethargy or complacency in an area where the least let-down could be disastrous. It could be disastrous because the temptation of news sources to manage the news for their own advantage is resisted most successfully in the presence of competitive reporters.

What I have said about Washington I could say of scores of other news-producing centers. It applies to competition between the war correspondents in Viet Nam, to the diplomatic runs in London, Paris and Moscow, to the science-and-space reporters, to the men covering state legislatures.

Newspapers and radio stations which have access to both news services obviously are in a position to give their readers and listeners the whole fruit of this competitive striving, and many of them do. However, some use only one. Obviously I have my favorite logotype. But regardless of a newspaper editor's choice of services he can be sure that the one he does choose is alert and dependable because an aggressive rival is challenging it minute by minute in every area.

The center of gravity in newspapers has shifted from editorial dominance to news dominance, and this has marked a decline in the highly personalized kind of newspapering that we knew in the heyday of William Allen White.

Journalism practiced mainly to persuade, and to mold public opinion, has become the role of the professional editorial writer and the syndicated columnists. There are very few dailies which do not subscribe to several columnists, and these are not always chosen because their views are the same as the editors' views. I've never known an American editor who wanted to monopolize opinion.

He has at his command and for the use of his readers what I have described as the fruits of the intense competition that exists between the wire services, and he has a wide choice of famous columnists.

It is unfortunate, I think, that syndicated columnists often command more attention on national and international issues than the local editor does. However, that's another story, and it would be a digression to talk about it today.

Now I would not cite the competitive balance that has emerged between the news services or even their physical growth as important milestones in my time if I could not tell you that they have also achieved new standards of editorial maturity.

In 1922 or 1923 I covered a national railroad strike from the headquarters of the railroad brotherhoods in Cleveland. I knew almost nothing about the economic issues of that strike or the rights of labor or of management. My dispatches dealt mainly with violence and the inflammatory statements of union leaders. If that strike was a chapter in an economic revolution, I had no grasp of what it meant. Yet there was nothing exceptional about my ignorance in the context of what newspapers demanded in those days. My stuff was getting printed in a competitive market. What impresses us now is that I could get away with it, that the AP man there could get away with it too, and that the newspapers accepted this kind of superficial coverage.

Shortly afterward I was sent to Cincinnati to cover a meeting of the American Association for the Advancement of Science. A delegate reported that for the first time science had changed a rooster into a hen or a hen into a rooster. I've forgotten which way it went. But I have not forgotten that this breakthrough on the hormone front was on the press wires the feature of the meeting. Surely more significant things happened at the A.A.A.S. that year, but only the scientists knew they they were.

After that I boned up on thoroughbreds and crossed the Ohio River to cover the Latonia Derby in Kentucky.

No doubt I was a versatile fellow. But it was a superficial versatility that today neither wire service would tolerate. Our newspaper subscribers are more mature now, and a wire service cannot be far behind its subscribers in recognizing that labor and science and even horse racing require reporters with special qualifications. Think of all the other areas that the news services cover nowadays in depth and with understanding.

The racial revolution is more than a series of riots. We must have reporters who have lived with it, men who are competent to evaluate it in print. Aviation has become a full-time specialty, as have many other topics — the country's spiritual life, atomic energy, medicine, education, outer space, the arts. Even what people are thinking is news nowadays, and so are the changing mores.

One of the most widely published surveys the UPI has carried recently was a comprehensive report on the problems of teen-age drinkers and their drinking parents. Another was about changing religious attitudes.

This kind of reporting was rarely undertaken in the days when we could cover a railroad strike in terms of bricks crashing through the windows of locomotives.

Where do we get the specialists who can dig below the surface and illuminate these complexities of modern society? That question was asked at a national convention of UPI editors last October in Washington. Reviewing a few examples from our own list of specialists, I found that most of them had started as all-around reporters. After mastering the disciplines of that profession, they began to specialize because their own interest in special topics led them to qualify by intensive study. They were encouraged by their bosses, but the reporters themselves took the initiative. They are all excellent general reporters, but their public recognition is usually based on their work as specialists.

I have said that the wire services are the chief sources of news for the press and for broadcasters, and I should add now that this does not mean they operate the same way as a newspaper, and certainly we cannot expect them to be as well known or well understood by the public as newspapers are. You often hear people say that they "see by the paper," but rarely that they "see by UPI or AP."

The chief difference is that the wire service is a wholesaler, an importer, exporter and distributor of news. The newspapers and broadcasters are the retailers. They serve the public directly. The wire services do not. The wire services deal almost exclusively with the professionals among the retailers. On newspapers these pro's are the telegraph editors; and in broadcasting stations, the news editors or program directors. These are the gate-keepers.

There is a gate-keeper on eac hof the more than 6,000 publications and broadcasting stations that the UPI serves. They are the men who decide how much of our news report to pass along to their audiences and how it should be displayed. They make their decisions on the basis of what they know about the interests and tastes of their own communities. If they conclude that a dispatch from Wichita is more useful to their readers than one of the same length from Tanzania, then Wichita wins over Tanzania.

As the editor of a news service I am glad that we do not have to write the headlines on our own dispatches. It would not be practical anyhow, because we could not devise one headline for one story that would be appropriate in all news markets. Last month there was a dispatch from Paris about Elizabeth Taylor seeking British citizenship. Since her husband was British this did not raise our cable editor's blood pressure or temperature very much. To my surprise, if not to his, the dispatch came out under eight-column banners in two afternoon newspapers in New York. One paper then conducted a poll to see how the man in the street felt about Miss Taylor's latest switch.

Another difference between a newspaper and a wire service is that a wire service cannot cater to the diverse policies of individual newspapers but must have its own style and its own standards. We cannot, for example, deprive Dr. Martin Luther King of his doctorate because there are newspapers which want him called only M. L. King.

We cannot omit news of revolutions from our world circuits although we know that in some countries it is verboten to publish news of a revolution anywhere, especially if the revolt has been a success. Saudi Arabia uses no pictures showing the Star of David, no descriptions of prizefights or other sports which may involve bloodshed.

As we have seen, there is much more to a world news report than bare bulletins. Each service delivers dozens of special dispatches each week by some of the most skillful reporters and writers in the craft.

In our own news report explanatory backgrounders, analyses, surveys, distinctive treatment of meaningful spot news, trend stuff and dug facts occupy from one-third to one-half of our transmission time.

The wire service must not swamp the retail gate-keepers with a glut of unevaluated news. Our biggest continuing problems, like those of the gate-keepers, are in selection and emphasis. How to recognize the kernels of important and significant news. How to point them up so the newspaper editor and broadcaster too will recognize their importance and find them digestible, even if not appetizing, as much of today's news certainly is not.

Already modern communication systems swirl news around the world at the speed of electricity, and communications satellites will only amplify the flow. More dispatches are coming in from more places than ever before. Many of them throb with urgency. Others are shocking and ominous and some seem improbable, or would have seemed so yesterday. In our business the world is not getting smaller, as the cliche goes, but is getting larger. In the last few years the UPI has opened 13 new bureaus in Africa. Previously this was a part of the world that barely existed in our pattern of news coverage. And still there is the vast area of Red China which remains a blank on our coverage map. That will be about the last frontier.

The picture of these world news agencies as giant communications machines linking hundreds of large staffs which pour their sometimes literary product onto the agencies' domestic and world circuits day and night is not a wholly valid picture. True, there is a constant hum of activity in the major centers. There is seldom a pause in the chattering stream of dispatches, directives and inquiries of varying degrees of urgency flying back and forth between the regional relay bureaus. But high tension is not every man's daily lot. The picture is incomplete if it does not include the hundreds who are merely on guard in the out-of-the-way places.

I don't know if you have ever thought of Port Stanley, or even remember where it is, but there is someone in Port Stanley who is, in a way, thinking of you. His name is Forrest McWhan. He is UPI's stringer in Port Stanley, which lies east of Cape Horn in the British-owned Falkland Islands in the South Atlantic. Forrest McWhan also is the local minister. As he goes about his clerical affairs he is alert for anything that might interest the UPI and the newspapers and radio stations it serves.

Truth to tell, not much happens in Port Stanley and weeks go by when nothing is heard from the Rev. Mr. McWhan. But we have a feeling not only of confidence but also of pride that a man of his stature is our representative in this very remote place; and his pride is equally great in playing a role, however small, in our globe-girdling operation.

Yes, behind the impersonal teletypes and picture machines which represent UPI in the newsrooms of 114 countries are thousands of men and women who are not constantly feeding the communications monster. But their skills are always on call to bring you an orderly account of a sometimes disorderly world.

Although we work on a wider canvas than the local newspaper does, and think in broader terms geographically perhaps, we still conform to the same standards of fairness and honesty in reporting the news as the good newspaper does. In many parts of the world, not excluding Washington, we must dig harder for newsworthy facts because we encounter many strange barriers; government restrictions at the source of the news, censorship, the reluctance of foreign officials to accept the American concept of free access to public information and their refusal in some cases to grant communicatioins facilities open to all on equal terms. The fact that we regularly prevail over these barriers, tomorrow if not today, is due in great measure to the fact that UPI men and their counterparts in AP are striving constantly to be first with the best information from everywhere.

Thus, in conclusion, I revert to my original thought:

On the news fronts of the world you will find wire service men and women trying ceaselessly to excel in the pursuit and capture of what is new and significant; and I hope you will agree that you, as the ultimate consumers of news, are the beneficiaries of this now firmly established pattern of competitive checks and balances.

17

THE WONDERFUL NEWSPAPER BUSINESS

By GARDNER COWLES

I had the privilege of knowing William Allen White in the years of the Great Depression and the New Deal. He was an original thinker. He had courage and imagination. Those qualities are not in over-supply today, unfortuantely, in the journalism profession.

This afternoon I want to make some critical comments about various phases of editing and publishing, in the hope that my remarks may stimulate the thinking of some of the young people just starting in the wonderful world of newspapers and magazines.

But before I assume the role of critic, perhaps you will pardon a quick sketch of my publishing career — just to illustrate that I have had a wealth of experience — a career filled with failures as well as success — so I feel entitled to a few opinions, whether you will agree with them or not.

My father was a first-rate newspaper man who started with a country weekly in northern Iowa. About the time I was born he bought a struggling daily in Des Moines, which was then as hotly competitive a newspaper market as one could find. Twenty-five years later the competition had thrown in the sponge, the Des Moines *Register and Tribune* had become superior, important statewire newspapers and the *Des Moines Sunday Register* had a circulation in excess of 500,000.

My older brother, John, who has been a life-long associate of mine and to whom I owe much for his advice and guidance over the years, moved to Minneapolis in 1935 and duplicated in that much-larger market exactly what our father had done in Des Moines. I am very proud of the *Minneapolis Star and Tribune,* which my brother and his great organization have built.

So, from early childhood I was steeped in the newspaper business. It was as if I had gone to journalism school all of my life.

Shortly after graduating from college, when I was a neophyte in the news room of the *Register and Tribune,* I heard that a George Gallup at the University of Iowa was trying to perfect a technique for measuring accurately what the public reads or skips in a newspaper. I became greatly intrigued. From his studies it became obvious to me the public in large numbers doesn't read long, gray, unbroken columns of type. Makeup, the style of heads and sub-heads, having each page look inviting and interesting, were extremely important.

Gallup soon convinced me of the universal reader-interest in pictures, if well handled, and especially the reader-interest in a sequence of pictures that tell a story. His research also proved that the public can be interested in almost any subject if that subject is simply and attractively presented.

The rotogravure supplements of Sunday newspapers were then — as now — pretty dull affairs. I originally thought of starting *Look* as a new kind of Sunday picture supplement, but the arithmetic of such an operation didn't seem attractive, so I launched it as a separate magazine in 1937.

This was a brash move. I had not had a day of experience in magazine editing and publishing. Nor had anyone on the original staff. I made horrendous mistakes. I almost went broke. But gradually, with a lot of luck and sweat and tears, and with the help of some extremely able people who had joined me, *Look* became an established success. 1965, I am happy to report, was its best year, with its circulation averaging 7,600,000 per issue and its gross advertising revenues about $79,000,000.

But I want to admit to some failures along the way. Sixteen years ago I tried a very posh and expensive magazine of fashion and the arts — *Flair* — with many printing and binding innovations, but after a year I gave up the ghost. *Flair* was ahead of its time.

I tried another kind of magazine — *Quick* — a pocket-size newsweekly which a busy reader could go through in ten minutes. It was a remarkable circulation success at 10c per copy — reaching 1,300,000 within two years — but I never could persuade advertisers adequately to use its small page size. Splendid as *Time* and *Newsweek* are, they are getting long and sometimes ponderous. I think some daring young journalist could succeed with a smaller, more concise newsweekly. Sometimes I wish we were still publishing *Quick*.

Later, I started *The Insider's Newsletter* (a poor title, but the best we could think of at the time) to see if it were possible to make a success of a newsweekly without advertising. I am happy to report this little publication has a circulation above 150,000, continues to grow, and is modestly profitable.

Three years ago we purchased *Family Circle,* a monthly for homemakers, because I felt it had extraordinary editorial vigor and reader loyalty. It has no subscriptions. Its circulation of better than 7,500,000 monthly comes from the voluntary purchase of the magazine by housewives, primarily at the check-out counters of supermarkets. It has the largest single-copy sale of any magazine in the world. *Family Circle* is still growing in circulation and advertising.

With a British partner we successfully launched *Family Circle* in England last year [1965] and it will be introduced in Germany, in German, next month.

Recently we started *Venture* — The Travelers World — because I believe the interest in travel is growing so rapidly that there is a place for a superbly-edited and printed modern magazine devoted to travel. I have high hopes for *Venture.*

During this somewhat checkered, but exciting, magazine development period I never lost my interest in newspapers. I continued to help guide the *Des Moines Register and Tribune.* I started from scratch the *San Juan Star,* the only English-language daily in San Juan, Puerto Rico, with the help of a very able editor, William Dorvillier. We bought the *Lakeland Ledger* and the *Gainesville Sun* in Florida. The *Star* and the *Sun* have both won Pulitzer Prizes recently. We are considering further expansion in publishing and broadcasting.

So much for what I fear has been an over-long recital of my own career. I think the record shows, however, I have dared, or been foolhardy enough, to try new paths in journalism. When I failed, I had the sense to swallow my pride and bury my mistakes.

Now, what conclusions have I come to after 40 years as an editor and publisher and operator in the hectic, but exciting, world of newspapers, magazines, radio and television? I'll name a few:

I think that the tremendous asset of daily newspapers over all other forms of communication is their role of public responsibility.

Radio and television inform within a dramatic, popular and limited scope, but their primary motivation is entertainment.

Magazines inform, stimulate thought and entertain, again within the scope of their facilities and the intervals at which they are published.

Daily newspapers not only inform and entertain, they are invested with responsibility for truth, fairness, balance, completeness and newness, coupled with their responsibility as the monitor and conscience of their communities and the nation.

Responsible newspapers thus have a public character. Those which lack this public character, or shun it, ignore their greatest asset and this will eventually show up in the balance sheet.

Too many issues of too many newspapers are just plain dull, dull, dull! To be dull is the cardinal sin of any publication. This does not need to happen. It comes about from lack of advance planning and from too narrow a concept of what is news.

You and I know the habits in the news room of the average middle-size daily: the editors rely heavily, too heavily, on that day's news report from the AP or the UPI or both. In addition, they are counting on news breaks from the police department, or the city hall, or the county court house, or the school board, or the state house. Inevitably, on some days when not much of importance comes in from any of these sources, the editors have little to work with. The news editor puts to bed that day a dull paper and says to himself, "well, I did the best I could."

I contend any real newspaper needs several good reporters and photographers who are not tied down covering spot news in the conventional sense, or covering a set beat, but who are free to dig out and work up material that is topical, but can be held for a week or a month until desperately needed on an otherwise dull news day. But this takes advance planning. It takes ideas. It takes imaginative leadership from the top editor running the news room.

The *Wall Street Journal* does what I am talking about superbly. So does Jack Knight's *Miami Herald*. Some of the most interesting issues of the *Miami Herald* are those published on days when really little spot news, in the conventional sense, is breaking. It is evident someone did a lot of advance planning and had prepared material which could be finished up fast for just such a contingency.

Too many newspapers still don't do an adequate job of digging in their own communities for the fascinating things and rapidly changing developments going on in the fields of education, medicine, science and the arts. Even in religion there are new ideas and trends rarely reported on the local level.

To make my point about advance planning, let me refer to *Look*.

At *Look* we do not cover spot news because of our long dead-lines. We take no wire service. So in effect, the editor starts each issue with a blank sheet of paper in front of him. All he has to work with is a large and extremely competent staff of reporters, writers, photographers, and researchers. The whole operation is built around fresh ideas for stories — we need dozens of ideas each week — and the most careful kind of long-range planning. Several of the staff are working on editorial projects now that won't be used in the magazine until next year.

Newspapers need this same kind of advance planning, on a smaller scale to be sure, to avoid so many dull issues.

A second and related point I want to make is that a good news-paper needs a good art director. When I say this, most editors don't know what I am talking about.

Newspaper pages today — with few exceptions — are made up, or "designed," by an old-time journeyman-printer and a make-up editor who may, or may not, know much about typography and the thousand and one methods for making pages look readable and exciting. On successful magazines, the art director ranks right below the top editor in importance and authority. He has a strong voice in helping decide how a story idea is to be developed. He suggests ways to give it maximum visual impact. He knows how to blend type and photographs so that each helps the other. His responsibility is to make each page come alive and intrigue the reader. Newspapers need this kind of talent. Too few have it.

If newspapers were as well edited and as well printed as I think they could be, particularly the great Sunday newspapers, then I doubt whether *Life* or *Look* and other leading magazines could have attained their present size and strength. *Look*, for example, edited in New York, printed in Chicago, has over 900,000 circula-tion per issue in California. This is a larger circulation than any California newspaper except the Sunday *Los Angeles Times*. Isn't this pretty convincing evidence that *Look* has something which too many newspapers lack?

I am afraid newspaper publishers feel it isn't too important how their product looks or feels. But it is important. Magazines have found this out.

Each magazine publisher tries to use the best grade of paper he

can possibly afford and buys the best printing he can find. It seems
to me too many newspapers reverse this process by looking for
the cheapest newsprint and being satisfied with sloppy printing.

Fortunately, great advances have been made recently in newspaper equipment. Important research now under way may bring
vast changes in production methods. The newspaper of the future
will achieve a printing quality, both in black and white and color,
comparable to the best magazine printing today. And this will
come about without large increases in operating costs.

A third, and critical point I want to make is this:

It perplexes me why big and important editorial material usually
appears first in some leading magazine. I'm thinking of things like
Sorenson's book on Kenndy, the by-line stories of the Astronauts,
Truman Capote's thriller *In Cold Blood*. The fact is, magazines
work harder in spotting this kind of material early and are willing
to pay big prices.

But if the top newspapers in each of the largest 50 markets
should band together to go after these high-interest features, they
could out-bid any magazine. The cost would not be tremendous
to any one of the 50 newspapers. But first, enough newspaper editors and publishers need to care, need to be concerned that they
are missing these features and be determined to do something
about it.

Too many newspaper editors today are too careful, too cautious,
too fearful of being controversial, too worried about ruffling the
hair of some readers. I don't think any man can become a great
editor unless he is willing to become meaningfully involved in the
important issues of his community, his state, the nation and the
world. And he needs to *care passionately*.

Dan Mich, a great editor, who died two months ago after heading the *Look* editorial department for nearly 25 years, had a favorite quotation which went like this: "The hottest places in hell are
reserved for those who, in time of moral crisis, maintained their
neutrality." I think William Allen White would have liked that
statement.

If I were teaching today in the Journalism School here in Kansas, I would say to budding young journalists:

"Dare to be unpopular. If you win a popularity contest, you
probably aren't doing your job. You can and should be respected
— but not necessarily popular.

"Always edit just a notch over the heads of your readers. They want to read a publication they can look up to and one which stimulates them to think — even if they are occasionally annoyed.

"If you are in doubt on a particular issue, lean over backwards to prevent adequately the less popular side. To help make this country truly civilized, we need to make it safe for diversity in thought, in morals, in customs, not try to force everyone into the same mold."

I think I would also say to the journalism students: "When you become an editor never get completely in bed with any politician. You will become a captive. You will lose your objectivity. And chances are eventually you will find your idol has clay feet.

"Learn to be very skeptical of government statistics and government press releases. They are frequently designed to lead a reporter away from the real news.

"Part of the job of an editor is to keep the temper of the country on an even keel. When the public gets too optimistic, warn it of possible troubles ahead; when it gets too pessimistic, remind readers that the country isn't really going to hell, that it has come through hundreds of past crises."

The public has a tendency to believe many things that aren't true. This needs to be pointed out. For example, today:

The public thinks the divorce rate in the U.S. is rising. It is actually lower than twenty years ago.

The public thinks we are increasingly living in ramshackle houses in slum areas. The truth is the typical American family has twice the chance to live in good housing than it had in 1950.

The public thinks narcotic addiction is growing. It is actually declining dramatically.

The public thinks a southern Negro in the U.S. has little chance of any college education. Actually, he or she has more chance than the average white youth in England.

I could go on endlessly with examples of misinformation widely believed to be fact.

And lastly, I would tell the journalism students:

American newspapers, with all their faults are, by and large, the best in the world and better on the average than they were a generation ago.

There is nothing wrong with American newspapers that couldn't be cured by a few more editors and publishers like William Allen

White — editors who care, really care, about the editorial quality of their products, and who are courageous enough to demand the best of their associates and of the leaders in the areas they serve.

Journalism is a business. Journalism is a profession. It can be frustrating. It is an intoxicating mistress. But it performs a vital service and if you dedicate your life to it with fervor, it will be truly rewarding. You will never be bored.

18

PERSPECTIVE REPORTING VERSUS HUMBUGABILITY

By WES GALLAGHER

When I started preparing this talk I planned to point out the difficulty of communication today by saying something like this:

"When man lived simply and primitively, the business of disseminating the news was done simply and primitively. But now in this complex civilization among people highly sophisticated, the job has become complex."

That's what I planned to say, but I found that William Allen White said exactly that in 1932, talking to journalism students at Drake University. That makes him either 35 years ahead of his time or me 35 years behind.

But Mr. White lived in an age of relatively small government, and image-making was not the industry it is today. The problems of the journalist then, as Mr. White pointed out, were the same as they are today — to be the conscience of the public, the defender of its rights, its spokesman, its protector against malfeasance in government, and the people's voice whenever it needs to be heard.

All newsmen should make brief speeches, but before I begin to be brief we'll have to go into some background.

First, the audience of the journalist today is quite different than even 20 years ago. Robert Ardrey, anthropologist and a playwright who wrote *"African Genesis,"* reflected on today's audience in his new book *The Territorial Imperative.* He said he has become aware that "a new human force — a force anonymous and unrecognized, informed and inquisitive, with allegiance to neither wealth nor poverty, to neither privilege nor petulance is silently appearing on earth and this class is massive."

"Informed and inquisitive" — these are the key words.

Statistically they are young — 51 per cent under 29 — and over 10 million are college graduates.

It is an impatient audience — too impatient to waste time on trivia. Deluged daily by the highly sophisticated techniques of Madison Avenue, it has become cynical and critical. It is eager for information but suspicious that it is being taken in by one device or another. It swallows up vast amounts of information and entertainment, but it hungers for the significant. It hungers for perspective. It hungers for understanding.

The audience is only half of the problem. The journalist stands between the audience and the sources of news. The sources of news have changed as much as the readers and listeners. First, the size and influence of government — local, state and federal — have been enlarged enormously so they affect the lives of every individual in the world. Whether big government is good or bad is in political dispute, but big government seems inevitable. Republican or Democrat, Socialist or Conservative, the powers of government have constantly changed everywhere in the world. The sheer bulk has become a problem in itself.

The Agricultural Department employs 80,000 people, the State Department 43,000, Justice 33,000 and Defense 1,222,000. No individual citizen or group of citizens could begin to hope to find out what all those people are doing with the taxpayer's money, or with your lives or your freedoms, on any given day, let alone year after year. Even trained reporters find it difficult to cope with such huge organizations.

The image-makers have been very busy in government. Press relations departments have grown even faster than other branches of government. We have reached the point where the federal government alone now spends scores of millions of dollars every year on sheer press agentry. The jobs of these press agents is to make disasters appear insignificant and molehills of success appear mountains of achievement.

Journalism's problems do not rest with government alone. The past three decades have seen an explosion of education and knowledge. The journalist of today, especially the specialist, must know a hundred times as much as his predecessor — just as the doctor of today must know a hundred times as much as the doctor of yesterday. Science has put spaceships around the moon, unleashed the demons of atomic weaponry, practically stamped out tuberculosis and infantile paralysis in the western world. It has brought a higher standard of living for everyone and a greater chance of dying by violence.

Is it any wonder then that this vast new public looking at the

huge apparatus of government and the contradictions of science
is hard to satisfy?

The agitation of this society is expressed in many ways.

"You can't believe what you read in the newspapers."

"There is a credibility gap in government."

"Television hides more than it shows."

"No politician ever tells the truth."

"All politicians are humbugs."

These are just a few of the phrases that you will hear daily.
They are reflections of our time.

This society doubts the credibility of almost everything and is
immune — if I can pronounce it — to humbugability.

And they have reasons for this attitude. In our time, the Vietnamese war has probably been the greatest contributor to the
cynicism in this country as far as the press is concerned. To cite
a few examples of what they have heard:

"The war can only be won by the Vietnamese themselves and
the United States will pull out more troops even if the war falters."

"Our responsibility is not to substitute ourselves for the Vietnamese but to train them to carry on the operation that they themselves are capable of."

Author — Secretary of Defense McNamara in 1963 and 1964.
These are just as few of many such government statements made
over five years of the war and proven wrong by events.

Within a week last fall, we had Secretary McNamara saying that
the troop buildup in Vietnam would be slowed up and level off.
Meanwhile, General Greene of the Marine Corps, in an off-the-
record Tokyo press conference, said they would need 750,000 men
in Vietnam. At the time we had about 350,000, Senator Stennis
set the figure needed at 600,000. Confusion multiplied!

The latest furor has been set off by the reporting of Harrison
Salisbury of the *New York Times* and Bill Baggs of the *Miami
News*. But the stage for Salisbury was not set by the *New York
Times* but by the statements of U.S. government officials during
two years of bombing in North Vietnam. Assistant Secretary Arthur Sylvester recently challenged anyone to say that the Defense
Department has claimed that *"all"* bombs fell only on military
targets in North Vietnam. It is true that the Defense Department
did not make a sweeping claim. But there was a concentrated effort

on the part of every arm in government, including the Pentagon, to make it appear that this was true.

Questioned about the bombing accuracy in June of 1966, when the bombs were close to Hanoi and Haiphong, McNamara emphasized at a press conference that the pilots were carefully instructed to confine themselves to military targets. He said the pilots were told "not to destroy the Communist government of North Vietnam nor destroy or damage the people of North Vietnam."

A Pentagon spokesman said that the bombs fell "right on target."

McNamara added, "The pilots were especially briefed to avoid civilian areas." "We have not hit Hanoi or Haiphong, we have hit oil storage facilities."

Senator Dirksen, a Republican who seems to echo the administration, chimed in to say, "We are absolutely astounded at the real precision result."

On June 30, General Myers said that fuel dumps were hit by a "surgical type of treatment — this means holding civilian casualties to an absolute minimu mand putting the bombs right on the money."

On the same day, Ambassador Goldberg said the bombings hit petroleum facilities "located away from the population centers of Hanoi and Haiphong."

On July 1, Vice President Humphrey in Detroit said the raids were carried out "so as to avoid civilian casualties." July 2, an administration spokesman said, "No more than one or two civilians — perhaps none — were killed in Wednesday's bombing of oil targets at Haiphong and Hanoi." The administration spokesman said that this conclusion was based on aerial photographs of the raid. Just how such an exact count of civilian casualties could be deducted from photographs was not made clear, since the administration first announced that 80 per cent of the oil facilities were hit, then revised this a few days later to 40-50 per cent. Then a few days after that, Secretary Cyrus Vance said that 66 per cent of the oil facilities had been destroyed.

Those aerial photographs seem to be the most flexible in history —they provided any kind of an answer for anyone.

At any rate, the administration's own attempt to convey the impression that bombs fell only on military targets set the stage for Salisbury's articles. He pointed out the inevitable—that bombs fall today, just as they did in World War II, on most any place — on civilians and military installations alike, particularly if the bombings are heavy.

Flying at 600 or 1,000 miles an hour with only split seconds over a target — shot at by ground fire and rockets and possibly attacked by Migs — it is a wonder that the bombing is as accurate as it has been. As a matter of fact, the bombings probably were more accurate than the statements made about them.

How much different the picture would have been these past two years if the administration had said the bombs were directed toward military targets but "inevitably some of them fell outside the area and probably caused civilian casualties." Such repeated statements would have been accurate, truthful and believed. And Salisbury's and Baggs' articles on the bombings would have not had the world impact that they did.

In this continuing furor over the credibility gap, the reader associates the untrue statement of a public figure with the paper or broadcast station that publishes or airs it. This is like getting mad at the local editor because the weatherman goofed. But it undoubtedly has a lot to do with public disbelief of journalism.

There is a remedy for this I will come to shortly.

Some critics already believe journalism has lost its influence because of this lack of credibility.

But I don't think so. I don't think we have reached this point because this vast audience *is* being influenced and *is* being influenced in such a way that it is still making the right judgment as far as the U.S. and the world is concerned.

What influences this new class?

Scotty Reston, a resident Washington skeptic in his own right, discussed in the magazine *Foreign Affairs* the influence of the journalist on diplomacy. He said, "The Lippmanns and Krocks have followings, but news is more important than opinion."

I do not believe that an individual column, an individual editorial, an individual television program influences to any significant degree this new sophisticated society.

But the *flow* of news does influence. If reporters in Vietnam write day after day, as they did in the early sixties, that the war in South Vietnam was going badly for the Vietnamese government, this is what the public believes. If today, the same hundreds and thousands of newspaper stories and broadcasts from South Vietnam point out that militarily the war is at least a stalemate, this is what the public believes.

The flow of news, accurately reported, influences the public. And I stress *accurately.*

Facts presented logically have a ring of authenticity that over a period of time convinces the vast majority or the reading and listening public regardless of their cynicism. There are still the extremists who believe nothing but their own preconceived ideas, but they are a small minority.

This does not mean the new "informed and inquisitive" public seeks to have heroes and villains clearly designated in the news. This more sophisticated class realizes that there are greys and various shades of grey in every situation. The trap the journalist must avoid is presenting a situation as black and white when the reader knows differently.

What tools do we need for our job? We have developed many and they have gone under different names — enterprise, reporting in depth, backgrounders. Now the emphasis should be on detailed "investigative reporting" and, what I like to call it, "perspective reporting." Investigative reporting is certainly not new, but we cannot do investigative reporting as it was done a few years ago. Then the classic technique was to take a few facts and flail away at the malefactors editorially. Today's problems are much more complex and investigation of them takes a lot more time and effort. It is a rare case when one reporter can gather enough facts in a short time and come up with a story that will be authentic enough to convince and hold the attention of our new readers. Investigative reporting must be done with enough resources to match and overcome any obstacles — and there will be many. We can convince only by the most detailed presentation of facts, for facts alone have the ring of truth — opinion alone is useless.

Indicative of the resources that you need to throw into such a situation was the *New York Times'* worldwide analysis of the operations of the CIA, which was months in preparation with scores of reporters working on various facets of it. In the same category was the Associated Press' own investigation into graft in Vietnam, which ran on virtually all front pages late last year. This story, too, was months in preparation. While the main burden was carried by two men, many others contributed to it over a period of time.

Investigative reporting is not the type you can hit just once and drop. You must come back again and again until the *flow of news — the flow of facts,* if you want to put it that way — convinces our new audience and gets something done.

The other great weapon that we have is *perspective* reporting that can and must be used on the daily flow of news.

Perspective reporting is the tool we need to use to keep the reader from associating a lack of credibility on the part of a news source with the medium that is carrying his statement.

The dictionary defines perspective as "the art of depicting on a flat surface, various objects, architecture, landscape in such a way as to express its dimensions and its relation of parts one to the other and to the whole."

Perspective reporting is presenting news in its proper relationship to the whole and in relation to other news in its own time.

Perspective reporting dissects the situation today and compares it with the past.

For example, in doing an article today on General De Gaulle, do you portray only the man who has been raiding our gold supply, throwing ou rtroops out of France, keeping Great Britain out of the Common Market, attacking our policy on Vietnam? Or do you put this complex man in perspective with the hero De Gaulle of the fories, who rallied France, saved it in the post war years and then came back again a decade later to save France from anarchy?

Perspective reporting sees both men and evaluates both for the reader. It presents a complete picture. It is cool. Much cooler and more objective than the former Secretary of State I met in Washington some months ago and asked if he felt General De Gaulle had ever been right on one single political question.

"Never," he replied looking me straight in the eye, and he wasn't joking.

Trying to put one man, even a General De Gaulle, in perspective is a simple problem compared with writing about the emotional problems today such as integration and segregation, China versus Russia or for that matter China versus China.

Perspective reporting requires a cold, logical approach to the news. It requires dogged pursuit of facts until the writer is convinced that he has everything he can possibly dig out. The facts must then be sorted and logically presented, devoid of conclusion-jumping or emotionalism. An emotional phrase in a story can destroy your credibility with a reader — particularly the new reader.

If these precepts are followed, the reader — no matter how cynical or sophisticated — will find himself convinced. The article will have that feel of authenticity.

Perspective reporting can and should be used everywhere not just on complicated situations.

Recently our Hugh Mulligan had a long story on just how pilots felt in flying and bombing over North Vietnam. It was a fascinating article — many times better than those first person stories of riding on bombing missions in World War II or Korea. I had given orders to the Saigon staff that the day of the reporter flying on bombing missions had been overdone since World War II, and I certainly didn't want anyone flying over North Vietnam, no matter what the opportunity was. Hugh's story had so much detail and such feeling of participation that, in reading it, I became disturbed he perhaps had violated this order. So I wrote him a letter, and this is what he wrote in reply.

"No, I didn't go, but neither did I get all that detail just by interviewing. Would you believe that the original story was twice as long? I have no complaints against my editors — whoever cut it in half did a superior job." Mulligan went on to say: "The point is that you don't get that kind of detail just from interviews. I lived with these guys in their barracks for almost a week, went to the movies with them, ate with them. It took me four days to find a communicative guy like Greene. On the day of the flight, I got up with them, attended all the top secret briefings, rode out to the flight line, watched the pre-flight, went by jeep to the armament pit, then to runway control point. I watched them take off, waited on the strip, Ann Sheridan-style, until they returned an hour or so later. I talked with the crew chiefs, attended all the top secret briefings and then got Randy and Duff to tell me in simple English, minute by minute, exactly what happened. We did it over a beer at the officers club. Then I wrote, discarded and wrote until I had it all in. Sometime you may be interested in reading all the details."

That is how Mulligan got his story.

I think this illustrates the difference between ordinary reporting and perspective reporting. Mulligan took a week or ten days to get his carefully detailed account of a pilot's experiencs over North

Vietnam. I cannot remember any reporter, including myself, who spent more than a few hours in World War II on similar stories. Mulligan did a far better reporting job. When you read his story you felt you were sitting right behind the pilot in a way that story from previous wars made you feel.

Everything Mulligan presented was true and was in relation to other facts and to the whole mission — this was perspective reporting. There could be no doubt in the reader's mind that this was the way it happened.

It is not always as easy to get the facts as it is in this particular type of war reporting. But by the relatively simple device of admitting that we failed to get the facts in a certain situation, or that a public official refused to comment on a critical point, we can convey authenticity to the reader. Most reporters hesitate to put such phrases into their stories, but when they leave gaps unanswered, their stories are not blieved.

The government, too, would be far better off if, in advocating its programs, it admitted failures from time to time. This, too, would give the reader more confidence in the credibility of what is being said. But this has never happened in the past — or present.

Every day I see stories — by AP as well as others — where the reporter accepted statements without question and didn't go deep enough or ask enough questions — perhaps embarrassing questions — to obtain the real perspective. You may say that only an editor would realize that these are missing, but if you do you misjudge our new society—"informed and inquisitive with allegiance to neither wealth nor poverty nor privilege nor petulance."

There is no doubt the flow of news can and does influence the most sophisticated critic. Even the doubters must take their arguments from the news itself.

If we, as journalists, use the tools we have at our disposal to put the news in perspective, then the news will have that ring of authenticity, and we won't have to fear any credibility gap. Nor will the lack of credibility of some news sources rub off on the journalist.

The public will have confidence in the journalist not only as a conveyer of vital information, but as the principal guardian of its freedom as well.

BIOGRAPHICAL NOTES

JAMES B. RESTON (1950). The winner of two Pulitzer Prizes, Reston has reported national and international events for the *New York Times* for more than 25 years. After two years with the London bureau, he returned to the U. S. in 1941 to work in the *Times* Washington bureau. Early in 1943 he was made assistant to the publisher, Arthur Hays Sulzberger, and later that year he became acting head of the London bureau. In 1953 he was made director of the Washington bureau, and in 1964 he assumed his present position as associate editor of the paper. Reston started his journalistic career as a sports writer. After graduating from the University of Illinois in 1932, he worked for the *Springfield* (Ohio) *Daily News,* served as sports publicity director for Ohio State University, and later was traveling secretary for the Cincinnati baseball club. He was writing sports and features from the Associated Press New York bureau in 1937 when the wire service sent him to London, where he subsequently joined the *New York Times* staff.

ERNEST K. LINDLEY (1951). Reporter, columnist, author, and now a diplomat, Lindley is perhaps best known for his 24 years as chief of *Newsweek* magazine's Washington bureau. He headed the bureau from 1937 to 1961, when he left to become a special assistant to the Secretary of State and a member of the State Department's Policy Planning Council, a position he still holds. He began his journalistic career while still in college as the editor of a small-town daily newspaper. Then, after attending Oxford University as a Rhodes Scholar, he joined the *Wichita* (Kansas) *Beacon.* Later he reported for the *New York World* and the *New York Herald Tribune.* During his years with *Newsweek,* Lindley's signed column was a regular feature in the magazine, and for 15 years he also wrote a syndicated newspaper column. He is the author of several books on world affairs and American foreign policy.

ERWIN D. CANHAM (1952). Editor-in-chief of the *Christian Science Monitor,* Canham is largely responsible for the paper's reporting prestige and leadership in appearance. He joined the *Monitor* in 1925 and, after a three-year leave-of-absence as a Rhodes scholar, returned to the paper as its Geneva correspondent. Then, from 1932 to 1939, he was the *Monitor's* Washington bureau chief; later he was transferred to the home office in Boston, where he rose from general news editor to managing editor and, in 1964, to his present position. Through the years, he has been appointed to various Presidential commissions and boards and as an alternate U. S. delegate to the United Nations. He is a former president of the U. S. Chamber of Commerce, an honorary fellow in Sigma Delta Chi, and the author of several books, both religious and secular.

PALMER HOYT (1953). The editor and publisher of the Denver Post, he has been a newspaperman for 45 years. He began his newspaper career in 1923 as a copy desk man for the *Portland Oregonian* and by 1946 had worked his way up through the ranks to publisher. He left the *Oregonian* that year to become *Post* editor and publisher. A former director of the Associated Press and national president of

217

Sigma Delta Chi, Hoyt was the first recipient of the University of Arizona's John Peter Zenger Freedom of the Press award in 1954.

GROVE PATTERSON (1954). Best known as editor-in-chief of the *Toledo Blade,* he also traveled extensively for the newspaper in Europe, Asia and Latin America before his death in 1956. Highlights of his career included interviews with Italian dictator Benito Mussolini and British Prime Minister Winston Churchill and a tour of Stalin's Russia. Patterson received numerous awards, was named honorary president of Sigma Delta Chi, and served as president of the American Society of Newspaper Editors.

NORMAN E. ISAACS (1955). The vice president and executive editor of the *Louisville Times and Courier-Journal,* he has been in journalism since 17, when he wrote sports for the *Indianapolis Star.* By age 27 he was managing editor of the *Indianapolis Times* and eight years later he became editorial director of the *Indianapolis News.* In 1945 he went to the *St. Louis Star-Times* as its managing editor. After that paper died he became *Louisville Times* managing editor. In 1953 he was president of the Associated Press Managing Editors Association and is now second vice president of the American Society of Newspaper Editors. A frequent traveler, he has served on several overseas missions for the State Department.

ROY A. ROBERTS (1956). Affiliated with the *Kansas City Star* from 1900, when he was a newsboy, to 1967, when he died as its board chairman, Roberts established himself as a top-notch political reporter who covered every presidential nominating convention between 1912 and 1964. He has been credited with a key role in the presidential candidacies of Alfred M. Landon, Wendell Wilkie, Thomas E. Dewey, and Dwight Eisenhower. He served as president of the American Society of Newspaper Editors, a director of the Associated Press, president of the Washington correspondents' Gridiron Club and an honorary president of Sigma Delta Chi.

IRVING DILLIARD (1957). During his 30 years on the editorial page staff of the *St. Louis Post-Dispatch,* his initials appeared on approximately 10,000 editorials. Although he retired from his post as editorial editor in 1960, he is still recognized as an expert on constitutional law and civil liberties, receiving awards from such groups as B'nai B'rith and the American Bar Association. Now a member of the faculty of Princeton University, he has also served as president of Sigma Delta Chi.

JENKIN LLOYD JONES (1958). A nationally-syndicated columnist and editor and publisher of the *Tulsa Tribune,* he has traveled to more than 90 countries to gather information for his newspaper and his weekly column. A leading figure in Oklahoma journalism since the mid-1930's, he is also vice president of the United States Chamber of Commerce and the author of a book entitled *The Changing World.*

BEN HIBBS (1959). Although his journalism career started with jobs on Kansas newspapers, he moved into the magazine field early. At age 28 he became associate editor of a Curtis publication, *The Country Gentleman* and stayed with Curtis for the next 34 years, gaining fame as the circulation-raising editor of *The Saturday Evening Post.* Since 1963 he has been a senior editor of *The Reader's Digest.*

JULES DUBOIS (1960). For 36 years prior to his death in 1966, he covered the Latin American beat for the *Chicago Tribune* Press Service. Once referred to by Argentine dictator Juan Peron as "the number one gangster of Yankee journalism," he was especially noted for his exclusive interview with Fidel Castro in the final days of the Cuban revolution.

HODDING CARTER (1961). From his editor's desk at the *Delta Democrat-Times* in Greenville, Miss., he has become one of the South's leading spokesmen for progressive race relations. Now a writer-in-residence at Tulane University, Carter has published newspapers since 1932. In 1940, he worked for the experimental and short-lived New York daily, *PM*. He is the recipient of the 1961 William Allen White Foundation citation for journalistic merit.

BERNARD KILGORE (1962). The spectacular successes of the *Wall Street Journal, Barron's*, the Dow Jones News Service, and the *National Observer* can be attributed in large measure to his efforts as a reporter, editor, president, and board chairman of Dow Jones and Co. An innovator in the newspaper business, he joined the *Wall Street Journal* in 1929 and rose rapidly through the paper's ranks, becoming its managing editor in 1940. In 1945 he became president of Dow Jones, the parent company. Cited often for his genius, Kilgore was an honorary president of Sigma Delta Chi and recipient of the society's Fellow award and Wells Key. He died in 1967.

PAUL MILLER (1963). Now president of the Gannett Company and the Associated Press, he began his newspaper career at age 18 in Oklahoma. In 1932 he left the state to work for the Associated Press, advancing from reporter to Washington bureau chief to assistant general manager. He became an executive of the Gannett Company in 1947 and has been its president since 1957. Under his leadership, the Gannett papers have won many awards, including a 1964 Pulitzer Prize. In 1963 he was the honorary president of Sigma Delta Chi.

CLARK R. MOLLENHOFF (1964). A Washington correspondent for the far-flung Cowles publications, he began his journalistic career as a police and court reporter for the *Des Moines Register*. Now widely known for his Washington exposes, Mollenhoff has won several awards for his reporting, including the Pulitzer Prize. The author of five books about the vagaries of the federal government, he now serves as chairman of the Sigma Delta Chi National Freedom of Information Committee.

EARL J. JOHNSON (1965). Retired since 1965 as vice president and general manager of United Press International, Johnson has had a distinguished journalistic career. Before he went to college, he was already city editor of the *Winfield* (Kan.) *Courier*. After graduation, he joined the old United Press in Chicago and rose rapidly in the ranks of that news service. Now commuting between homes in Southampton, N.Y., and Morelia, Mexico, Johnson is a veteran reporter of news events ranging from the plight of Floyd Collins, trapped in a Kentucky cave, to Hitler's blitzkrieg.

GARDNER COWLES (1966). For four decades, he has cut a pioneering swath across the mass communications media. Beginning as a newsman on the *Des Moines Register and Tribune,* a publication he now heads as president, Cowles later turned his skills to the magazine field with the establishment of *Look.* As editor-in-chief and board chairman of Cowles Communications, Inc., Cowles has also entered electronic journalism with the acquisition of several radio and television stations.

WES GALLAGHER (1967). From his New York office, Gallagher directs the flow of the world's news as general manager of the Associated Press. An AP man since 1937, he gained fame as a European correspondent during World War II. He returned to the New York office in 1951 as general executive in charge of personnel and became assistant general manager three years later. He assumed his present position in 1962. Author of *Back Door to Berlin,* a book about World War II, Gallagher is a fellow of Sigma Delta Chi and recipient of the 1967 William Allen White Foundation citation.